Trauma and Healing Under State Terrorism

Andrea Northwood

Inger Agger received her Ph.D. from the University of Copenhagen. She was active in the women's movement in Denmark in the 1970s, when she published her first book on the psycho-social dynamics of consciousness-raising groups (1977); in the 1980s she worked as a clinical psychologist for political refugees, and thereafter as a researcher. In 1993 she was appointed Coordinator for Psycho-Social Projects for the Humanitarian Office of the European Commission (ECHO); she is now based at ECHO/ECTF's task force in Zagreb, where she supervises psycho-social NGOs in Bosnia and Croatia. She has published extensively on women's studies, refugees, human rights and mental health, and her book *The Blue Room: Trauma and Testimony Among Refugee Women: A Psycho-Social Exploration* was published by Zed Books in 1994.

Søren Buus Jensen received his doctoral degree from the University of Copenhagen. A specialist in psychiatry, trained as a psychotherapist for work with couples, families and groups, he is an internationally recognized expert in the field of sexology. During the past decade he has also been involved in clinical work, and in research on refugees traumatized by human rights violations. In 1994 he took up duties as WHO Consultant on Mental Health, based in Zagreb, with responsibility for the first WHO intervention in this field under war conditions; in 1995 he took charge of the WHO Humanitarian Assistance to the Countries of Former Yugoslavia. He has published extensively on alcoholism, sexology, refugees, mental health and human rights, including (with Leslie Schover) the textbook *Sexuality and Chronic Illness: A Comprehensive Approach* (Guilford Press, New York, 1988).

Trauma and Healing Under State Terrorism

INGER AGGER
&
SØREN BUUS JENSEN

ZED BOOKS
London & New Jersey

Trauma and Healing Under State Terrorism was first published in 1996 by
Zed Books Ltd, 7 Cynthia Street, London N1 9JF, UK, and
165 First Avenue, Atlantic Highlands, New Jersey 07716, USA.

Typeset in Monotype Bembo by Lucy Morton, London SE12
Printed and bound in the United Kingdom
by Biddles Ltd, Guildford and King's Lynn

A catalogue record for this book is available from the British Library
US CIP data is available from the Library of Congress

ISBN 1 85649 383 0 (Hb)
ISBN 1 85649 384 9 (Pb)

Contents

Preface

This book is based on a research project which was initially entitled 'Human Rights and Mental Health: The Chilean Human Rights Movement as an Exemplary Model for Mental Health Work in Developing Countries'. The project was supported by grants from the Danish Research Council for the Humanities and the Department for Evaluation, Research and Documentation of the Danish Ministry of Foreign Affairs. The results were presented in our preliminary report: *Trauma and Healing Under State Terrorism: Human Rights and Mental Health in Chile During Military Dictatorship: A Case Example* (Agger and Jensen, 1993b). The Danish Ministry of Foreign Affairs also supported our seminar in Casa de la Paz, Santiago de Chile, in April 1993, where we had the opportunity to share the preliminary results with our Chilean colleagues.

We are very grateful for this valuable and generous support, which enabled us to study the Chilean human rights movement in detail and to share the outcome of the study both with our informants and through the publication of the book. Through this work, the grant also offered us a chance to develop our theories and professional skills in a way which has been very useful in our practical work under war conditions in the countries of the former Yugoslavia.

We would also like to express our utmost gratitude to our Chilean colleagues, members of the Chilean human rights movement, and all the other people we met during our fieldwork in Chile. Without their participation and open-hearted invitation to share their experiences this project could never have been realized. We hope that our map of their territory can contribute just a little to the further development of the field of mental health and human rights – and allow others to learn from the Chilean work. Seen from our position as we finish this book, in the midst of a war in Europe, these themes have not lost their importance.

Inger Agger and Søren Buus Jensen
Zagreb, Croatia, January 1995

Introduction

'Because of the bird in the cage...'

THE COMMITMENT

A rumour flew in a whisper over the tables in the cafés in front of the Vicarage of Solidarity on Plaza de Armas. We are in the incipient Chilean spring, Santiago, November 1989. The Sebastián Acevedo Movement will soon demonstrate in front of the barracks at No. 1470 Borgoño Street, one of the torture houses. During the walk to Borgoño Street, one of our companions wants our exact names and the numbers of our passports. 'Just in case,' she says. Another gives us a quick lesson in how to hold a slice of lemon in front of our nostrils against the tear gas, and instructions about which direction to run: 'Run towards the police, not away from them,' he says.

In front of the barracks, everything is as usual: heavy traffic in five lines, and the omnipresent buses sending their black smoke vertically into the air, thus adding to the already heavy smog. A swarm of people are on the sidewalks.

We are 'parked' in a bar across the street. It has heavy doors which could be closed in a hurry: 'to protect us if they use the "Guanacos" [the lorries mounted with water cannons],' we are told. 'They have come,' someone says, although the world outside, to us, looks the same. A 'now!' is heard and everybody leaves the bar to join the others. A moment later, the traffic is stopped by a chain of close to fifty people. An inferno of noise breaks out when the hundreds of buses and cars start honking their horns – in protest or in solidarity. A great banner has been attached to the wall of the villa, saying 'En Borgoño 1470 se sigue torturando' ('In No. 1470 Borgoño Street they continue to torture'), and the demonstrators are singing their litany:

'Queremos una patria sin torturadores' ('We want a fatherland without torturers').

A confetti of small pamphlets are blowing in the wind. The first policemen park their motorbikes. The passers-by pick up, read and put the pamphlets in their pockets and bags, and seconds later the traffic is moving again. The demonstrators have disappeared. If the banner had not still been on the wall and the pamphlets in our pockets, we would not have been sure that this had really happened.

'We can't leave the place together,' they say. 'Just walk naturally away and look like tourists.' Minutes later, we are sitting at a table in a restaurant at the fish market. A guitar player arrives and begins singing love songs. It's just too much. The emotions are so overwhelming that it's impossible to look like tourists any more.

A few days later, we are walking along the beach of the Pacific Ocean. The place is called Isla Negra. The skies are grey and the waves crash against the huge black rocks. We have just attended the First International Seminar on Torture to be held on Chilean soil. The cars of the CNI, the secret police, were parked in front of the entrance to the congress building. There had been presentations of scientific papers and dramatic testimonies by priests, therapists, judges and survivors. We could still feel the astonishment from suddenly being in the midst of a storm in our first real meeting with the Chilean human rights movement. The opposition against the dictatorship was outspoken. Everybody expected the regime to lose power at the election the following month.

We are approaching the house of Pablo Neruda, here in Isla Negra. There are poems and drawings on the black rocks 'naming freedom'. Nobody else is out here. We did not get permission from Santiago to enter the house. So we walk along the hoarding of this strange house. On every plank poems, slogans and names are written. We realize that we are in a holy place – a place of pilgrimage for the resistance.

Thousands of voices are naming freedom. Thousands of signatures confirm the bond of commitment. In a corner, we write our signatures to commit ourselves to this project:

> Because of the bird in the cage
> Because of the fish in its bowl
> Because of my friend who is in prison
> Because he spoke his thoughts aloud
> Because of the flowers that were torn up
> Because of the grass that was downtrodden
> Because of the trees that were pruned
> Because of the tortured bodies
> I name thee freedom.[1]

THE PURPOSE

Psychological warfare is an integral part of state terrorism. Resistance to state terrorism, therefore, also includes psychological weapons of self-defence. This book, then, is a map of the psychological strategies of terror and of the counter-strategies against them, seen through the Chilean 'prism'.

State terrorism, in different variations, is a common phenomenon in the world today. This raises the fundamental question of how people in these societies are able to take their fate into their own hands, resist the abuse of power and heal the traumas following violations of their basic human rights.

What is the nature of those psychological and social processes which facilitate the empowerment of politically repressed people? From where did the demonstrators from the Sebastián Acevedo Movement Against Torture get the courage to defy the terrorist system in front of the torture houses?

In this book, we attempt to give *our* answers to these questions on the basis of a total of six months of fieldwork in Chile. We were lucky enough to be able to follow the development in Chilean society during three important phases: in 1989, just before the election of the democratic government; in 1991, just after the publication of the report by the governmental Commission of Truth and Reconciliation about the violations of human rights committed by the former government; and in 1991–92, when the transitional process towards democracy had become more stabilized but had also begun to show its contradictions in a more clear-cut way.

The purpose of this study is thus to document and analyse, on the basis of the experiences of the Chilean human rights movement, how people develop new ways of resisting that abuse of power which is an inherent element of state terrorism. More specifically, we want to understand how concepts of trauma, therapeutic strategies and therapeutic relationships are developed under state terrorism. From this Chilean case example, we have attempted to develop a model which is 'transferable' to other societies in which human rights are also abused.

The object of our research is the community of a human rights movement in a certain societal context. This community is different from and more than the sum of its individual members. Therefore, we could not limit ourselves to interviewing individual members of the community. A human rights movement consists of social *relations* between people, and it was the *collective consciousness* and the *moral community* of this movement which were our prime targets. It is this collectivity and this moral community which has – we assume – a certain resisting and healing quality. We see the typical themes of the Chilean human rights movement – the emphasis on the close relation between the private, the professional and the political levels, and the linkage of human rights and mental health – as another way of expressing the importance of collectivity and moral community for individual and societal healing and resistance to abuse of power.

However, the body of our empirical material comprises interviews with forty Chilean therapists from the human rights movement. Three-quarters of these professionals had themselves been traumatized in various ways by the strategies of political repression. We draw heavily on the experiences of these mental health professionals who had to develop their work under the hardships of state terrorism.

We believe that the knowledge which has been gathered by these therapists is valuable for other mental health professionals who have to work in places where human rights are violated. The stories and writings of the Chilean therapists about how it all began can thus teach us a valuable lesson about the quality of psychological resistance and resilience in survivorship.

THE REASON

It was the meeting with political refugees in our own country which started our commitment to this field. Through psychotherapeutic work in an exile context with survivors of organized violence, we realized that there was a need for more knowledge about the traumatic consequences of state terrorism. The individual refugees felt a severe 'private' pain and at the same time were survivors of political violence – a 'political' pain.

In this work, we found that our traditional therapeutic attitude, which excluded the political dimension, did not give a sufficient understanding of the situation of the refugees, who needed our assistance. The pioneering work of the Chilean therapists Elizabeth Lira and Eugenia Weinstein[2] about the use of testimony as a therapeutic tool gave new meaning to our work, and little by little we modified their methods into a psychotherapeutic model for therapy in exile (Agger and Jensen, 1990a).

Because of our experiences with this work in Denmark, we participated in the first seminar about torture in Chile in November 1989. The dramatic encounter with the Chileans, the country and the spirit of the human rights movement developed into our first 'astonishment' (Hastrup, 1992).

The Chilean therapists' constant combination of the private and the political dimensions struck us, and opened our eyes to a new kind of cultural knowledge. Although worlds are different, they are all populated by people, who are universally able to imagine the positions of each other. Cultural knowledge, however, cannot always be transformed into words. To use the words of the anthropologist Kirsten Hastrup (1992), culture is not something we talk about, but a position from which we talk.

In the meeting with the culture of the Chilean human rights movement, we tried to sense their meanings and rationality through a foreign language and a foreign environment. However, we also shared at least one major position with them – the belief in fundamental human rights. Coming from an outside position and invited into this new culture, we got the chance through our research to develop a dual vision. Our aim was not to translate their culture into our language, but to extend our language to encompass the new reality we met.

The concept of 'the bond of commitment' ('el vinculo comprometido') gave us a new understanding of the therapeutic role. How could you be 'neutral' in the meeting with systematic and deliberate evil committed with the objective of breaking down other human beings? However, if you were not 'neutral', how could you remain 'professional' as a therapist or a researcher?

The concept of 'ethical non-neutrality' offered a position from which it was possible to show the solidary commitment to human rights without forgetting one's professional role. From this concept, we have developed our map of the Chilean experience: 'the Chilean model'. In this model, we extend the concept of ethical non-neutrality to encompass the interaction between the private, the professional and the political dimensions.

We have attempted to include the committed relationship and ethical non-neutrality in a new understanding not only of the Chilean work, but of post-traumatic work in general. The Chilean therapists themselves were not, and maybe are still not, convinced that a Chilean model does exist. They see the differences between their work, while we, from our perspective of a dual vision, are impressed by the similarities in their positions which are obvious and different from our local variation of therapeutic life.

We are convinced that there are, in the Chilean model, important elements which can be generalized and transformed for use in other social contexts – in local variations. We are also convinced that the

Chilean mental health professionals from the human rights movement would be those who are most qualified to disseminate their knowledge to their colleagues in other state terrorist societies.

In November 1994, the Chilean therapists Elizabeth Lira and David Becker from the Latin American Institute for Mental Health and Human Rights (ILAS) visited Zagreb and gave a seminar on 'Families of the Disappeared and Killed'. The seminar was attended by mental health professionals from Bosnia, Croatia, Macedonia and Slovenia. The Chilean therapists were able to share their experiences of trauma and human rights violations with their European colleagues in a solidary way which originated in a deep feeling of mutual understanding.

In a situation when the war in countries of former Yugoslavia seemed without solution and the task of mental health professionals over-whelming, this seminar gave a different perspective to the work of therapists under war conditions: the linkage between private and political suffering – a perspective which was new to many of the professionals from former Yugoslavia. However, this perspective also seemed to be received with interest, fascination and a wish to meet again with the Chileans.

No recipes exist for 'how to do it in the right way'; however, the narrative of the way the Chileans developed their own path under difficult circumstances is testimony to human creativity and the capacity to survive. It is also testimony to how new strength can be gained through the sharing of feelings, and how such sharing can turn pain into inner strength.

The seminar in Zagreb in the middle of hopelessness and despair constituted such testimony.

NOTES

1. Hymn of the Sebastián Acevedo Movement Against Torture. This Spanish text and all the following have been translated by the authors.
2. They published their now famous article under the pseudonyms of Cienfuegos and Monelli in 1983.

2

The Fieldwork

A journey through the field

We visited Chile over three periods. Our first visit took place in November 1989 and it lasted for three weeks. This visit we now consider to be our pilot phase, because of its later importance for this research project.

When we arrived in Chile in November 1989, we did not know that this would be the beginning of a long and committed relationship with the country. It was during the first visit that we conceived the idea of this project, and it was also during this first meeting with the Chilean human rights movement that we established a mutual trusting relation with people in the movement. No doubt this enabled us to collect the type of data that we did. This first visit made the subsequent passage of 'La Cordillera' (the Andean mountains) more easy: we already had a provisional map of the route and the people we met during the passage knew us, and they were benevolent and helpful in our search.

The following two visits to Chile were made in connection with this project, which included two periods of fieldwork: the first lasted two months (April and May 1991), and the second lasted three and a half months (November 1991–March 1992). During the first period of fieldwork our permanent base was in Santiago, while during the second period of fieldwork we chose to base ourselves in a provincial town, Concepción. By living in both a metropolitan and a provincial context we could experience different aspects of the human rights movement and of Chile.

Some of the answers and some unspoken things that we did not recognize or know how to interpret in the metropolitan setting became understandable and audible while we lived in the provinces. Here, somehow, we got closer to the experience of poverty and of fear. In this smaller social context, the significance, extension and limitation of the human rights work became more visible compared to our experiences in the metropolitan setting of Santiago.

During our first period of fieldwork, we travelled to the north of Chile and visited Iquique. During the second period of fieldwork, we went south and visited Temuco and also Punta Arenas, the latter in the extreme south of the country. The vanguard of the human rights movement – the theoreticians, the political leaders and the mental health teams – originated in Santiago. In the provincial towns we got closer, however, to the feel of a repressive society as it is experienced by the ordinary people, and we could, more directly, get an impression of the problems of building up mental health work with more limited resources.

THE INFORMANTS

Interviews with people in the human rights movement were an important method of data collection during fieldwork. We had to realize, however, that the culture of the movement was something through which people in the movement *saw* the world. This culture was not something that they normally talked *about*; it was a position from which they talked.

In our interviews we could not just ask people about their thoughts and then be sure that their answers would express the very truth about the human rights movement. Their answers were to questions that *we* posed. During the fieldwork, we gradually began to get a feel of the collective consciousness and moral community – began to sense the content of those answers to which we did not know the questions in the beginning.

In total, we interviewed (with tape-recorder) 76 people: 40 therapists, 23 members of survivor groups, 13 others (6 members of the Sebastián Acevedo Movement Against Torture, 2 lawyers, 2 priests and 3 people with connections to the Mapuche Indians – 2 anthropologists and 1 political leader).

The 40 interviewed therapists comprised 13 men (33%) and 27 women (67%); 24 were metropolitan (60%) and 16 from the provinces (40%). According to profession we interviewed: 13 psychiatrists (33%), 6 other doctors (15%), 13 psychologists (33%), 4 social workers (10%) and 4 others (a nurse, a physiotherapist, a pastor and a child therapist).

A total of 11 therapists (28%) had themselves been exposed to torture; of the doctors, 10 out of 19 (53%) had been tortured; 14 therapists had been in exile (35%) and 8 therapists (20%) had both been tortured and in exile.

THE INTERVIEWS

Our reflections are not primarily focused on 'how we felt', but on how the interaction between ourselves – the researchers – and the Chileans influenced the data that we gathered. How did the interaction, for example, influence the 76 interviews, or the observation of group therapy – the empirical part of our investigation in which both we and they became participants. We as subjects – as researchers and Danes, as psychiatrist and psychologist, and as man and woman – had to recognize this subjectivity, but also to see ourselves from the outside – as objects. We are, however, familiar with this process from therapy and supervision of therapy in which it is of paramount importance to recognize transference and counter-transference reactions.

Our position as researchers was important. We had a position as '*outsiders*', foreigners who were only living in their community for a transitory period. We were, however, also '*insiders*' who had been accepted as solidary members of the professional society in the field of human rights and mental health. We had an *independent* position because we were not evaluators from organizations providing funding, and at the same time we had a *professional background* in the university/psychiatric hospital. Moreover, we had our *own research funding* through a Danish governmental structure.

Our position as a married *couple* placed us in a recognizable category, where our collaboration and mutual presence needed no specific explanations. The three-person setting of the interviews reduced problems of talking about intimate themes and created an atmosphere which reduced 'seductive' elements on all levels. However, some very emotionally loaded themes (for example, about sexuality), which could only be discussed with a researcher of the same sex, were possibly not raised.

We emphasized that we had come to Chile to learn from the interviewees – not to evaluate or rank them in any way. We stressed the fact that the book which would come out of the project would be *our* narrative of what we had experienced, and that *their own version would probably be very different*.

By emphasizing that we came to learn from them, we wanted to counteract the asymmetrical power relationship between them and us.

There is a great sensitivity with regard to European – and especially North American – imperialism, also on the scientific level. At the same time, many of the non-governmental institutions receive financial aid from Europe and North America. It was thus unavoidable that an asymmetrical position was introduced between them and us, and this demanded moral reflections on our part. It was also unavoidable that our interviews could be experienced as a sort of 'violence' committed against them.

In the name of science we have the right to ask questions of, to talk about and to analyse the interviewees, but when we do that we are also introducing a relation of asymmetry. On the other hand, *if it is not sufficient to ask in the name of science* (Hastrup, 1992, p. 57), what would then be a good enough reason?

We are aware of the fact that, by emphasizing certain elements of what we called their 'model', we also led them to talk about those elements in the interviews. This was, however, also our purpose, because those were the elements we wanted to learn more about. However, by doing this there were also important areas which we did not get very deeply into (for example, the problem of having 'talked' during torture). We realized this in the subsequent writing process, and have attempted to make up for it by studying the literature and those interviews in which the interviewees, on their own initiative, mention this important topic.

The Reactions of the Interviewees

In order to learn about the conditions of the interviewees' work and the culture of the movement, we had to maintain a certain level of pressure during the interview. This involved an intrusiveness and, in some instances, arousing pain on the part of our interviewees. Some reacted with such painful emotions when we asked them about their trauma story that we chose not to go into more details about it. Others were relieved to tell it.

We, as interviewers and researchers, had to employ our intuition and background as therapists to monitor the reactions of the interviewees closely as to how much pressure we could exert. This occasioned a continuous process of ethical reflection on our side before, during and after the interviews. Our choice of primarily interviewing professionals made it a bit easier. As colleagues and professionals, we could expect that they would also take responsibility themselves for what they chose to tell us.

We had to accept that we were seen as 'objects' by our interviewees, that the people we interviewed created their own picture of us, and that we could not just change that picture and become our private selves. This objectivity that we attained, however, also involved a responsibility towards the interviewees: when we took upon ourselves the authority to conduct an interview, we also had to accept the responsibility of leading it in an ethical way.

Some interviewees told us, later on, that they had been very tired after the interview, but also that it had given them something to think about. We never heard about or received any negative reactions from our interviewees.

The Reactions of the Interviewers

We were already acquainted with the interviewing role as both researchers and psychotherapists in Denmark. We were familiar with the use of our subjectivity as a tool in the testimonial process. In such a process the interviewer or the therapist can experience a whole range of counter-transference reactions towards the interviewee – from feelings of avoidance at one end of the spectrum, to feelings of enmeshment and over-involvement at the opposite end (Wilson and Lindy, 1994).

In this process you are never 'objective' in the sense of not being emotionally or intellectually engaged with the interviewee, but partici-pate empathetically in the interviewee's story as redefining (reframing) subjects. In order to do that in a professional way, the researcher or the therapist must go through a process of *counter-identification*: that is, to identify with the interviewee or patient (*empathy*), but also have an observing part of yourself outside of the emotional process. This dual vision is what distinguishes a therapist or a researcher from a sympathetic listener.

The observing part of the researcher (or the therapist) redefines and reframes the story of the interviewee in the perspective of professional theory and practice. In this process the world of the interviewee is changed – and so is the researcher's world. The researcher or the therapist must, however, be aware of how his or her private vulnerability influ-ences the communicative space, how the counter-transference interferes.

By entering the world of the people we interviewed, we learned not only from what was spoken in words. There were also areas of silence which could never be put into words – for example, the emotions associated with the experience of torture.

During the interviews, we felt a whole range of counter-transference reactions: feelings of being drawn into the interviewee's world with a temporary loss of boundaries; feelings of denial and avoidance in the face of horrible trauma stories; feelings of guilt and anger towards the interviewee; and sometimes even a feeling of complicity – maybe we in turn were traumatizing them through our interviews.

We could usually discuss these different types of reaction with each other after the interview, in this way acting as supervisors for each other. The fact that we were two researchers (and therapists) together during the interview was a great advantage in the management of these reactions that invariably emerged in the confrontation with trauma stories of death, severe loss and torture.

Such debriefing talks were often held immediately after the interview in a nearby café – sometimes accompanied by a highly needed glass of *pisco* to reduce the level of emotion after an intense interview. Sometimes we felt an urgent need to sleep. Sometimes we experienced how the confrontation with evil was transmitted into our own relationship due to what could be called *projective identification*: although we might have been in a good and peaceful mood prior to the interview and without any external reason throughout the interview, we could end up in a dramatic quarrel a few minutes after we had left an emotionally loaded interview.

The recognition of these processes made it clear to us, once more, that researchers in this area – as well as therapists – must have debriefing talks and/or supervision simply to stay alert and receptive; in order to survive, on a symbolic level.

OBSERVATIONS

One of our main tasks was to register important *events* in the movement. An event is an occurrence that is significant from the point of view of the human rights movement. How did the movement dramatize itself? What could we learn from the field of tension between the dramatic events and the simple occurrences? It is in this field of tension that we can find the key to insight. *Every time something is said there is something else which is not said* (Hastrup, 1992).

Could we find the structural elements of the movement? Our task was to get to see and understand both those aspects of the human rights movement which were spoken about and those elements that were unspoken because they were self-evident, part of common knowledge or repressed – the 'subconscious' of the movement. It was important for us to learn to recognize significant events and to distinguish them from simple occurrences.

We lived for nearly six months in a developing country and were confronted with poverty and social contradictions. We saw and heard about street violence. We saw the heavily armed police in the streets and experienced the terror of looking into their machine-guns at close range. We got the feel of fear into our own lives. We experienced the confusion between reality and fantasy: were we over-dramatizing it? Were we developing a paranoid position? Was it realistic to feel fear in this situation?

We felt how it was to struggle between giving in to the fear and denying it – to find the point of balance between the 'fear of the fear' and a realistic cautious attitude. We felt the mistrust against neighbours: were they Pinochet supporters? Could we tell them why we were in Chile? On several occasions, we heard ourselves make up outrageous explanations of our presence in Chile: we were just on vacation for a couple of months – a rather unlikely explanation when the neighbours saw us every morning leaving the house with tape-recorder and papers, looking very business-like. One major bridge to reality was our Spanish teacher, who came daily. We could test our thoughts and feelings against her matter-of-fact answers.

Life in the public space of fieldwork also involved following the news and the discussions in the mass media during important phases of democratization. The news was often quite dramatic, with detailed stories and close-up photos of murders, terrorist attacks and new revelations in the aftermath of the dictatorship.

THE FIELD DIARY

During our two periods of fieldwork, we kept a field diary to monitor our observations as well as our own reactions and reflections. This text (166 pages) was written daily by one of us (S.B.J.). The diary also had several other functions: to create at least a little distance from the intensity which was experienced especially by the main interviewer (I.A.); to share our experiences more explicitly; and, to a certain degree, to keep a dual vision of events and experiences.

We became our own informants: what astonished us led us into new and unexpected roads in the process from discovery towards understanding. The field diaries were the first step, on location, to monitoring this research process. A second step was taken when these documents were consulted, retrospectively, after return from fieldwork. Events and occurrences, thoughts and emotions were recalled and re-experienced.

Nevertheless, a new perspective was now part of the process. The temporary encounter between 'them and us' was over. A new distance from the experiences had developed, the recorded data in the field diary were processed, and a new dual vision of what happened became part of reality. The field diary told us one story; it was our first draft of a map of an unknown territory. We listened to our voices, but we ourselves had changed.

In the following, we will present excerpts from our field diaries followed by our later reflections (in italics).

Excerpts from Field Diary I:
Fieldwork, April–May 1991

2 April

This is the first day of official fieldwork (after having found an apartment and dealt with other practical things). We feel that we were received quite well in the first institution. It seems to us that there are some aspects the Chileans themselves apparently are not so aware of in the middle of their own very nationalistic commitment: the relation between the private and the political, and the theme of 'the wounded healer'.

The fact that they do not seem to think that their experiences can be of value outside of Chile can maybe also be attributed to the old discussion between cultural relativism and universalism. We shall, of course, not write their story, but we shall attempt to listen and understand – find out if we can extract something general from the specific which can be applicable to other places. The Chileans underline the advantage of the situation in Chile, where there is one language, one culture or one religion, and a rather well-defined social and cultural situation.

We were astonished this very first day when a rather central member of the human rights movement questioned what, in fact, was the major purpose of our research project, namely to document the 'Chilean model' and to find ways in which their experiences and skills could be developed into general hypotheses concerning trauma and healing under state terrorism. Our disappointment had elements of ethnocentrism: here we came, and told them that, from our perspective, their model was very useful to learn from in other parts of the world. They insisted that there was no model and that they were unique as a nation. It is fascinating that we, on the very first day, ended up in the midst of the central debate between cultural relativism and universalism. We made strenuous efforts to be more convincing.

We both think that we must try to strengthen our description of what exactly we want to do in those places we visit before we meet the leader of the next institution tomorrow (we are both a little intimidated by her impressive personality).

Do they really understand what we want to do? Language is difficult and the translation done for Søren's sake today was not perfect. Have we overcome their mistrust and the old bad experiences of being evaluated by Europeans? Will it give us problems to interview some staff members and not others? Will we be able to create a contact with 'the wounded healers' that enables us to perceive the dynamics of the therapeutic strategies? How do we incorporate in the project the current events that are described in the press – by intuitive newspaper reading and clippings?

It feels as if we are beginning a therapeutic process. The first assessment interview was a success, the 'patient' will return, but have we also succeeded in establishing a viable contact and working alliance? If we want to collect significant testimonial material here, we must allow the necessary preparatory time before we can really start to work.

How much will we be restricted by language problems? How will the interviewees react to the tape-recorder? We must be clear about the ethics around the interviews, questions of anonymity, the framework.

Inger is constantly afraid of doing something wrong, of breaking unknown rules. Søren is worried about how he can overcome his language problems, which reduce the possibilities of his establishing contact.

Thousands of questions came up; it was an overwhelming experience to start fieldwork. We were still not quite sure whether we really had a project.

3 April

We are received very warmly in the next institution. When we tell the director that we have come not to evaluate them but to learn from them, she emphasizes that they have complete trust in us. The presentation of the project works better today.

We have made it! We are on track! We are quite confident now. We have already arranged about ten interviews for the next week and have been invited to participate in several events. The project will come off!

The relief, the enthusiasm, the engagement – we were on track, and we were sucked into a whirlpool. We were unable to say no – the impressive leader and our own strong wish to get the project going made us schedule too many interviews. We did not realize the risk of exhaustion when we entered the powerful space of the 'wounded healers'. This over-involvement created the basis of our own first research wound.

4 April

Today we do our first interviews. We start with 'the ritual' – her name and her voice is heard in the room. Our first interviewee is Danish – she works at one of the institutions; it is good training before the interview with the Director in the afternoon.

The Director is waiting for us and appears to be motivated and obliging. It seems important to him that we bring a tape-recorder. Apparently it does not arouse mistrust. On the contrary, it seems to indicate that something important is happening. The tape-recorder has the role of 'the significant other' – as the witness.

The interview lasts three hours and this is maybe the maximum time that we and the interviewee can endure. All of us are very tired afterwards. It is evident that we created a good contact with him and that our questions started a process of reflection on his part. By asking our questions, we are actually influencing the process that we are investigating.

A small first feeling of triumph? A few days ago, he did not accept our thoughts about the Chilean model; today, he reflected and told us that he had been thinking about it. We were fascinated and listened for hours.

5 April

We discuss with each other what we want to get out of this project. The testimonial method that we are using is unique. This method enables us to use our professional backgrounds in a combination of data collection and establishment of contact. We are really on to something. We get some very moving and insight-giving stories. This 'qualified interview' is a very interesting way of doing research. Maybe we have, however, underestimated the amount of energy that this method requires.

Maybe we will have to take some time off after the interview, postpone our reflections about the interview a bit and then write the most important thoughts into this field diary – use it as a form of research diary.

We were just great – was it narcissistic omnipotence? Between the lines, one senses that we were beginning to feel exhaustion and the need for debriefing.

8 April

We take a taxi to be sure to be on time. We do not dare to be late for the interview with this other director. When we arrive we have to wait for a few moments, but it is evident that we are expected. We are taken seriously and feel all right with that. We have already formulated a number of questions for her. We feel the necessity of being well prepared for this interview. The questions are in Danish, but maybe we can later elaborate them and have them translated into Spanish for the next interviews.

In the evening, we interview a woman whose husband was murdered. She has been in exile in Denmark, so this means that both of us can be active in the interview process. It turns out to be an intense experience, and afterwards we discuss ethical questions. How far can we go when we do not have any therapists' contract – and she apparently needs to talk?

Here we are in touch with an important problem in our research method. Our training as therapists and researchers allowed us to create an atmosphere of trust. Our position as 'outsiders' who had been invited into this culture offered the interviewees a setting in which they felt safe to tell their stories. From their own work, they recognized the importance of the testimony method and it was meaningful to give testimony to us, as researchers, also from a professional point of view. However, the strength of the encapsulated traumata on some occasions caught all of us (including the interviewee) by surprise, although we all should have expected this as professionals. During our interviews, we often appreciated the fact that we had a therapeutic background, that we knew about trauma, that we were trained in containing heavy emotional material.

According to Hastrup (1992, p. 68), the collection of data during fieldwork often involves a certain element of 'violence'. However, most times we felt that we did not have to exert pressure on our interviewees. We got the feeling that we removed the lid from years of bottled-up emotions. Of course, this required ethical considerations, when no therapists' contract existed. Were we offering a certain relief, although it was a difficult process, or were we re-traumatizing the interviewee? Many times during our fieldwork we had doubts about these questions. At a distance we think that we mostly offered relief, seldom pain.

9 April

After the interview today, with a psychiatrist who suffered torture during the dictatorship, we discuss how we shall handle the torture stories of the professionals in a proper ethical way. Into how much detail shall we go with their own stories, and how can we follow them up? What is it especially that the tortured professionals can contribute to the project in comparison with patients? Maybe it could be expressed in the following way: by interviewing the professionals we can, hopefully, benefit from informants who are able both to tell us their private stories and to see these stories from a clinical and political perspective.

We discussed the problem of the wounded healer with our interviewee, and we sensed that he feels that *he* has a greater healing power towards those symptoms that he recognizes from his own experience. This question of the wounded healer seems relevant, but the 'wounds' are not specifically from torture, for example. We are confronted with so many variations of organized violence and repression, so much fear. To isolate the torture experience from this makes no sense in this context.

We must not forget about sexuality. We must not forget (be afraid) to ask about this although we are in Chile – it still seems relevant to explore this area, which we have already written so much about.

10 April

When we start the interview we understand that they have talked about us in the institution and discussed what it is like to be interviewed by us. From the way our interviewee tells us about it, we understand that they think the interviews are all right. The director has told our interviewee to tell us 'everything'. We seem to do to them what they themselves do in relation to their patients. They are not, however, accustomed to that. They appreciate being asked about their story, but expect to be asked about other things, maybe to be questioned on theoretical issues.

We were evaluated by them. We were placed in certain roles. A transference process was developing between the community of the institution and us. We, ourselves, were developing counter-transference reactions in the balance between over-engagement and the fear of being rejected by them.

We are a bit exhausted by now. It is hard work with too many terrible stories. We must learn to respect our own tiredness. The project is, by now, working so well that we will, no doubt, get a lot out of it. The risk is that we exhaust ourselves and privatize our pain from listening to all these trauma stories – that we direct the anger from this pain against ourselves or each other.

The aim of our project is to understand the interaction between the private, the professional and the political levels. We have adjusted our research method to their own way of working clinically. Also, we are on our way towards working within the 'bond of commitment'.

11 April

Today, we were on a tough job. Our interviewee – a psychiatrist – was sceptical. We have not met that reaction before. We knew, beforehand, that she had been terribly tortured (the director had told us), and she was clearly defending herself – primarily by intellectualization. She did not want to go into her private story. We knew that the director had told her to 'tell them everything'. At last, we understand that we have not been precise enough about the aim of our project.

We took something for given. We had interviewed others from that institution and we expected them to tell each other about our project. For the first time, we did not give our presentation. We committed a well-known elementary error of institutional psychology: the contact and working alliance established with one person cannot just be transferred to another person in the institution.

She did, however, tell us parts of her story about prison, torture, flight and exile. She did loosen up at last when we asked her how she was feeling right now. Maybe she could have told us another story if we had started all over again. We are wondering how to interpret this process. Was she only looking after herself? Defence mechanisms are not created to bother therapists – or researchers. At last she symbolically offered us a cigarette and talked in a more relaxed way. Maybe she did not understand our aim until the interview was over. Maybe the analysis of her reactions can open up an understanding of central aspects of the project, although we in no way were idealized by her. Her reactions could be interpreted in many ways. Something also has to do with our method. We must reformulate and structure our aim and our method in a better way. We already know much more than we did a week ago. By now, we know much more about what it is that we want, and we must follow that up.

This interview was a landmark in our interview process. Many times during our fieldwork we returned to this interviewee, to her reactions and our reactions. We clearly experienced that she had been severely traumatized and that she was still very vulnerable. Her anxiety and lack of confidence must be seen in the perspective of the request from the director to 'tell them everything'. This was a request which had been given in solidarity with our work, but at the same time it created a trauma-symbolizing situation. She felt forced to offer information which she was not ready to share with us. Her taking care of herself was interpreted by us as directed towards us, and we felt narcissistically wounded when she did not readily idealize our aim and work. Our over-involvement and fear of rejection provoked our emotional reactions. Her perception of us as violators and transgressors of her boundaries made us feel – and maybe even act – as transgressors or violators, although we from the 'outside' could have been seen as a 'neutral', considerate couple doing a very empathic interview. When the tape-recorder had been turned off and the trauma-symbolizing situation was over, all three of us were able to develop another relationship. We were back into a professional exchange situation into which the strong emotions did not interfere.

Maybe we could have restarted the interview at this point. Maybe we would have been back in an equivalent situation if we had tried.

Now, we have interviewed several clinicians from this institution, and we are beginning to wonder if they maybe are developing aggressive feelings towards us: could we possibly become 'scapegoats' for problems that we sense this institution has? They talk with each other. They know that we question people closely. It is probably OK, but we have to be aware of what happens. Are we doing any harm to them? It is probably impossible to go into this process – in the way we do it – without influencing the life of the institution. Maybe we should send them a thank-you letter to round off the process?

We were struggling with the problem of complicity: did we ourselves become violators when we asked them to disclose their trauma stories? Maybe most of this was our imagination – or was it real?

We must soon reformulate our introduction and questions. We must also monitor our own sensations and reactions. Counter-transference phenomena will probably also arise in us.

One circle into another circle into another circle: the private, the professional, the human rights movement, the political context. Our focus must be on the boundary areas and the interaction – a sort of focal point analysis.

13 April

We are observing group therapy of Family Members of the Disappeared. It is exhausting for us to listen to all these stories about loss of close family members. Inger gets in contact with feelings from her own past and part of the exhaustion is suddenly verbalized. We must pay extra attention to our own counter-transference reactions. Inger's reaction here must be seen as a clear reaction of subjective counter-transference, while the fear that is slowly invading us during the interview process has more to do with projective identification. Other times our reactions are maybe more a natural consequence of listening with empathy to difficult stories about life.

Our thoughts at this moment were massively concentrated on emotional interactions between them and us. We now interpret that our struggles were part of the reality of the therapists who work in this area. The over-involvement combined with exhaustion. The guilt combined with anxiety. Outbursts of anger were directed towards ourselves and each other. The problem of the wounded healer had become part of our daily life. Our own old wounds came closer to the surface, and we were brought into contact with feelings that contributed to a deeper understanding of ourselves and why we were there doing that kind of research. The universalism of the problem of the wounded healer became clearer. We felt, in our own bodies, that the empathy of the wounded healer deepens the understanding of the wounded patient. We were, however, also confronted with the continuous dilemma of the wounded healer: either to be sucked into feeling powerless without the resources to take a step back and go into a process of counter-identification; or to be overcome with grandiose feelings of being a specially gifted healer – or researcher.

14 April

We must be more precise about empathy, counter-transference and projective identification. Does our tiredness come from listening to all these stories about torture and death?

16 April

We are going to visit another institution today, and we get our introduction reformulated and corrected by our Spanish teacher on the basis of what we imagine the intellectual demands of this particular institution to be.

Apparently, our new introduction works well. They listen and take notes. They cut down on the standard programme they have for visitors after having heard our introduction. They understand that we want something different. We also sense that the two psychologists are a little nervous about being interviewed by us – they imagine that they will be examined. Should we just let it pass? Maybe it does not matter if they make an effort and afterwards feel relieved that it was not so bad after all.

17 April

Today we write a thank-you letter to the other institution. We try to counter the resistance that we imagine, 'stabs in the back' or whatever. Anyway, it is a nice letter. Maybe we ought to meet them once more before we leave?

24 April

During the interview with the two psychologists who insisted on being together during the interview, we note that it is the first time that they hear each other's story. Our method also influences what is happening here in the institutions.

Researchers are not neutral observers. We have an impact on the people that we interview. The research process changes the object of research.

25 April

After an interview with a therapist couple: it was an impressive and powerful session. Inger is worried that we questioned them too closely – she feels that *she* could not contain more, and that Søren seduced her into persisting and going too close. How traumatized does the listener become by just listening? In this couple, the wife was trying to take care of the husband because she feared that he would break down, but she also felt that they should talk about the difficult things. In the interview, Inger was trying to take care of both of them because she feared that they would break down. The omnipotence of the man, of us. Søren feels that he is able to contain the fear and ensure that we keep on track without getting too tired.

In couples therapy it is well known that the problems between the individuals in a couple will be expressed in the interaction between the couple and the therapists in the therapeutic room. Often the problems will also be transmitted into the interaction between the two individuals in the therapist couple. Through this process – for example, the observation of the interaction between the couple and between the two individuals in each couple – we can often understand key elements of the problem. In this interview, Inger was angry at Søren for having no empathy for her pain, nor was he taking responsibility for the couple's pain, although on the surface he was being very nice. The man in this couple had insisted on returning from exile. The wife was so dedicated to him that she agreed to accompany him, although she was afraid of what would happen to their young children. She was angry at him for not giving priority to her pain, and his lack of responsibility for their children. At the same time, it was difficult for her to blame her husband, who was so committed, who wanted to fight for justice in his country. Their actual existential dilemma was transmitted to us.

2 May

We have both had dreams about how to manage sexuality. We begin wondering about what they do *not* tell us: 'the really forbidden'; the secret spaces; some of the strange things happening in the torture houses, for example in the one called 'La Venda Sexy' ('The Sexy Blindfold'). Our fantasies begin pouring out. Something happens during torture that we do not understand – maybe they could avoid other types of torture by agreeing to the sexual part. We read an article in one of the magazines about the torturers in the tower of Villa Grimaldi: one of them raped, the other always obtained a 'consent' to sexuality but never used it!

We know about sexual torture. Part of our professional background has been to bring this theme to the surface (Agger, 1989, 1994; Agger and Jensen, 1993a).

We nearly 'forgot' about it here in Chile. It was too difficult to ask the questions and maybe to listen to the answers. The sexual undertones were still part of the 'conspiracy of silence', part of the unspoken; maybe words can never express it. The brief hints about what happened in the tower of Villa Grimaldi or 'La Venda Sexy'[1] *fertilized fantasies about the universal female condition. Maybe a key was hidden here to a deeper understanding of the repressive strategies.*

We also, however, 'forgot' about another theme: the process of turning into a collaborator during torture. The theme of 'talking' during torture, of giving information, of betraying your comrades and your ideals. Forgetting this theme was even more noteworthy, because retrospectively we can see that we struggled indirectly with it throughout our interviews: the problem of how much pressure we could exert on our interviewees to get information.

At home, and at a distance, we begin wondering if the problem of having 'talked' during torture is not the real trauma, the real conspiracy of silence, and that the sexual torture methods – although deeply traumatizing – are somewhat manageable in comparison. Maybe it is an illusion, on the part of the European or North American therapist who is not familiar with the strong ideology of a resistance movement, that you get to the deepest layers of the trauma when the sexual part is disclosed and integrated. Maybe the patient will even disclose this part to avoid getting into that which really damaged his or her soul.

3 May

We know from one of his colleagues that the psychiatrist we interview today had been imprisoned and tortured. He does not tell us this; neither has he told it to his team. How credible, then, is the rest of what he tells? We have come to expect that they will tell us everything – including things they haven't told other people.

Maybe his reaction was an adequate way of protecting himself. The dramatic testimonies we had been listening to illustrated a need for therapy and supervision among the therapists, since most of them had never been through that process. The research situation gave to some of them a chance of debriefing.

He tells us that the therapists accompany the relatives of the disappeared to identify the corpses. It must be a rather onerous job. For the first time we get through all the questions. Maybe as a consequence of his reservation – and ours – the interview becomes more of a question-and-answer business than the testimonial type we usually produce. Actually, the interview ends up being rather informative.

8 May

We attend a staff meeting in one of the institutions. We have to leave before the meeting is over, and those of the staff whom we have not interviewed seem a bit frustrated about our 'observing' position. We need to have a very short version of our presentation. It is frustrating with observers if you do not know why they are there. We also felt a bit uncomfortable at the meeting – we felt both inside and outside of the situation. Our position was not well enough defined.

14 May

When we returned from the visit to the former concentration camp, Pisagua, they told us in an offhand way that they had informed the PRAIS team[2] at the hospital and the Association of Ex-Political Prisoners of Pisagua that we would visit Pisagua today – just in case. There are still right-wing paramilitary groups; those groups do not ask for the 'To whom it may concern' paper from the Danish Ministry of Foreign Affairs before they shoot. Maybe it was lucky that we didn't know about that beforehand.

That day we really felt collective fear. Walking around in Pisagua, this feeling of fear became a living reality to us while in this ghost town. We saw the pain of our two companions who were revisiting their old place of trauma: we saw the grave of the disappeared. We felt the fear and kept on working, interviewing, asking and taking photos, and were concerned with taking care of our companions. We forgot to take care of ourselves. We did not really believe that this situation could be risky also for us. Retrospectively, as we heard so many times from the therapists that we interviewed, our own anxiety became part of reality.

23 May

Today the interview was a bit too short: we could have gotten much more valuable material. We broke the interview off by reminding *them* of the time-limit they had told us about when we started the interview. Who is responsible for keeping an eye on the clock, them or us?

Retrospectively, we realize that this is a pseudo-problem. We were simply exhausted, couldn't take any more. Our preoccupation with keeping the interviewee's timetable was our way of ensuring that the interview ended fairly soon – maybe there were also other mechanisms at work.

27 May

We are leaving in a few days. We have a hard programme today catching up on the last things we should get done before leaving. The atmosphere between us is tense all day long – maybe it is also coloured by the process of separation which we are now into. We conduct our last interview late in the afternoon. It is raining and we sit for a while waiting for our interviewee. We are wet. Both she and we are a bit defensive. She tells us that she only has one hour, which in some way is a relief. We end up with the feeling that the interview was only a 'starter', that we must follow it up – there is much more material.

Excerpts from Field Diary II:
Fieldwork, November 1991–February 1992

20 November

We still have a hang-over of guilt feelings towards two of the institutions. We attend a book presentation arranged by one of them. The psychiatrist who was so defensive during our first 'landmark' interview writes a dedication for us in a copy of the book: 'For our colleagues who are dedicated to the same wish for knowledge as we are,' she writes. It seems as if we are forgiven – but maybe we never did anything wrong?

We meet representatives from the other institution at a conference and feel that we are able to re-establish contact. Nothing is wrong. The contact and working alliance are still there, and we can proceed with the project.

6 December

We have moved into our house in Concepción. It is a bit cold, and Inger is beginning to get ill. We are both tired. It is rather hard to adjust oneself to life on the other side of the globe. We begin doing 'telephone work' to make appointments and contacts. We construct the time-schedule and plot in the first appointments. The field diary is started, and we have hired a Spanish teacher to come every morning. The daily life of fieldwork has started!

21 January

We try to organize the material we have collected. We begin discussing how to organize our data. On one of the coming days we will begin to lay down the framework of our report on the basis of our data and field diaries – find the main themes – and find out how to give priority to the remaining collection of data – find out what is missing while we are still here.

25–27 January

How do we organize and analyse our data? We divide it under trauma, therapeutic strategies and therapeutic relationships. We want to reflect on the private and the professional in a political context. We establish a model for organization and analysis of our data, and we propose chapter headings. We then try to consider which kind of material we have for the individual chapters – and especially for the chapter on our method. We categorize the different types of data we have. We decide to work in English from the beginning, and during these first days we gradually get this first organization of our report [this book] outlined on the computer. It is a rather painful process involving quite a lot of discussions, but at last we reach a provisional solution that we both can agree on.

28 January

We are still working with the structure of our report, but we break off to do another interview. We have not finished the data collection yet, although we have a certain feeling of being 'full'. We have observed that the interviews do not reveal many new things any longer. Sometimes we feel that we now have knowledge which many of our interviewees do not have – especially in the theoretical field. Sometimes we have had to explain what 'the bond of commitment' was – but maybe that has more to do with Concepción being a provincial town. In Santiago everyone talked about 'el vinculo comprometido'.

2 February

We are a bit tired; it is reflected in our relationship. Of course, we are still influenced by all the hard stuff that we experience here and our life together is somewhat isolated twenty-four hours a day. It requires a strong relationship to endure all this. Apparently we have such a relationship, but it seems as though we have to pass through a number of trials.

7 February

We are leaving for a week's stay in Punta Arenas in the extreme south. We have packed a security suitcase, and have brought all our data and collected material with us. We are afraid that it will be stolen while we are away from the house.

We already have an appointment scheduled for the afternoon when we arrive in Punta Arenas. It is really helpful now that we know so many people in the movement. It was no problem getting this appointment by phone, long-distance from Concepción. It is evident that it opens new doors for us: the fact that we at this moment have talked with so many important people from the movement gives other professionals the urge also to join the project. Also the people from the survivors' groups receive us with openness when they hear that we have visited people from their association's other places.

The people in the institution in Punta Arenas receive us in a friendly way, but they have not prepared any programme for us as we thought they would. We give our presentation of the project. We have given it many times before, but it is still valuable, although we now improvise a great deal. If we were to continue fieldwork for a longer period here, it would now be the time to rewrite it.

This town is so small that people know who the torturers are, and they still walk around the streets. The humiliation and the shame are lurking everywhere in the midst of the provincial atmosphere. The visibility and maybe also the massive, collective repression which was carried out here have brought about a sort of collective learned helplessness among those who stayed. On our first walks in the town we receive the emotional impact of life in a 'tortured town' – the terror continues in many ways with a visibility that we gradually also can register from our own level of fear. Very quickly we also become quite visible here.

9 February

We do some tourist work. In the bus together with other foreigners we feel how close we usually get to people and life here in Chile in contrast to the surface seen with the tourist's eye.

11 February

Representatives of the survivors' groups are eager to be interviewed. We realize that they consider us to be economic resource persons. It is difficult for us to explain that we are just researchers. We end up feeling guilty about taking their time 'in the name of science'. They want us to raise money for a foundation to help young people get an education, especially for children of ex-political prisoners.

12 February

We interview a woman representative of the ex-political prisoners. We find out that she has checked up on us before the interview. In the tortured town, our interviewees are careful to find out if we are on the right side. The woman tells us that while she was in prison someone came and said they were from the Red Cross, but they were not.

After the interview we learn that she has told another of our interviewees that she felt good talking to us. It was helpful to tell her story to some strangers who listened and could use it for a good purpose. We sense that we are taking her suffering with us when we leave.

During the evening, we interview another ex-political prisoner. The family of our interviewee seems disappointed that we do not stay after the interview and do some social talking. The professional closeness which develops during the interview can be misunderstood as personal friendship. After three interviews that day we are simply too tired to stay for tea and conversation. We do succeed in leaving in a proper way, however.

13 February

We end our visit in Punta Arenas by interviewing two therapists in the local institution. The contact is a bit formal. It is as though it does not develop. Are they a bit afraid of us? They know that we have been around interviewing their 'patients' from the survivors' groups. Are they afraid that we know something incriminating about them?

We close the field diary. While listening to our own voices from that time, we have become aware that we are not the same any longer. Researchers have an impact on the object of research. Likewise, the research process will have an impact on the subjects doing it.

NOTES

1. Two well-known torture houses in Santiago.
2. The PRAIS is the governmental mental health team for victims of the dictatorship. The programme is described in Chapter 11.

3

General Background:
Before and Around the Coup

At the eleventh hour

Queueing in front of the international police in Santiago airport requires patience. A Chilean couple are being checked; maybe they are returning from fifteen years of exile. We are not on the computer and are let in. The Chileans, however, are still negotiating when we see the sun rise for the second time this early November morning in 1989.

The presidential election is due in one month. Posters along the road to the centre of Santiago announce the different options: Hernán Büchi (Pinochet's former Minister of Finance); Francisco J. Errázuriz (an independent businessman) and Patricio Aylwin (Christian Democrat and candidate for the Concertation for Democracy). In a few weeks, a historical change may take place and bring an end to seventeen years of dictatorship. But at this moment, the situation is still full of uncertainty and anxiety.

Three years later we are drawing our map of the Chilean territory. During two periods of fieldwork, we have been living in the midst of a historical change. Aylwin took office in March 1990, but nearly three years later the former dictator is still the Commander-in-Chief of the armed forces.

The official story of those in power is changing. The new authorities have created space for the reconstruction of history, although there are some stories that still cannot be told. *Truth* and *justice* are the key words in the demands of the people in the human rights movement. However, in the 1988 plebiscite, 42% of Chileans voted 'yes' to continue the dictatorship of Pinochet. Chile is a divided nation – a 'nation of enemies' (Constable and Valenzuela, 1991). Those who benefited from the dictatorship still have difficulties in believing that the human rights violations really happened.

Constable and Valenzuela (1991, p. 10) comment on this:

> Often we were struck by the vast psychological and cultural gap between these two types of Chile – the winners and losers of the Pinochet years. The coup had frozen society at a point of great trauma and divisiveness, and all sectors – right and left, rich and poor, military and civilians – remained locked within separate microcosms, nursing their mutual fears and private dreams. Chile had become a nation of enemies.

CHILE BEFORE 11 SEPTEMBER 1973: FROM COLUMBUS TO ALLENDE

Vignettes

Don Eusebio, the Mapuche chief, 1992

'When *we* discovered Columbus and his men, it was already too late!' Don Eusebio, an old Mapuche Indian, pushes the military cap back and wipes his old sunburned face. We are close to the 500th anniversary of the arrival of Columbus in South America. Don Eusebio's wife is serving *maté* (herbal tea) and a boiled egg while he tells us his version of history, here in the cottage in Chol. He continues:

> The dictatorship did not change things much for us – the Mapuche. The main difference was that this time, with Pinochet, the foreigners [that is, the non-Mapuche] were also hit by the repression. First our people were repressed by the Spaniards, then by the Englishmen, followed by the North American gringos, and then the 'Pinochistas' took over. All of them want to take our land. We have been repressed since the days of Columbus, it has become part of our life.

From O'Higgins to Arica

'Los Heroes' ('The heroes')

The liberation from the Spanish colonization was initiated by armies based in Argentina. From there, General San Martin ordered Bernardo O'Higgins to liberate Chile from the Spanish. Later, he became the first president ('Director Supremo') of the Chilean nation.

On the maps of most Chilean towns today, the military touch is evident: a central square called Plaza de Armas and streets named after the military heroes – O'Higgins, San Martin and Cochrane. In wars with its neighbouring countries, Chile extended its territory. Most battles and victories seem to have their own memorial days, location and parades.

The parade in Arica

In 1991, we visited the former concentration camp of Pisagua and carried out some moving interviews with members of the camp's survivors' group: ex-political prisoners and relatives of the disappeared and executed. We listened to terrible stories about death, torture and disappearances. We felt like visitors to Hades and had an urgent need to get out of this world of evil.

On the way to the peaceful resort town of Arica, we shared our mutual astonishment: How could they get away with it? Why did people let it happen? How were they able to accept that the military and the police continued in their former positions, while the survivors of human rights violations were still kept out of jobs – stigmatized by the fact that they had been prisoners in the Pisagua camp? What did they think on both sides when they met today in the supermarket?

On this Sunday, Arica had one of its great celebration days. We joined the crowd: thousands of people in their best clothes were standing in the burning sun. Small boys wore sailors' blouses and small caps with 'I love the Navy' in the midst of a world of ice creams, cokes, beers and small Chilean flags.

At last, the parade started and the crowd was shouting with joy and waving their flags. The peak experience was the heavily armed police (the *carabiñeros*) in Nazi-like uniforms. They went by in a goose-step march, and everybody clapped enthusiastically. Our image of black and white, good and evil, was shaken. The distance from the statue of the liberator, O'Higgins, on the local Plaza de Armas, to the world of Pinochet was not as far as we had expected.

One Map of the Chilean Territory: A Journey North, South, East and West

Entering the Chilean world is not that easy with the Andean 'Cordillera' to the east, the Pacific Ocean to the west, the Atacama desert to the north and the icy Antarctic to the south. Foreigners sometimes do cross 'La Cordillera', but a certain isolation is part of Chilean history, nationalism and tradition.

In some of the towns we visited, people felt that they lived on an island. Each town, in consequence, has its own specific history and tradition, and such differences were also mirrored in the political repression after the military coup in 1973. Local variations were typical, especially in the 'first wave' from September to December 1973.

Nearly half of the approximately 12 million inhabitants live in the metropolitan area of the capital, Santiago. During our fieldwork, we also observed significant differences between daily life in the metropolitan and provincial areas. There was a long distance between Santiago and even some of the larger towns such as Concepción/Talcahuáno, Valparaíso, Valdivia, Temuco, Iqique and Punta Arenas (sometimes in kilometres, sometimes in culture). Also among those major provincial towns there were marked differences.

Iquique in the north is a fishing town at the edge of the Atacama desert, and it has many similarities to the more Indian-dominated cultures of Bolivia and Peru. It is located close to the old mining towns. A five-hour drive from Iquique through the desert will bring us to the natural jail and former concentration camp of *Pisagua*.

When we travel south from Iquique along the Pacific coast through the cities of *Antofagasta, Coquimbo* and *La Serena,* the desert disappears and we meet the fertile valleys in the metropolitan area, where vineyards and agriculture set the scene of a rich, green and beautiful country.

Further on to the capital, *Santiago*: a southern European touch gives this capital a more familiar atmosphere than expected. It is hot, polluted and poor in its central parts, but rich and green in suburban sectors like Providencia and Las Condes.

In the centre of Santiago, on the Plaza de Armas close to the Cathedral, we find the Vicarage of Solidarity, and a short walk from the main street, the Alameda, brings us to the headquarters of the Social Aid Foundation of Christian Churches (FASIC): the Vicarage and FASIC were two of the first organizations to lead the fight for human rights and mental health after the coup.

Dispersed in older villas in the Providencia area we find the other non-governmental organization (NGO) human rights and mental health centres which were created later. To the south and west the enormous suburbs will end up in extremely poor shanty towns – among these La Victoria.

A one-hour drive to the west will bring us to *Valparaíso*, where the parliament is located, and if we follow the coastline we will meet the resort town of *Viña del Mar* and more humble places like the village of *Isla Negra,* where the summer residence of the national poet Pablo Neruda is a symbolic memorial of the resistance.

Here, 2,000 kilometres from the northern border, we can still travel 2,000 more kilometres south. On our way towards the south we will pass the landowners' large haciendas. If we go slightly west we will end up in *Concepción*, with the university in which the MIR (the Revolutionary Movement of the Left) originated. We will meet *Talcahuáno,* with its harbour from which coal and fish are exported, and with the

Navy peacefully stationed at the delta of the Bío-Bío river. From Talcahuáno we have a view of the 'naval' *Quiriquina Island*, once the site of a concentration camp.

A bit further south, along the Coal Coast, we will meet the polluted coal mine towns, for example *Coronel* and *Lota*, where Sebastián Acevedo lived until he burned himself in front of the cathedral in Concepción. Later, this act gave the name to the Sebastián Acevedo Movement Against Torture, which from 1983 played an active and important role in demonstrations against torture and other human rights violations.

From here, we pass the invisible borders to the land of the Mapuche. This ethnic minority is, today, concentrated in the IX Region, in which *Temuco* is the most important town. The markets of the Mapuche, the large shanty towns (such as El Progreso) and the ox-carts set the scene. Many Mapuche live in villages like *Chol*, where we met Don Eusebio.

Today, close to 1 million people identify themselves as Mapuches. Often their number is underestimated in national statistics. Some 90 per cent of the Mapuche have an income below the UN poverty line, and close to one-fifth of the poor people in Chile are, in fact, Mapuche (close to 5 million Chileans live below the UN poverty line).

When we go further south, we pass through the Lake Region. Here, a German influence is noticeable. Many immigrants came here in the nineteenth century, and this is evident in towns such as *Valdivia*.

In our interviews, another German influence was also felt. We heard about Germans in the role of professional helpers in the development of the concentration camp structures. The 'German republic of Dignidad colony' near *Parral* is still not open to or safe for travellers, and especially not for human rights researchers.

During the dictatorship, there was a close connection between the inhabitants of the heavily guarded colony and the secret police – or the DINA – as reported by the Commission of Truth and Reconciliation (1992). In 1991 blurred newspaper photos showed prominent members of the regime as honoured guests in the colony.

From the town of *Puerto Montt* near the beautiful island of *Chiloé* we still have to travel 1,000 kilometres more to the south to arrive in *Punta Arenas* at the Magellan Straits. Among the inhabitants here are a large number of military people due to the strategic importance of this place. The town has remnants of former prosperity – from the time before the Panama Canal, when ships had to pass through the Magellan Straits to reach the western coasts of North and South America.

Although 'only' five people were killed in Punta Arenas during the first months of repression, approximately one thousand people were detained and tortured (Commission of Truth and Reconciliation, 1992, p. 58). From Punta Arenas, one can nearly catch a glimpse of *Dawson Island*, where another concentration camp was located. Here, the high-ranking Allende people were imprisoned to 'strengthen their health and minds in the fresh air', as one of our informants told us.

Four Important Chilean Cultures

The military culture – before the coup

Prussian military culture was always an important inspiration for the Chilean armed forces. However, the Germanic-inspired discipline and hierarchy was mixed up with Chilean nationalism. The culture of the armed forces also involved a powerful separation between civilian and military worlds. In spite of this, until the coup, the Chilean democratic tradition was quite strong and differed from the widespread military dictatorships in neighbouring countries (Constable and Valenzuela, 1991).

A look through the window into the military barracks might add to our understanding of military thinking, which was later extended to military rule and dictatorship. We might understand why a man like Augusto Pinochet could pass through the military hierarchy and become the 'Supreme Chief of the Nation' and how he was able to stay in power through a manoeuvre based on an intimate knowledge about individuals and rules of military hierarchy.

'I remember Augusto from school. He was not very bright, I always wondered how he was able to climb up through the military system,' an old human rights activist told us. Nevertheless, through these activities Pinochet was able to change his position step by step from a four-person junta, where all were equal, into a leadership where he was senior and without serious competition from any other military officials. Potential rivals were outmanoeuvred by different tactics.

Vertical obedience, disrespect of civilians – especially of politicians – suspiciousness against the academic world, and a massive, paranoia-like disgust of communists and the 'reds' were basic elements in the military spirit, and – we may surmise – in the minds of Pinochet and his aides (Constable and Valenzuela, 1991).

The military culture could be described according to different frames of reference. Theories and concepts from sociology, anthropology and political science would all be relevant. However, one could also analyse the military spirit according to a psychological frame of reference.

Maybe this perspective could add to our understanding of the psychological warfare of state terrorism.

Concepts of borderline pathology seem applicable to the meanings and rationality of the military culture; that is, some of the characteristics of Chilean state terrorism resemble a 'borderline position' (Kernberg et al., 1989). For example:

- The mechanism of *splitting*, by which the world is perceived in its extremes: as either black or white, good or evil.

- The *paranoid tendency*, which makes all opponents resemble communists, terrorists or just 'reds'.

- *Projective defence mechanisms*, which place the blame on everybody else but oneself. This can develop into a dissociation which allows disagreeable events and realities to be 'forgotten' or denied.

- The *narcissistic aspect*, which is characterized by sudden switches between omnipotence and extreme vulnerability. The constant evaluation which is part of the hierarchical structure of the military implies the threat of suddenly being turned down by inferior up-comers.

- The *sado-masochistic position*, in which humiliating others and being humiliated yourself is an interdependent source of satisfaction. In the military, where it is necessary to lick upwards and spit downwards, this position is obvious.

Although we find the borderline position to be a useful model for the understanding of the collective repressive strategies, we have no intention of extending this perspective to an individual labelling of those in power. However, the psychology of the collective structure has made a blueprint on the individual perpetrators. This military culture has developed other meanings of the term 'normality' than the one which, for example, is expressed in the UN World Declaration of Human Rights. In this culture, people could be pushed into roles in which they acted as psychopaths (seen from a 'usual' perspective), but in which they – from their own military perspective – acted as heroes.

The similarity to a 'narcissistic position of omnipotence' is noteworthy when General Pinochet sees himself in a 'Jesus-like' position: '*I was not looking for this job. Destiny gave it to me*,'[1] and later, when he had received the 'NO!' from the 1988 plebiscite: '*Don't forget that in the history of the world, there was a plebiscite, in which Christ and Barabbas were being judged, and the people chose Barabbas.*'[2]

While the Army culture gave birth to the repression, the cultures of the *church* and the *political parties* shared a commitment to a democratic tradition. However, they also shared a deep inner dilemma – a split between a section that defended human rights and a section that supported the use of violence.

The church and ambivalence

The Catholic church contained (and still contains) a wide spectrum: it is the church of the rich, of the landowners and the businessmen, of the military, and of its former 'Supreme Chief of the Nation'. However, it is also the church of the poor. An internal conflict in the church has also been waged between a left-wing group of priests, who were (and are) inspired by liberation theology, and the right-wing, who defend ultra-conservative Catholic ideals (Constable and Valenzuela, 1991).

The priests who supported liberation theology wanted the church to take a more active stand in theory as well as in daily practice in favour of the poor: 'I'm sure that the future and the truth is found in the life of the poor,' said one of our interviewees, a former priest who is now working with NGO educational programmes in the shanty towns. The priests should leave the churches, their privileged life, and go out into the shanty towns to live with the poor, and be their advocates against social and political discrimination and violations of human rights. As one priest told us:

> I have been a professor of ethics at the university since the beginning of 1950. I wanted to join the poor people and I got leave from the university and lived in Concepción for two years. Here I lived as a construction worker when the coup started. I belonged to the left wing of the church. We did not have real problems with the hierarchy, but we were always pressing them to be more committed to the people – to defend the poorest people. In general the church hierarchy is far away from the people. We thought that the church should be constructed not from the top down but from the bottom up. So we tried to learn about the real situation of simple people and how the Gospel should be given to them. To me it was a challenge, intellectually, to find out if it makes a difference whether you teach in social and moral matters based on books or on personal experiences. I think it is not the same to talk about truth and to make truth in your own life – it is important to be consistent as a professional teacher and as a human being.

This attitude was shared by some of the Protestant churches also, for example by the Methodists, who were actively involved in social aid programmes.

Seen in retrospect, this wide spectrum of the Catholic church seems to be very important. The church was important to General Pinochet in his need to legitimize the regime. He needed the church to convince the population about his views and versions of the truth. The respect for church authorities, however, also made it possible for the church to shelter the first organized mental health support of victims. The social engagement from the liberation theologians and many Protestant organizations, and the traditional confidence offered the priests as solidary advocates of the poor, created a useful network for the establishment of the resistance from the very beginning of the repressive period.

Thus, ambivalence was a central factor in the position of the church. The ability to contain this ambivalence was a powerful factor in the creation of a shelter for the resistance.

From the barracks of Humberstone to La Moneda palace: some elements of the left-wing culture

The Spanish conquerors came to Chile to search for gold. According to myth, one of the commanders, Pedro de Valdivia, was killed by the Mapuche, who poured red-hot gold down his throat. In fact, the mines in the north were rich not in gold, but in copper and nitrate. The wealth was, however, mainly poured into the pockets of foreigners: the Spanish, the English and the North Americans.

The massive concentration of poor labourers in the barracks of towns such as Humberstone in the north was an excellent base for the development of organizational structures. A similar tradition grew out of the coal mining areas in the southern and western parts of the country. As Manuel told us:

> I was born in a miner's family in one of the barracks towns near Humberstone in 1944. We lived under very poor conditions and my father was engaged in the Communist Party. To me, independence was always a strong theme, I wanted to become a fisherman, and from my adolescence I was a member of the communist youth groups.

In 1973 Manuel was arrested as a board member of the fishermen's trade union and sent to the Pisagua concentration camp.

In 1948, twenty-five years before, the young Captain Pinochet was the commander of the Pisagua camp, already in use at that time. The Communist Party was outlawed in 1948 and more than four hundred party activists were banished.

Manuel was held for some months in Pisagua, was exposed to torture and passed through several prisons in Chile before he was sent into exile. Now, he and his family have returned. He is without any job due to his old 'criminal records' as a prisoner in Pisagua.

We accompanied him during his first visit to Pisagua since then. On our way back from this strange location, we followed the tracks back through the desert and passed the ghost town of Humberstone, where rusty, abandoned machines, locomotives and tools radiated feelings of emptiness and an impression of something lost. The winners took it all.

Another important element in the development of the strong socialist organizations were the confrontations between the landowners and their employees. A massive migration went from the countryside to the larger towns in search of better living conditions. Here, new concentrations of poor people grew up. These people lived under sometimes very deteriorating conditions in a constant struggle for survival.

Still another group were the academics to whom the Marxist ideology became a strong alternative during the fifties and the sixties. The revolution in Cuba was a key event, and Fidel Castro and Che Guevara were ideological heroes for the students and intellectuals in their demand for an ideal and equal society. There was also a general acceptance of the necessity of the armed revolutionary struggle in order to reach this goal (Constable and Valenzuela, 1991).

Many young people were drawn towards these ideals and the student revolts in Europe and North America also reached Chile. Thousands of young people were engaged in the Popular Unity (Unidad Popular) movement with the doctor Salvador Allende as their most outspoken leader.

At the edges of this front, the more revolutionary groups were found. During the period before the coup, and later on, during the development of the resistance against the dictatorship, the left-wing parties were constantly confronted with their two options: Allende's peaceful 'third way to socialism' and the more revolutionary – and armed – strategies of other groupings.

The left-wing position also contained another inner conflict (which is found in most socialist movements): the academics and the students on one side, and the labourers and the poor on the other. To the military leaders, however, academic socialist leaders such as Salvador Allende, Carlos Altamirano, Clodomiro Almeyda and Orlando Letelier personified their strongest aversions: they were 'communists', 'academics', 'politicians' and 'civilians' – all in one (Constable and Valenzuela, 1991).

An important element related to the mental health area was a strong Chilean tradition for social and preventive health care. Most doctors and public as well as mental health workers felt that work in the shanty towns was a natural element in their tradition. This tradition was not only followed by left-wing professionals and students. As one psychiatrist told us:

> The medical tradition in Chile is social-medical, directed at the health problems of the majority of the Chilean people, a poor majority in a poor country. This is an old tradition shared by physicians from the left, to the centre, to the right.
>
> A doctor such as Hernán Alessandri, son of the former president and brother of another president, was a right-wing sympathizer. He and others developed this model which was influenced by a humanitarian Christian thinking. At that time, the government put much emphasis on problems of health and education in the shanty towns. This was the dominant model until 1973.
>
> In 1952, a law was passed which was proposed by Salvador Allende, who, at that time, was Minister of Health. Through this law a National Health Service was established. It was an important year for me, because this was the year in which I started working as a physician. Medical doctors and students had jobs in this service with salaries which were not high, but we were able to live from them. It was a kind of philosophy that the doctors should assist those who needed help most badly, and many good programmes were initiated. I think it was an important development that doctors started their careers by working in the shanty towns for two or three years as general practitioners and in cross-disciplinary teams. My interest in social-psychiatric problems developed from this work, in which alcoholism was the most important problem.

New collaborative structures were created and in some shanty towns very well organized communes developed. Such structures were later of great importance as environments in which people who were persecuted by the regime could hide. From this perspective, politically oriented socialist ideology and liberation theology obviously shared many views.

The Christian Democrats and the right-wing culture

A political alliance between the leftists, the radicals and the right-wing parties was, for decades, a core element in Chilean democratic tradition (Constable and Valenzuela, 1991). Through compromises and negotiations it was possible to rule the country without having to lean on military power. As many of our interviewees told us:

> We were (and are) the 'Englishmen of Latin America'; that is why the dictatorship was such a shock to all of us. We just could not believe that it happened here in our country. In politics people were debating, yelling at each other and then went and had a glass of wine together.

When the Christian Democrats arrived on the political scene, they were seen by the US government as the democratic alternative to the threat of one more Marxist revolution in Latin America. A Christian Democratic President, Eduardo Frei, was the central figure in the sixties (while the socialist leader, Salvador Allende, was Chairman of the Senate).

But in the 1970 election, the Christian Democratic Party and the Radical Party could not reach an agreement about a mutual candidate. In a three-candidate contest Allende had 38% of the votes in his fourth run for the presidency. Big efforts politically and economically were made by the US administration and the CIA to support the continued presidency of Eduardo Frei, and, later on, in attempts to keep Allende out of the presidential office (Constable and Valenzuela, 1991).

The National Security Advisor in the Nixon administration, Henry Kissinger, is cited as making the following remark:

> I don't see why we need to stand idly and watch a country go communist due to the irresponsibility of its own people.[3]

The efforts to foment a military coup did not succeed in 1970 and Allende took office on schedule.

During the presidency of Allende, similar interventions from the USA helped produce economic and political chaos. These initiatives, combined with Allende's direct attacks on the economic establishment, the take-overs of industries and land, the attempts to nationalize the copper, tin and coal mines (involving large international economic interests), set the scene for dissatisfaction, strikes and pleas to the Chilean military to intervene and bring back law and order (Constable and Valenzuela, 1991).

Armed revolutionary groups like the MIR and radical socialist political orators gave further support to fear of a Cuba-like revolution. Gradually, parallel right-wing groups of para-military organizations like Fatherland and Liberty (Patria y Libertad) developed, and the conservative side of the political spectrum became divided.

Some politicians wanted to use democratic and peaceful negotiations, but others wanted to employ the armed forces to change the political situation. Some even wanted to carry out their own armed activities and acts of provocation.

Finally, in 1973, a majority of politicians – even the Christian Democrats – agreed to ask the armed forces to take over. However, later, the Christian Democrats were the only party on the right to take a clear stand against the violations of human rights committed by the armed forces, once these became known.

Similar to the Catholic church, the Christian Democrats contained a wide spectrum of views, including businessmen, lawyers and conservative Catholics, along with Christian leftists and those inspired by liberation theology.

On the way back towards democracy, this mid-position and spectrum was an important element in the creation of a platform on which socialists, human rights organizations and the Christian Democrats could organize an alternative 'NO!' to Pinochet in the 1988 plebiscite (Constable and Valenzuela, 1991).

The ultra right-wing parties accepted and supported the military take-over, and even today these parties act as an opposition in favour of the former regime, with what some perceive to be a lack of distance from its methods.

At the Eleventh Hour

In early September 1973 many people expected a coup to come. The church called for a dialogue between Allende and the new Christian Democratic leader, Patricio Aylwin, in the hope of establishing a compromise which could save the government. But it was too late. While the politicians talked, the armed forces took action.

NOTES

1. *Newsweek*, 19 March 1984, cited in Constable and Valenzuela, 1991, p. 64.
2. *La Epoca*, 26 October 1988, cited in ibid., p. 296.
3. *New York Times*, 11 September 1974, cited in ibid., p. 23.

4

Historical Background:
The Coup and What Followed

'Because of my friend who is in prison...'

THE DAY OF THE COUP AND THE FIRST MONTHS OF REPRESSION

11 September 1973

At noon two jets fired their first rockets into the presidential palace, La Moneda. A few hours earlier, Salvador Allende had given his last speech by telephone to a local radio station:

> They have the strength; they can subjugate us, but they cannot halt social processes by either crime or force. History is ours, and the people make it. (cited in Constable and Valenzuela, 1991, p. 16)

Allende was found with his head demolished by machine-gun fire. The death of Allende remained an important issue for years. His companions insisted that he died fighting, while his detractors insisted that it was the suicide of a coward.

To the surprise of the military, the resistance had been much weaker than expected. Years later, in 1980, Pinochet admitted this, although his conclusion was that they 'fled like rats when it came to pass'.[1]

Late in the afternoon, the armed forces had taken total control and a 24-hour curfew was declared. The same evening the four-man junta took over 'to restore the institutional structure and character of Chile'. During the next days, the junta statements encompassed rhetoric like:

- 'It is a moral duty to overthrow an illegitimate government.'
- 'This is not a military coup, but a military movement which will salvage the country.'

- 'There will be no victors or vanquished, only Chileans united in the brotherly task of rebuilding the nation.'

On 12 September, the junta declared a state of siege, and one week later the whole country was declared an emergency zone. Mass raids continued day after day and close to 45,000 people were held for interrogation. More than 7,000 were herded into the National Stadium in Santiago. The radios were broadcasting lists of political figures who should report for interrogation. The most common impulse was to obey.[2]

11 September – From the Other Side

On the day of 11 September, most doctors in the hospitals were on strike. Those on duty that day were primarily those who supported Allende and who, therefore, refused to go on strike. Due to the curfew, doctors who were in the hospital when the coup began had to remain there for three days. As one female psychiatrist told us:

> A few of us stayed there the whole time. We thought that victims, wounded people would arrive, but nothing happened. Well of course the military arrived and searched all of the hospital. When they lifted the curfew every one of us went off to find out what had happened to the rest, to our family, to our friends. To find out who needed help, take care of security cases, transfer people. We practically kept on by doing this all the rest of September and October.

Other professionals, such as psychologists and social workers, heard the news of the coup on the radio in the morning and many stayed home. When they returned to their places of work, they found out that they had been dismissed. A psychologist who worked in a psychiatric clinic for children told us:

> I went to the hospital to work like every other day, in spite of all we had heard, and when I arrived at the hospital, I saw colleagues whom we considered to be our friends arrive in military clothes. The situation was terribly confused. We sat in a group together and heard Allende's last speech on the radio and we did not know what to do. People did not go home, we did not know whether to go home or to stay, or if this situation meant a complete rupture. In reality we were in a state of terrible shock. It was strange, but at the same time the people at the hospital who were connected with the military also organized themselves, and our clinic – the psychiatric service of the hospital – was accused of having hidden arms and of having a political function. It was a psychiatric clinic for children. We saw children and nothing more.

They accused people who worked there of being terrorists, communists and of being highly dangerous people. Before the curfew was imposed we went home without knowing what would happen to us. This we found out when the curfew was lifted again, because on the lattice entrance gates of the hospital there had been put up lists with names of people. There was an A-list, a B-list and a C-list. The A-list contained names of employees of the hospital who had the confidence of the new regime. The B-list contained the names of the employees towards whom they were doubtful. And the C-list contained the names of the employees who were terrorists and very dangerous. Well I was on the C-list.... The clinic was closed. This meant I could not work any longer, and the same happened at the university where I had a teaching post. It also happened to my husband. We had a feeling of complete defenceless-ness. After a month we succeeded in getting away into exile in Europe.

Many were arrested in their homes on the day of the coup. Among those were several doctors and other mental health care professionals.

The Initial Stages of Repression

The highest-ranking military officer on each location was assigned to be the supreme political, governmental and administrative authority. The governor (*intendente*) of each province was appointed as chief of the emergency zone and also to the post of military judge. He held the power to ratify death sentences which had been dictated by war tribunals. The secret police, the DINA (Dirección de Intelligencia Nacional), was organized in November 1973 and it had an important role in the repression.

Detention and torture

Based on the report from the Commission of Truth and Reconciliation (1992) (in Chile, called the 'Rettig Report' ['Informe Rettig'] after the chairing judge), some of the initial repressive strategies of power were as follows:

- Edicts requiring named persons to present themselves before military authorities. After doing so, they were arrested.

- Specific searches for a person in his or her house, his place of work or on the streets.

- Round-ups in rural areas and searches in large cities.

The arrests were carried out by patrols of uniformed police (*carabiñeros*), sometimes assisted by members of the secret police in plainclothes and civilians. Regiments, police stations and police barracks were used as concentration camps (for example, Pisagua, near Iquique in the north, Tejas Verdes in San Antonio, Quiriquina Island near Concepción and Dawson Island in the south of the Magellan Straits). Other places of detention were ships (*Esmeralda* and *Lebu*) and sports stadiums (for example, the National Stadium and Stadium of Chile in Santiago and the stadium in Concepción).

The Commission Report names some principal torture places and concludes:

> The commission, in conscience, concludes that the accusations which are the source of the before-mentioned descriptions [that is, of torture methods and places] have not been devalued or mitigated by any of those – from the other side – who should also know the same facts. The aggregate of facts gathered, due to their huge number of virtual uniformity, seems to compose an undeniable reality of torture which, as atonement and example, cannot remain secret or forgotten. (Commission of Truth and Reconciliation, 1992, p. 47)

The initial deaths and disappearances

The Commission Report records the deaths and the disappeared. The official record from 11 September to 31 December 1973 showed 1,213 deaths due to government agents. The distribution of deaths across the country was quite varied (see Table 4.1). The territories of most severe repression were the metropolitan area (40% of deaths) and the Concepción area (17%).

It does, of course, give us a false impression of the violations in this period if we only count the deaths. For example, the Commission Report has only recorded five deaths in the XII Region of Magellanes and Chilean Antarctica. Four were executed and one died due to excessive use of force. The Commission Report comments, however, that

> in the Magellanes region, torture was practised regularly and it is estimated that approximately 1,000 persons were detained and subjected to this treatment in 1973. But counting torture is outside the aim of the commission. (p. 58)

The Initial Reactions to Human Rights Violations

The situation in this initial period elicited practically no public criticism in Chile. This absence of reaction can be explained by several factors: fear, surprise or ignorance about what was happening. Even

Table 4.1   Deaths produced by violations of human rights (HumRight) and by political violence (PolViol), regional data

Region	HumRight	PolViol	Total	%
Metropolitan (Santiago area)	445	48	493	(40.5)
Tarapaca (Iquique area)	35	0	35	(3)
Antofagasta	71	0	71	(6)
Atacama	19	0	19	(1.5)
Coquimbo	22	0	22	(2)
Valparaíso	38	3	41	(3.5)
Lib. B. O'Higgins (Rancagua area)	8	0	8	(1)
Maule (Linares area)	59	1	60	(5)
Bío-Bío (Conceptión area)	206	2	208	(17)
La Araucaniá (Temuco area)	112	1	113	(9)
Los Lagos (Osorno area)	126	2	128	(10.5)
Aisen Gen. Ibanez (Coihaique area)	10	0	10	(1)
Magellanes (Punta Arenas area)	5	0	5	(0.5)
Total	1,156	57	1,213	(100)

Source: Commission of Truth and Reconciliation, 1992, p. 30.

when the facts later became known, vast sectors of public opinion permitted, tolerated or even supported the violations of human rights. To this, the Commission Report says:

> There did not exist in our country the profound conviction that the human rights of all persons must be respected ... it is not our role to determine the moral responsibility which society as a whole might have as a consequence

of its lack of a timely and strong reaction to what was taking place. We believe, nevertheless, that what occurred must make every Chilean reflect on the serious omission incurred. (p. 57)

Among the leaders of the new regime, there was no self-criticism. The press was under absolute governmental control and the communications media – for example, the major newspaper *El Mercurio* – supported the regime strongly and without any criticism. Left-wing political parties were declared illegitimate (Decree Law 77, 1973) and were not able to organize a response.

The Christian Democrats reacted in February 1974 with a statement published abroad. No reactions were given from the right-wing parties in this period. The family members of the victims had, at this time, not begun to organize and coordinate their efforts. Organizations such as the trade unions and students' organizations were not permitted to publish any type of criticism.

Outside Chile, some reactions were published from international organizations. Amnesty International and the International Commission of Jurists requested UN intervention on 15 September 1973 in view of the threats to life in Chile.

Inside Chile, the only significant resistance came from the churches and the two critical structures of psychological resistance developed already in these very first months after the coup: the National Committee for Refugees and the Committee for Peace.

The Resistance: The Development of Mental Health Organizations

Mental health under state terrorism

When a dictatorial system seizes power, this affects all the institutions of the country, no matter whether they are governmental or non-governmental. Therefore, the situation will also influence the institutions that normally help people with psychological or psychiatric problems. It will become difficult or even impossible to find a supportive institutional context where victims of the dictatorship can receive treatment. Therapists in the existing institutions may commit an act of treason if they help people who are defined as enemies of the regime. It therefore becomes necessary to create new institutional settings – maybe in the form of underground networks – to help victims.

The particular historical circumstances of how such networks or institutions are built up under state terrorism will, of course, vary from country to country. We do, however, find it important to show how a system of therapeutic assistance is gradually born in the midst of chaos. Before therapy can even begin, there must be a setting for it.

The National Committee for Refugees and the Committee for Peace

In the days following the coup, hundreds of people approached the churches to ask for help. Most of the priests had tried to do everything possible, but the task was so great that their efforts were inadequate. Therefore they decided to coordinate their work.

The Catholic Archbishop of Santiago in conjunction with Protestant and Jewish leaders established two committees: the National Committee for Refugees (Comité Nacional de Refugiados) and the Committee for Peace (Comité por la Paz).

In the beginning the primary purpose of the *National Committee for Refugees* was to protect the lives of Allende supporters – from Chile and other Latin American countries – and offer legal assistance to those who were persecuted by the regime. The primary purpose of the *Committee for Peace* was to help Chileans who, as a consequence of the coup, had ended up in a difficult economic or personal situation. Between September and November 1973, the government detained ten of the members of the Committee for Peace.

The word of the existence of the committees spread quickly and an increasing number of people began arriving with their burdens of anxiety and uncertainty. They were looking for their relatives: husbands who had been arrested during the night, sons or daughters who had disappeared. Everyone thought that this situation would only be transitory.

Among the people who worked in the committees were priests, lawyers and social workers, and every day they thought that this was their last day of work. They worked as volunteers and some of their most important practical tasks were to help look for people who had disappeared, to identify corpses and to go to funerals.

As one lawyer who had worked with the Committee for Peace told us – visibly moved:

> The military coup was a traumatic experience for me. I remember sitting at a small, wobbly table with a typewriter and with a queue of people which was so long that I could not see where it ended, a waiting-line of people that continued around the corner. I was manufacturing series of *habeas corpus* and trying to find time, afterwards, to go to the court and present the many

habeas corpus. It was a horrible experience, but it is strange, because those times were very influenced by the urgency of the situation. I had to make those *habeas corpus*, and I had to assist all the people who were waiting there – together with my lawyer comrades. Therefore, I did not have much time to think about the meaning of all this, and I had to react, I had to act towards all this.

The work continued as the requirements grew, and the lawyers in the committees began to take on the defence of prisoners in front of the war tribunals (*consejos de guerra*). A social worker told us that the best she could do was to give people space to pour out their anxiety. But at the same time she had the feeling that the situation was a complete horror. It was in every way a new experience for the professionals who worked for the committees. They had to build up a practice relying completely on their own resources in an attempt to confront the realities of the dictatorship.

In this type of emergency situation, there seemed to be a strong mutual support among the professionals. The work was innovative and flexible, and there was a great effort to find allied agencies to network with. Trustworthy people were contacted and asked to take care of emergency cases on a voluntary basis. The committees needed help from doctors for medical as well as psychiatric assistance. A female psychiatrist told us about how she got involved:

There was a group of psychiatrists who had a private clinic. They were members of a leftist party, now illegal, and all of them except one had sought asylum in foreign embassies. As I had been dismissed from my job at the hospital, they asked me if I would join their work in the clinic. Patients were sent anonymously to this place, without any record but with a letter of identification from which we knew that they were sent by the Committee. In the beginning they sent family members of prisoners, of people who had disappeared or of people who had been murdered. At the same time comrades who had been wounded in confrontations with the military began to come, and they needed medical attention. Later on people who had been imprisoned began to come, a good percentage with panic reactions. I remember the case of an ex-prisoner who had been almost mutilated and his panic reaction was so enormous that he wanted to shoot the first soldier he met so that the military would kill him. So what I did was to get him in at an embassy – so the treatment, if we can call it that, the therapy, consisted in getting him into a European embassy. We did this with many cases because we were not able to keep them or treat them. Some of them returned to their normal life in Chile later on when they felt better, others left the country to go into refuge.

Emergency aid

Aid during the first chaotic months developed out of emergency needs. Only two major structures, the churches and the international community, had any possibility of giving assistance to the resistance. Thus, regardless of their ambivalence towards the new regime, the churches took on a role as guardian spirits of this work. Somehow the regime accepted these activities. Although some of the mental health work was clandestine, it was not unknown to the military.

One of the most important roles of the international community was to exert pressure on the regime by the publication of information about the reality in Chile. Another was to shelter refugees in the embassies and assist people in seeking asylum and getting safely out of the country. Many stories are told about embassy cars being used as transportation to international airplanes – with an escort of DINA cars to monitor the process. Some ambassadors also supported the search for the disappeared people.

THE DINA PERIOD, 1974–77

The Repressive Structures

The DINA

The principal intelligence service in charge of political repression during the 1974–77 period was the DINA. The organization was formally created on 18 June 1974 (Decree Law no. 521)

> to produce the intelligence necessary to formulate policies and planning and to adopt measures to procure the safeguarding of national security and development of the country. (Commission of Truth and Reconciliation, 1992, p. 26)

Secretly, the DINA had also been given the authority to arrest suspects and to demand collaboration from all public agencies. In practice, the organization, which was headed by Colonel Manuel Contreras Sepúlveda, was already functioning from the autumn of 1973. From their barracks in Tejas Verdes, the several hundred selected DINA agents participated in a crusade against Marxism with permission to carry out any order they received.

In Tejas Verdes, they learned to spy, to deceive and to kidnap, to interrogate and torture, and to do what was needed to break down any resisting opponent. Their secret symbol was a clenched, armoured fist (Constable and Valenzuela, 1991). The international supervision which they received during the programme makes it more understandable why rather similar torture strategies are used across cultures.

The DINA on the international scene

Manuel Contreras created a web of import–export firms to fund his operations. He planned to create an international political network (the Condor plan) and developed ties to fascist terrorist groups in Italy, Argentina and Brazil, and exiled groups from Cuba based in Miami, Florida (Constable and Valenzuela, 1991, pp. 102–5).

General Carlos Prats and his wife were assassinated in Buenos Aires. The Christian Democrat politician Bernardo Leighton was shot in Rome. Although natural targets for the Chilean intelligence service, no hard evidence of the involvement of the DINA was found. A final blow occurred in Washington, DC, when Orlando Letelier (a former foreign minister and ambassador to the United States for the Allende government) and his secretary were murdered.

The investigations discovered the involvement of the DINA and in August 1977 Manuel Contreras had to leave his position (although in fact was promoted to general) and the DINA organization was dissolved and replaced by the CNI (Central Nacional de Informaciones).

Additional intelligence services

The Commission Report refers to the existence of a network of different intelligence services:

The Joint Command

The Joint Command operated from the end of 1975 to the end of 1976. The establishment of this command can be interpreted as a protest against the unchecked operations of the DINA. Participants were people from the intelligence of the armed forces: from the DIFA (the Air Force), the DICAR (the armed police), the SIN (the Navy) and the DINE (the Army). The command operated primarily in Santiago and its primary aim was the repression of the Communist Party.

Intelligence services of the armed forces

The Air Force

The SIFA (1974–75), and from 1975 the DIFA (the Intelligence Directorate of the Air Forces) were primarily engaged in the repression against the socialist party – the MIR.

The armed police

The SICAR was replaced by the DICAR in 1974. Its specific task was to be in charge of detention. The organization had sophisticated surveillance equipment.

The Navy

The SIN operated in the Valparaíso area in collaboration with the DINA in the persecution of the MIR organization; and in the Concepción area the SIRE, a regional intelligence service, was involved in a similar fight against the MIR.

The intelligence community

This was an organization with the purpose of centralizing the administrative aspects of intelligence work – such as, for example, the exchange of relevant material and the training of personnel.

Each directorate or intelligence service worked independently until late August 1975.

Deaths due to violations of human rights and political violence in the DINA period, 1974–77

The Commission Report records the number of deaths in the DINA period (see Table 4.2). The largest group of recorded deaths is constituted by the 'disappeared' (80%).

The Resistance: The Development of the Mental Health and Human Rights Network

The second generation of mental health institutions in the human rights movement

FASIC

On 1 April 1975, the *Social Aid Foundation of Christian Churches* (Fundación de Ayuda Social de las Iglesias Christianas, FASIC) was founded. This organization was based on the activities of the National Committee for Refugees. It was (and is) an ecumenical organization. At that time FASIC was the implementing partner of the United Nations High Commissioner for Refugees (UNHCR) in Chile. Perhaps for this reason, its activities were not stopped. The aim of the organization was to support political prisoners who had been sentenced and were going to leave the country for exile, but it soon extended its activities to the assistance of political prisoners and their families in general.

Table 4.2 Deaths produced by violations of human rights and political violence, 1974–77

	In Chile	Outside Chile
Detained and disappeared	449	15
Chilean/Argentinean couples detained/disappeared	–	16
Executed	65	1
Deaths due to torture	14	–
Deaths due to political violence	10	–
Deaths due to terrorist acts	–	4
Deaths due to induced suicide	5	–
Deaths due to abuse of power	5	–
Deaths due to excessive use of force	2	0
Unclassified deaths	10	3
Total	560	39

Source: Commission of Truth and Reconciliation, 1992, p. 71.

The Vicarage of Solidarity

At the end of 1975, Pinochet put pressure on the church to stop the activities of the Committee for Peace. However, its work was continued shortly after by the *Vicarage of Solidarity* (Vicaría de la Solidaridad).

From its establishment in 1973 until its dissolution (31 December 1975), the Committee had offered legal aid to 6,994 persecuted people in Santiago and to 1,908 people in the provinces. It had recorded 6,411 cases of people who had been dismissed from their jobs for political reasons, and 16,992 people had benefited from its medical assistance programme (Vicaría de la Solidaridad, 1990).

On 1 January 1976, therefore, the Catholic church established the Vicarage of Solidarity with a similar purpose to the Committee for Peace. As part of its work, the Vicarage soon formed a medical team ('el Equipo Medico'), which primarily offered emergency help to victims. A leading member of this team was the social worker María Luisa Sepúlveda, who has continued to play a central role in the work of the Vicarage. This team also referred patients to the private practice of psychiatrists and psychologists who were part of a network of solidarity.

The survivors' groups

In 1974, the first survivors' groups ('Los Agrupaciónes') of family members of the disappeared organized themselves. The experiences from their work served as an example for the creation of similar groups in other regions of Chile. In the beginning, their work was connected to the Committee for Peace, and after the establishment of the Vicarage they held their meetings there.

The survivors' groups developed nationwide and became a core structure of the human rights movement. These groups went out into the streets and demonstrated. They carried pictures of their disappeared family members, asking 'Where are they?' ('Donde estan?'), and they demanded the liberation of their relatives. Thus, these groups had a very important political function: they were the first openly to defy the dictatorship in peaceful demonstrations.

Moreover, these groups offered a new network for support on the emotional level – a space in which it was possible to share pain and to receive empathy from others who had had similar experiences. The group members could also receive medical, social and legal support from the professionals at the Vicarage.

All members of the groups had suffered violations of their human rights, but they divided themselves in relation to the specific type of traumatic experience they had suffered. In consequence, several people qualified for a membership in more than one group.

In 1976, the *Association of Family Members of Political Prisoners* also organized itself nationwide. The different associations often worked together. In the beginning their meetings took place under the shelter of the church; later they also found space in 'culture houses' in shanty towns such as La Victoria or acquired their own small premises. The work of these groups was an important inspiration for the further development of the professional institutions.

'In a cafe in Buenos Aires': the development of the FASIC medical–psychiatric programme

During 1976, the psychiatrist Fanny Pollarollo was asked to lead a mental health team which was being developed at the FASIC. At that time, she had just returned from exile in Argentina, and she told us:

> I remember we were sitting in the darkness in a small square in Buenos Aires. We had decided to return to Chile and had set the date to be at the end of 1975. We asked ourselves why we were going back. What were our reasons? Although I was a member of a political party, it was nevertheless the professional engagement which made me take the decision. The young psychiatrists would in the future ask us what we did and how it was to live under such conditions. The confrontation with torture is something in life you are never

prepared for. I knew by myself that I had to go back and explore, to find out what really happened – and of course to assist and treat victims of the repression. We discussed how these events might demonstrate new clinical findings – a new pathology.

In 1977, under the leadership of Fanny Pollarollo, FASIC started a medical psychiatric programme ('el Programa Médico Psiquiátrico'). Until then they had referred patients to an external network of clinicians. Dr Pollarollo continues:

> Before we left Argentina I had information from and contacts with Chileans working outside Chile against the dictatorship – in Latin America and even with some of our comrades in Paris.[4] In fact it was through their inspiration that we created the FASIC medical team, in reality a medical psychiatric programme aimed at assisting the victims. In the organizational phase we read a lot especially about crisis theory, for example the works of Bettelheim, and we tried to link this to an understanding of the political dimension. We wanted to understand more about the trauma – both on the individual and on the collective level.

The theoretical outlines of the work undertaken by FASIC were later published in an important key paper (Pollarollo, 1983).

The professionals working in the FASIC team did an outstanding job in formulating the first theories about psychotherapeutic assistance to victims of the repression. One of the leading members of this team, the psychologist Elizabeth Lira, recalls the emotional state of the team in the years of emergency following its creation:

> Our team was directly threatened many times, and we were only able to think of how we could protect patients and the information about them, but we were not aware of our own risk, and thus we were not able to protect ourselves. This threat generated a deep anguish in the therapists that invaded life beyond the therapeutic field. (Lira, forthcoming)

At the Vicarage, several members of the staff went on trial and some were imprisoned. One of the doctors was imprisoned and tortured, and a social worker was murdered. The government and the DINA put pressure on the church by accusing the staff of being communists, but the prestige of the church was great enough to let the organization subsist.

The therapists at FASIC observed that giving *testimony* in a meaningful context seemed to have a beneficial effect on the survivors. From this the testimony method as a psychotherapeutic tool was developed and was described in another key paper from the early days (Cienfugos and Monelli, 1983).

The Vicarage also became a repository for documentation. One important tool especially in this early phase was to collect testimonies about the violations to provide evidence for the subsequent judicial settlement. During these years, more than 40,000 testimonies were collected and stored at the Vicarage.

Reactions in Society to the Human Rights Violations from 1974 to 1977

During this period, Chilean society experienced a slow rebirth of the social habit of solidarity. The defence of human rights became more important as more became known about what had happened. Among the leaders of the regime, no important internal criticism could be discerned with regard to the problem of human rights. Some fractions tried to reduce the power of the DINA, but only after pressure from the USA following the murders of Letelier and Moffit.

The political parties were still without much impact. Christian Democrats complained about the censorship of a radio station, Radio Balmaceda. The result was detention and expulsion of party leaders, and the closure of the radio station. In 1977 a decree law dissolved all remaining parties, confiscated their goods and prohibited all partisan political activity (Constable and Valenzuela, 1991).

Communications media maintained a tolerant attitude towards the regime and did not use their influence to the benefit of human rights. The first critical publications appeared towards the end of the period (*Hoy*, *Apsi* and *Mensaje*), and included the Vicarage publication *Solidaridad*. Television stations were in the hands of the government and radio stations were either closed or exposed to internal and external censorship.

In November 1977, the *Peace and Justice Service* (Servicio de Paz y Justicia, SERPAJ) was officially founded. This human rights organization worked to promote non-violence and the construction of a democratic society with solidarity and respect for human rights. The intermediate organizations of society (trade unions, students' organizations), largely due to their disintegration, still did not have an official public position with regard to human rights.

Reactions on the part of the *international community* were mixed. During the first years of the military regime, it is estimated that about 20,000 people left the country for political reasons. The majority were received as refugees by foreign governments. Relations with numerous countries deteriorated as a consequence of the human rights problem in Chile. Relations with the USA remained relatively normal, however, and economic aid even increased from 1974 to 1976. A visit from a US government official coincided with the announcement of the dissolution of the DINA (Constable and Valenzuela, 1991).

At the beginning of 1974 the UN prepared special reports on the situation of human rights in Chile, and in the following years the General Assembly condemned the government of Chile for human rights violations several times.

THE CNI PERIOD FROM 1977 TO MARCH 1990

The Repression

The CNI

The secret police force known as the CNI was created in August 1977; it ceased to exist in February 1990. The organization was very similar to the DINA and had the same characteristics and functions. The main difference was its legal placement under the control of the Ministry of the Interior and a new remit to 'defend existing institutions'.

Between November 1977 and the middle of 1980, the CNI was primarily oriented towards political intelligence. Later, the organization systematically carried out illegal actions (for example, murders), and participated directly in the political repression until 1990. The power of the CNI was quite similar to that of the DINA, and minor differences were primarily due to the general political changes in the country.

In 1979, and more systematically from 1980, the MIR began to organize resistance, which involved the clandestine entry of its militants into the country to prepare themselves for an armed struggle against the military government. Other armed organizations were the Manuel Rodrigues Patriotic Front (FPMR) and later the 'Lautaro group' (1983).

In 1984, the law that defines terrorist conduct was promulgated, permitting the CNI to detain people without judicial warrant and through orders from the Ministry of Interior. The same year this mandate was expanded: the CNI was empowered to arrest and detain people in their own torture houses, when ordered to do so by the Ministry. This power was repealed in 1985.

On 7 September 1986, the Manuel Rodrigues Patriotic Front attempted to assassinate Pinochet. Five of his bodyguards were killed, but Pinochet got safely away. This attack, however, led to a furious assault on the left. 'CNI agents seized and brutally interrogated hundreds of activists, while unidentified armed squads kidnapped four known marxists and left their bullet-riddled corpses dumped beside a deserted road' (Constable and Valenzuela, 1991, p. 112).

The CNI organized complete teams for surveillance, repression and infiltration of the military/political organizations of the FPMR and the MIR. The Metropolitan Intelligence Division (DIM) and Regional Intelligence Division (DIRE), with an enormous staff, were involved in the creation of paramilitary organizations (Commando 11 de Septiembre and the ACHA) to cover up intelligence activities.

Another important project was the development of new political and labour organizations supportive of the government. Impressive sums of government money were secretly handled by the CNI, which could undertake these activities with an absolute certainty of impunity.

Other intelligence groups were formed, more or less connected to the CNI (CAS and COVEMA), and the armed police created their own intelligence organization named DICOCOMCAR after the dissolution of SICAR (in September 1983). The repression changed in this period. The victims were selected more carefully, and the vast majority of the murdered belonged to the MIR, the FPMR and the Communist Party. Massive violations of human rights occurred.

The deaths

The deaths recorded by the Commission Report are shown in Table 4.3. Deaths are also recorded in the Commission Report due to violent acts 'perpetrated by private citizens under political pretexts': ninety-three persons were killed in this period primarily through the acts of the MIR, the FPMR and, at the end of this period, the MAPU–Lautaro.

Although there were some cases of disappearances between 1978 and 1981, they did not have a systematic character and were not primarily the responsibility of the CNI. From 1981, however, a number of new disappearances occurred and the methods employed differed from those of previous periods.

A number of people were killed while they participated in protests and collective demonstrations. These types of manifestations started in 1983 and the fatal cases were essentially concentrated around the years of 1983 and 1985, on the 'Days of National Protest'. The protests and demonstrations were essentially peaceful. Nevertheless, there were severe expressions of violence, especially in shanty towns and during the evening and night.

Political and social leaders were taken by surprise by the public protests that began in 1984, and the degree of violence and disorder

Table 4.3 Deaths produced by violations of human rights and political violence, 1977–90

	In Chile	Outside Chile	Total
Executed	85	1	86
Detained/disappeared	23	10	33
Deaths due to torture	7	–	7
Unclassified	4	–	4
Political violence	30	–	30
Total	149	11	160

Source: Commission of Truth and Reconciliation, 1992, p. 81.

increased. Government measures and police actions were often excessive and generated a climate of confrontation in which the most unprotected social actors suffered the greatest consequences (124 deaths were recorded in the Commission Report due to these events). Besides this, 66 deaths were caused by 'excessive use of force' and 'abuse of power', with the tolerance of the authorities (Commission of Truth and Reconciliation, 1992, pp. 81–5).

In this period the total number of recorded deaths due to these events was 432. Based on data on about 2,279 individuals from the Commission Report, the population of victims could be characterized as follows: 98% were Chileans; 94% were men; and 52% were married. The age distribution is shown in Figure 4.1.

The Resistance: Mental Health and Human Rights

The further development of the mental health organizations

The survivors' groups

During the period from 1978 to 1980, new survivors' groups were organized: the *Association of Family Members of the Executed* (1978) and the *Association of Family Members of the Relegated and Ex-Relegated*[5] (circa 1980).

In the years after 1980, the following survivors' groups were also established or reorganized: the *Association of Ex-Political Prisoners*, the *Association of People Who Have Been Dismissed from Work for Political*

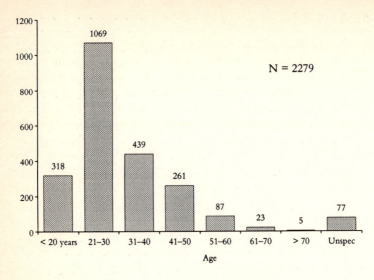

Source: Commission of Truth and Reconciliation, 1992.

Figure 4.1 Victims according to age

Reasons, the *Association of People Who Have Returned from Exile*, and the *Association of Witnesses* (1990). This last group is composed of survivors from different torture houses.

One of our interviewees explained about these recent groups of witness-survivors:

> I belong to a group of witness-survivors. It is not group therapy, but we act as witness-survivors. However, the communication in the group is rehabilitating, reparative. We act as witnesses of those comrades who have disappeared. We are divided into groups according to torture houses. So we have organized the group from Londres, the group from Domingo Cañas, the group from Villa Grimaldi, the group from Tejas Verdes. Basically, we have created the groups because of the Rettig Report – to verify that the disappeared have really been detained. So every one of us fills out a questionnaire: about where we have been, with whom we have been together, what clothes they were wearing, their physical characteristics, the last time we saw these people. It is because of the secret burial grounds – we think that they will keep on being revealed – so our information helps in the identification of the skeletons. So we are together because of this, and we have now given our information to the Rettig Commission.

Third generation of institutions

Until 1979, the two organizations FASIC and the Vicarage were the main sources of mental health assistance for the survivors. In this year, however, a new institution was created: the *Foundation for the Protection of the Children Who Have Been Damaged by the Emergency Situation* (La Fundación de Protección de la Infancia Danado por las Situaciones de Emergencia, PIDEE).

This organization was created as a result of requests by the relatives of the disappeared and also support by the Association of Family Members of the Executed. These families saw how their children were developing severe emotional problems and felt that they needed specialized help. The director of this new institution, Maria Eugenia Rojas, had previously worked in the FASIC team.

In 1980 the *Committee for the Defence of the People's Rights* (Comité de Defensa de los Derechos del Pueblo, CODEPU) was formed. It consisted mainly of professionals who had collaborated with the Vicarage. Some human rights groups like the Vicarage followed the Amnesty International standpoint of not engaging in the judicial defence of prisoners who had been accused of participation in armed confrontations. CODEPU, however, decided not to make this distinction.

Very soon after its creation, CODEPU also began offering mental health assistance on a voluntary basis. Their team was directed by Dr Paz Rojas, who had recently returned from exile in Paris. In 1984, this team began receiving financial aid and was, thus, 'officially' established. The team had three objectives: denouncement of the crimes of the dictatorship, investigation/documentation of the regime's repressive methods, and the treatment of the victims; hence its name – the *Team for the Denunciation, Investigation and Treatment of the Tortured and His Nuclear Family* (DITT-CODEPU).

The staff of CODEPU added a more militant dimension to the work. Consequently, they and their facilities were under constant observation from the CNI, and the institution was continuously harassed. Many of the therapists working in DITT-CODEPU were themselves damaged through personal repressive experiences of torture, exile and the disappearance of family members.

The therapists working in this team told us about constant threats from the CNI, about the CNI cars that were parked in front of the centre, about being followed when they left the office, and about their offices being ransacked during the night.

In 1985, a legal process was initiated in a military court against a physician and a lawyer from the Vicarage because they had given professional assistance to a person who was accused of being involved in terrorist acts. Both of these professionals were detained for two years and probably tortured. On 29 March 1985, a staff member of the Vicarage, José Manuel Parada, had his throat slit.

The fourth generation of institutions

In 1986, the *Centre for the Investigation and Treatment of Stress* (CINTRAS) was opened under the directorship of Dr Mario Vidal.

In 1988, the *Latin American Institute for Mental Health and Human Rights* (ILAS) was founded. The founding staff members came from FASIC, and the director was the psychologist Elizabeth Lira.

In 1988 DITT-CODEPU set up a special team for family therapy which in 1990 became autonomous under the direction of Dr Hector Faúndez: the *CODEPU Collective for Mental Health and Family Therapy.*

In January 1989, the military prosecutor tried to confiscate the medical records of the Vicarage, but because of the intervention by the Vicar and the US Ambassador, who appeared in front of the Vicarage, the operation was unsuccessful.

In November 1989, we observed CNI cars parked at the entrance of the First International Seminar on Torture in Chile arranged by CODEPU. The event was tolerated, although carefully watched.

The NGOs and the human rights movement

The explicit political purpose of all these non-governmental organizations (NGOs) is to fight for human rights. They denounce violations, document and investigate the strategies of the repression and its effects on the victims, and offer treatment for survivors of repressive political experiences.

For the survivors, this distinct political position of the institutions helped create the trust which was a necessary condition for a therapeutic process to begin to take place. The development of these NGOs from 1973 until 1990 seems to reflect a growing specialization.

The first institutions, working under the protection of the church, the Vicarage and FASIC, created mental health teams as an integral part of their general work. From the establishment of PIDEE in 1979 and onward, mental health work has been organized in autonomous centres, all of which have their own physical surroundings and rely on their own funding from abroad.

In the human rights movement in general, several new organizations were created after 1978:

- The *Committee for the Return of the Exiled* and the *National Commission for Youth Rights* (CODEJU): this last organization was established with the purpose of denouncing violations of human rights against young people and making the problem of human rights the responsibility of all youth organizations.

- The *Chilean Commission for Human Rights*: this was founded on 10 December 1978 with the basic objective of working in a pluralistic, free and autonomous way for the observance, respect, protection and promotion of human rights. The Commission had the scope to create groups nationally that could carry out activities in the defence of human rights.

- The Chilean section of *Amnesty International*: this worked against the violations of human rights outside of Chile, and a new *National Commission Against Torture* had as a main objective the elimination of all forms of torture.

- The *Sebastián Acevedo Movement Against Torture*: this was established in September 1983. It carried out peaceful demonstrations and had an important role in the denunciation of human rights violations.

The official mental health system

The official governmental mental health system paid little or no attention to the care of the survivors of human rights violations. The hospitals were, of course, part of the official system. In some of the provinces (as in the region of Tarapaca in the north and in the region of Los Lagos in the south) there were reports of doctors' participation in torture. Some of our interviewees pointed out that even today some of these doctors work in the hospitals.

One of the psychiatrists whom we interviewed told us that if a survivor had been admitted to hospital with a psychotic reaction to human rights violations, the real traumatic event that had precipitated it would not have been officially recorded in the files.

Reactions in Relevant Sectors of Society to Violations of Human Rights between August 1977 and March 1990

From August 1977 to May 1983

In August 1977, the state of siege was changed into a state of emergency. This made it possible to express reactions to the violations of human rights in a more organized way.

The opposition to the regime was channelled into two different and opposing positions: one sector that recommended armed struggle against the military regime and one sector that advocated a non-violent strategy. The MIR and similar organizations adhered to the first position, while the human rights organizations supported the non-violent strategy.

Among the general public, in this period, there were no significant reactions of solidarity with the survivors of the violations. Rather, public reactions were characterized by indifference or disbelief.

Thus, there was still no open criticism of those in power. The repression of dissidents was mainly carried out by prohibiting the exiled entrance to Chile. Moreover, critical labour or student leaders were relegated to different parts of the country, and some political leaders were sent into exile and were also insulted and abused. The number of disappeared and deaths decreased significantly during this period.

In 1977, the UN General Assembly again condemned the Chilean government for human rights abuses. The government called for a national referendum (4 January 1978) without electoral safeguards or systematic registration of voters. The result: 75% 'in favour of Chile' and supposedly 'against external attack' (Constable and Valenzuela, 1991).

On 19 April 1978 the amnesty law was decreed and many people thought that the government meant to put an end to the civil war that was supposedly in progress. This law permitted amnesty to some of the political prisoners, but in fact it also gave full immunity to the perpetrators of human rights violations committed until that date. On 15 July 1978, the Minister of the Interior claimed:

> with regard to the list of detained-disappeared, I categorically declare that the government has no information that proves the detention of any of these persons, and that is why it rejects the suggestion that they have been detained by the authorities. (Commission of Truth and Reconciliation, 1992, p. 86)

This was a statement from the formal leader of the CNI.

Although the press had a little more freedom, self-censorship was difficult to overcome. The magazines *Cauce* and *Fortin Mapocho*, nevertheless, carried out denunciations of human rights violations.

In this period the political parties still had no legal existence, but achieved a greater degree of organization:

• Rightist political parties condemned terrorist acts and theoretically condemned violations of human rights, without clearly recognizing that such violations were committed in Chile.

• Centre parties condemned human rights violations from both the right and the left – and from the government as well as terrorists.

- The left-wing parties continuously condemned the human rights violations, but they had no clear position on terrorist acts.

Among the international community, the Organization of American States (OAS) approved resolutions in 1977 and 1980 expressing concern over the human rights situation in Chile. In the United Nations, the General Assembly still condemned Chile every year from 1978 to 1982 for violations of human rights, and in 1979 a Special Rapporteur was appointed to investigate the development of human rights conditions in the country. In 1981, Chile suspended relations with the Inter-American Commission of Human Rights (Constable and Valenzuela, 1991).

From May 1983 to March 1990

The decree law 5720 of 16 September 1985 stated that communications media could not report or editorialize during a state of emergency on conduct described as terrorist crimes or on partisan political activities. Some improvement took place, however, though without creating complete freedom of expression.

As in the preceding phase, the two different positions on how to oppose the military government were maintained. The militant position led to a number of terrorist acts from armed groups of the left, and similar acts were carried out by ultra-rightists. People supporting the non-violent approach, meanwhile, favoured protests and public demonstrations. These were in fact often infiltrated by persons favouring the militant approach – from both sides. The non-violent organizations began to seek new approaches through reorganization of the political parties and professional organizations. The process culminated with the triumph of the 'NO!' verdict in the 5 October 1988 plebiscite with the approval of constitutional amendments. This led to a new plebiscite in 1989 and to the election of Patricio Aylwin on 14 December 1989. In all of these events the issues of human rights played a paramount role. Some sectors of the right wing developed a more critical attitude to the military regime's conduct, although this did not entail the withdrawal of their support (Constable and Valenzuela, 1991).

The Unexpected Effects of the Repression

A report from FASIC (Orellana, 1989, p. 104) lists those factors in the resistance against the dictatorship which those in power had *not* expected. Among these factors were:

- The constant pressure and demand from the survivors groups for the truth.

- The international solidarity to which the many Chileans in exile contributed actively. As part of this solidarity, an important body of research and practice in the field of human rights and mental health was developed by the exiled psychologists and psychiatrists (see, for example, Barudy, 1990a, 1990b; Bustos and Ruggiero, 1986; Corvalán, 1990; Riquelme, 1994).

In the following chapters, we will turn our attention towards the mental health work which was built up in the context we have just delineated. Maybe this was one more unexpected result of the repression – 'the Chilean model' for mental health and human rights.

NOTES

1. Pinochet (1980), cited in Constable and Valenzuela, 1991, p. 18.
2. This description of the coup is mainly based on Constable and Valenzuela, 1991.
3. The rights of someone in prison to appear in a court of law so that the court can decide whether they should stay in prison. It is a protection against unlimited imprisonment without charges (Longman, 1991).
4. The most important of these was Dr Paz Rojas.
5. Relegation: sent into 'internal exile' within Chile in a remote place.

Repressive Strategies and Experiences on the Individual Level

'Because she spoke her thoughts aloud...'

Under state terrorism the nature of the stressor has some characteristics which differ significantly from other types of stressor events. We will start our map of 'the Chilean model' by giving a brief overview of the wide range of stressors found in state terrorism in order to gain a better understanding of the mechanisms of psychological warfare.

CODEPU (1989) divides the stressor events into the following four categories: direct repression, indirect repression, social marginalization and individual marginalization. The final objective of all these instruments of terror is to create fear and disorganization (Lira and Castillo, 1991; Orellana, 1989).

Among the most important instruments of *direct repression* we can list the following nine items in ascending order of severity: (1) violent arrests; (2) forced exile; (3) threats; (4) arbitrary imprisonments; (5) torture; (6) the 'disappearance' of prisoners; (7) executions; (8) the killing of opponents under false precepts; (9) death during torture. Whereas the immediate aim of the first five instruments is to break the opponent psychologically, the aim of the last four is to eliminate her/him physically (Orellana, 1989).

Among the terror instruments of *indirect repression*, we find deprivation of food, housing and health care, dismissal from work, distortion of facts and manipulation of information.

Both direct and indirect repression start a process of marginalization on the social and the individual levels. *Social marginalization* describes the process whereby people are deprived of their social and political power. *Individual marginalization* describes the process whereby people, as a consequence of the other repressive strategies, experience a loss of skills and knowledge, cultural integrity and self-esteem (CODEPU, 1989).

As noted by Lira and Castillo (1991), these strategies of power result in a pervasive fear throughout society which is felt on all levels of human relationships. As one female social worker told us:

> We lived in that way for sixteen or seventeen years with a lot of shock, a lot of fear. All that time, I had fantasies about the death of my husband, always. During that period he was involved in one of the socialist parties. For me, therefore, it was a question of living in a continuous state of suspense. At any moment, something could happen to him, and this got even worse in 1989 when they assassinated one of the other leaders of the party. All this terror, all this panic was a permanent state, but we also – and this we were very sure of – would not avoid doing things because of fear. Neither did I demand that my husband stopped his activities, nor did I believe that it was my duty to tell him so. One obviously transmits all this fright and insecurity to the kids. Our children were extremely frightened by all this. At that time, we had two, and the oldest was aware of everything we went through, because we transmitted it to him. Personally, I think that I transmitted a lot of insecurity to my oldest son. Only recently has he begun to feel more safe, more relaxed when he sees armed policemen in the streets. Now he no longer automatically thinks that something will happen to him or his father.

Our own observations in Chilean society made us very aware of the necessity to extend our perspective on traumatization. We saw – and experienced ourselves – how efficiently the repressive strategies have been enmeshed throughout the society. We found that we needed to be much more specific in the analysis of the many different ways traumatization can occur on various levels.

Traumatization can, therefore, be described from different perspectives. One perspective describes the *distance* of the stressor from the 'object' (a person, a couple, a family, a group, a society). Another dimension describes the *frequency* of the stressor events. A third dimension describes the *context* in which the stressor events take place.

The distance of the stressor from the object describes how close the object is – physically, psychologically and/or socially – to the stressor event. In *primary traumatization* the object is the direct target of the stressor: for example, the murdered person, the executed, the disappeared, the tortured, the arrested.

In *secondary traumatization* the stressor event is the primary traumatization of another object: the object is traumatized *through* the traumatization of another. The secondary traumatized object has a close relationship to the primary traumatized object, emotionally or socially. Examples would be the husband, the close friend, the colleague, the political comrade (see Milgram, 1990).

In *tertiary traumatization* the stressor event is the primary or secondary traumatization of others. In tertiary traumatization the object is not directly connected with emotional or social ties to the target object. For example, the occasional observer, the rescuing professionals, the therapists, the neighbours.

This classification into primary, secondary or tertiary traumatization says little about the *degree or severity* of traumatization (apart from direct physical elimination of the object). The impact of the stressor must be balanced against the cultural context and the resources of the object, for example, personality structure, social network, political commitment and the degree of repression in society in general.

Under state terrorism, *the frequency of the stressor events* is characterized by an enduring, repetitive and chronic impact of stressors which take place in a *context* of power, where fundamental human rights are violated in a systematic and deliberate way. For people who live and work in this context of continuous stress, the nature of the stressor dimension can thus also be described from the following perspectives: you may become the object of direct and indirect repression, of social and individual marginalization, and of primary, secondary and tertiary traumatization. Under these circumstances of state terrorism, therapists have many personal factors in common with their patients – both categories being possible target-objects of the repression, and both being the objects of a whole range of other stressors.

People who identify themselves as possible target-objects of political repression (that is, leaders of political parties and trade unions, members of leftist parties, human rights workers – including therapists) experience a continuous social and political threat, a stressor that generates 'the paradox of chronic fear' (Lira, forthcoming). Fear, which is normally an emotion that arises in order to cope with a specific external or internal threat, becomes a permanent component of everyday personal and social life (Becker et al. 1990; Lira and Castillo, 1991).

What, then, were the manifestations presented by patients during the first years of the dictatorship?

> Fear, confusion, general distress, personal threat of death and harassment were some of the subjective consequences presented by the affected people. That was the rea son why psychological help was included very early. Those services were mainly conceived of as a relief under emergency conditions. (Lira, forthcoming)

From the beginning, the stressor events were described as 'traumatic political experiences' (Cienfuegos and Monelli, 1983) or 'repressive experiences'. We see the use of this terminology as an important feature in Chilean human rights and mental health work. The introduction of this discourse implies that the symptoms of the patient are caused by those in power: they can be explained by factors outside of the object. *'They are not ill, they are suffering from the dictatorship'*, as one therapist told us.

Here, we have chosen to focus on torture as one of the most traumatizing primary *repressive strategies*. First, we will examine objectives, agents and methods of torture. Thereafter, we will illustrate this repressive strategy by the case history of one of our interviewees, the psychiatrist 'Julia', who was subjected to severe torture.

PRIMARY REPRESSIVE STRATEGIES

Interrogation/Torture

Interrogation/torture is one of the repressive *strategies* of state terrorism aimed at destroying resistance to the system. The strategies of repression hit people as individuals, as well as relationships between people. Here, however, we will focus on repression from an individual perspective. Although people will always be interacting with other people and with society, we have for analytical purposes chosen to extract the individual perspective from the world of social relationships that are affected by state terrorism.

Repressive strategies such as interrogation/torture hit people at a deeply personal level. We therefore find it important for therapy and mental health work in general to get as close as possible to an understanding of the quality of this individual experience. To meet with the attempt of other human beings to destroy you in a systematic and deliberate way is a very lonely experience. Probably, it can only be fully understood by someone who has lived it him- or herself. 'We knew the concrete problems of the person, because we ourselves had been persecuted,' as one of the pioneers told us. Although the individual experience of going through interrogation/torture, therefore, can only partly be understood by most of us, it is nevertheless important for healing on the individual and social levels to attempt to understand this individual experience, even though much of its quality may be expressed in silences that can hardly be put into words.

We knew from the beginning that it was impossible to do any kind of psychotherapy at all if you did not know who the others were. It was not possible to do psychotherapy if you did not know what the repressive apparatus in Chile was doing: who the repressive apparatus was, what they were doing, how they were doing it and why did they want to destroy this person?... You were not able to understand the problems of the person if you did not understand what the other wanted to do to this person, how they wanted to do it and why they wanted to do it. Do you understand me?

This was explained to us by one of the pioneers of the human rights movement. Yes, we understood her. During our fieldwork we became increasingly aware of the truth of her statement: you were not able to understand the trauma of torture if you separated it from the political, ideological context in which the person had become traumatized.

To gain a deeper understanding of this 'other', we will list the most important methods and aims of the repression and give an unusual description of this other from a special viewpoint, namely from the perspective of the *resistor*. We will make use of parts of a historical document which was circulated, secretly, in the resistance movement in the 1980s: 'Resistir la Detención–Tortura–Interrogatorio' ('How to Resist Detention-Torture-Interrogation') (Rojas, 1981). The document was subsequently used by the human rights movement in South Africa. In an enlightening and indirect way, this document – which was written to inform possible prisoners about what to do if they were arrested – tells more about torture than any matter-of-fact presentation.

The Objectives of Torture

Very soon after the coup, professionals in the human rights movement began to analyse the strategies of repression. In 1974, from her exile in Paris, the neurologist Paz Rojas began a large research project about the methods and the consequences of the repression. 'It was just like throwing yourself into a swimming pool without knowing how to swim,' she told us. 'Many of the concepts we had to develop ourselves.'

In 1975 she was joined by two exiled psychiatrists (Katia Reszczynski and Patricia Barceló) and other professionals, and they set up a team for treatment of ex-political prisoners. During the following two years they conducted an investigation of 300 exiled Chileans who had been tortured, and they wrote a ground-breaking book – 'a combat weapon' as they say in the Preface – on account of their findings. The book, *Tortura y Resistencia en Chile: Estudio Médico-Político* (Torture and Resistance in Chile: A Medical-Political Study), was first written in French in 1978, but was not published in France until 1984 because of a certain 'accidental' delay. It was not published in Chile until 1991 (Reszczynski et al., 1991).

The knowledge that was gained from the investigation constituted the theoretical framework for the DITT-CODEPU team which Paz

Rojas started shortly after she returned from exile in 1981.[1] The findings of the investigation also formed the basis of the above-mentioned paper, 'How to Resist Detention-Torture-Interrogation'. This paper – which was generally referred to as 'The Fear' ('el miedo') – was the first teaching material developed for the psychological training courses held by the underground resistance movement.

In their early work, DITT-CODEPU developed its own concept of torture which corresponded to the reality in Chile. When the United Nations approved the International Convention Against Torture in 1984, CODEPU decided to adopt this concept as the basis of their work. Consequently, both physical and *mental* suffering is a part of torture. In fact, it is underlined by DITT-CODEPU that irrespective of which technique is used, torture *always* involves psychological suffering (see Pesutic, 1989, p. 109). This important psychological element of torture is a part of the *psychological warfare* carried out by the regime in conformity with the doctrine of national security. The overall aim is to terrorize the population into obedience to the state; but subordinate to this, the aim is also to destroy the detainee, who is considered to be an 'internal enemy', and to manipulate the population by demonstrating and displaying such power.

DITT-CODEPU lists eleven main objectives of interrogation/torture (Pesutic, 1989, pp. 72–3). These items are not necessarily considered to be exhaustive, and they do not only reflect the situation in Chile but also that of other Latin American countries:

1. To obtain information for a judicial process (investigation).

2. To obtain information for use in immediate or later operations in the 'war'.

3. To obtain information about the 'enemy':
   - type of people;
   - habits, working methods, language, organization, etc.

4. To obtain a confession (that is, to extract a confession).

5. To neutralize: to produce social and political immobilization:
   (a) of the detainee him- or herself;
   (b) of the groups to which he or she belongs: the political group; the social group; the family group;
   (c) of the social sector to which he or she belongs;
   (d) of the opposing population in general.

6. To obtain collaboration at once and/or permanently: to transform the detainee into a collaborator.

7. To destroy, to break the detainee down.

8. To punish the detainee.

9. To punish through the detainee the groups to which he or she belongs.

10. Secondarily, or later, the detention and the confinement (in all its forms, especially isolation) can be used to provoke mistrust and splits in the groups to which the detainee belongs.

11. The whole situation and the information which has been collected are used for manipulation of the population through the mass media, which is controlled by the dictatorship and which gives a distorted account of what has happened.

The Agents

Thus, in order to understand the trauma of ex-political prisoners it was necessary to recognize the aims of the torture they had suffered. It was also, however, important to know *who* the people were who carried out the torture. Were they maniacs, psychopaths, sadists or especially sinister types?

In her document on how to resist detention, torture and interrogation, Paz Rojas (1981, pp. 5–8) gives the following description of the agents of repression:

At the moment (1981) there are basically two types of services that detain people: the police (*carabiñeros*) and the CNI (Centro Nacional de Inteligencia).

The police: In former years, the intelligence service of the police (SICAR) made intensive use of a large number of torture techniques and they also even killed people. Now, however, it does not constitute so large a risk to be detained by the police. In fact, they have not equipped specialized centres for interrogation and torture (when they did have such centres, in 1974–76, they only imitated the techniques used by the DINA), and they have now returned to their usual techniques: harsh, rude treatment, language which sometimes is vulgar and humiliating, threats, isolation from the outside (together with other prisoners), no blindfolding, deprivation of food and water for 24 or 48 hours, occasional random blows. During interrogation they usually do not have any specific knowledge about the prisoner. They always make a complete police-record. Sometimes, in the case of women prisoners, the police women – who in general are ruder and harsher than the men – use obscene, humiliating language and force the women prisoners to take off their clothes for a body search.

Often the police arrange a medical examination of the detainee, especially if he is to be delivered over to the CNI. This fact shows – together with testimonies and information – that there is hostility and unrest among the detaining services (the police find that they are held to be guilty of deeds, tortures and assassinations that they have no part in).

Also, feelings of guilt have been detected in some policemen because of the crimes that have been committed by their institution. Many of them get uneasy if these crimes are mentioned. The resistor must try to use these feelings against them in a correct way during his detention.

CNI: At the moment [1981], all civilian cases are investigated by the CNI, unlike the first years of the dictatorship when the intelligence services of the Navy, the Air Force, the Army operated separately. The CNI is the present name of the ex-DINA organization created at the end of 1973.[2] In this organization participate intelligence people from different branches of the armed forces (predominantly from the Army) and also civilians. The organization has principally been developed and trained in this country, but concrete information exists about education and specialized courses abroad (the Canal Zone in Panama, Brazil, South Africa...). It has also been proved that the CNI collaborates and exchanges ideas with other repressive agencies in the world (USA, France, Italy ... and more specifically in South America, Salvador and Guatemala).

Their previous training is basically ideological: to fight the internal enemy (the doctrine of national security), to whom they attribute every negative trait which a human being can have: he is violent, aggressive, a traitor, without principles, and they call him 'terrorist, extremist, murder, immoral', sometimes they endow him with an almost demonic character (see the book by Pinochet, *The Decisive Day* [1980]). To eliminate the enemy which is defined in this way is an act of honour, of courage, there is no guilt: on the contrary, in this way you are saving the Western world, the values of society, the family, religion, the economy, freedom, justice. At the same time as they despise the 'enemy' and make him inhuman, they glorify the values of the official, the soldier, who defends and keeps the country free of Marxism–Communism–Socialism, 'inherently perverse' doctrines; while they themselves want to live in 'order and peace'.

Besides this ideological inculcation of values, there is also a special training for torture. Actually, the techniques which are used have been learned, developed, evaluated and perfected both from experiences with their use in this country, and by the exchange of ideas with other repressive agencies. There is a theoretical and practical training for the officials; it is known that there are specialized courses given by specialists on how to extract information by the use of physical and psychological torture techniques. It is also known that many torturers have themselves been subjected to various torture techniques.

Consequently, the torturer is not a sadist, a crazy person, a psychopath. He is an official from the system, the repressive system. He is doing his duty and he is convinced of what he is doing; to obtain information, to break down the enemy, is a 'normal' act which many times is rewarded and classified as 'heroism'.

In this teaching material, we see how the rationality of the torturers has been developed in the culture of the military. We see that in their culture torture is a normal act. It is important for the resistor, the opponent, to recognize this concept of normality – both so as to take precautions and for the healing process, later on. This is a way of de-privatizing the torture: it is not individual acts of craziness or sadism, but collective and systematic acts of destroying the enemy psychologically – in fact, not much different from the physical killing of enemies in a war.

The Methods

Testimonies about torture

The methods of torture have changed during the years of the dictator-ship. Maria Eugenia Rojas, who worked as a member of FASIC's medi-cal psychiatric team and founded PIDEE, has investigated the history of the repression in Chile from 1973 to 1983. In her book, *La Represión Política en Chile: Los Hechos* (The Political Repression in Chile: The Deeds), which was written between 1984 and 1986 and published in Spain in 1988, she describes, amongst other things, the different torture methods developed during the first ten years of dictatorship.[3] The em-pirical basis of her investigation consists primarily of testimonies and statistics which she collected at FASIC – that is, she documented and registered the repressive experiences of the people who received treatment in the institution. On the basis of their testimonies she carried out an analysis of the torture they had suffered. 'This was a terrible job, very demanding,' she told us:

> My colleague sometimes stopped taking testimonies and went to the bath-room to vomit – at that moment she had just taken too much in. Because the people who gave the testimonies were crying, it was terrible – and I cried afterwards when I read them. I often brought them home, and I went crying back and forth in my living room, and my daughter said to me: 'Mother, how long will you keep on doing this?' ... Sometimes I read five, six testimonies of torture per day. Also Fanny said to me: 'Does all this horror go into the cells of your body?' When I had written this book, I said: 'No more, I cannot anymore. Now it is time for the children.'

The book became her own testimony as a human rights profes-sional, but it also became a personal testimony: her ex-husband, the father of her three children, disappeared in 1976, and her son-in-law was murdered in 1985, while she was writing the book.

Maria Eugenia Rojas opens the doors to a cabinet in her office and shows us piles of papers. They are testimonies, typewritten manuscripts, enough for several books. It has not, however, been possible to finance their publication.

In her book she analyses testimonies of torture, disappearances and executions, and the subsequent distortion of these deeds in the state-controlled mass media. She claims to have evidence of the existence of psychologically trained employees within the CNI.

The principal torture methods

In the book *Violaciones a los Derechos Humanos e Información: La Experiencia Chilena* (Violations of Human Rights and Information: The Chilean Experience) published by FASIC, Orellana (1989, pp. 61–2) the following principal torture methods are listed:

Predominantly physical

- continuous blows;
- 'telefóno' (simultaneous blows on both ears);
- application of electricity;
- sexual torture;
- forced positions;
- water torture (pressure through the orifices of the body), named 'submarino';
- suspension combined with application of electricity;
- burns;
- deprivation of food and water for a long period of time;
- powerful spotlights;
- 'falanga': (blows to the soles of the feet);
- extraction of nails;
- others.

Predominantly psychological

- blindfolding – the detainee is kept blindfolded during the whole process;
- nakedness;
- rudeness and obscene insults;
- interruption of sleep;
- continuous strident music;
- threats of killing the detainee or his family or friends;
- threats of torture or rape of the detainee or of his family;
- mock executions;
- being forced to witness or apply torture to others;
- drugs;
- the signing of incriminating documents;
- continuous isolation.

There are many different classifications of the torture methods employed in Chile during the dictatorship. The above-mentioned list builds upon the classification made by Amnesty International. The Vicarage of Solidarity has another classification which is much more detailed (Orellana, 1989, pp. 163–6).

In her document about how to resist torture, Paz Rojas (1981, pp. 15–17) explains the methods as follows:

(1) Predominantly *bodily*: These techniques attack the human body through pain, exhaustion.... The principal among these are *blows* which are general or directed towards a certain part of the body, and also continuous blows; *electricity* which can be applied in a diffuse way ('the grill', some types of electric chairs...) or in a guided way with electrodes placed on the most sensitive places: the genitals, the ears, the tongue.... *Forced positions*: being tied up, being hung up, etc. Aggressions with *sharp instruments. Burns.*

(2) Predominantly *biological*: deprivation of food and water, obligation to eat filth. Restraint of respiration. Prevention of the realization of physiological functions, prevention of sleep.

(3) Predominantly *sexual*: sexual insults, rape, rape with objects. These aggressions are practised against the prisoner or his wife or other family members.

(4) Predominantly *psychological*:
- blindfolding;
- nakedness, insults, humiliations;
- obligation to witness the torture or murder of a family member or a comrade from the prison;
- false executions, dropping or burials;
- solitary confinement;
- sensorial deprivation;
- drugs: pentothal, drugs that produce addiction, hallucinogenic neuroleptics;
- hypnosis.
- In general, a constant watch is kept over the feelings, beliefs and values of every prisoner. There are good interrogators and bad interrogated. A specific watch is kept over a certain prisoner. This is done after one or several sessions of interrogation with or without specific torture until they have discovered deep emotional ties, values, psychological or biological weaknesses. When these 'weak points' have been found, they elect which specific strategy to use.
- Gratification-punishment. They gratify the prisoner by satisfying one of his or her necessities or wishes (to smoke, sleep, eat, hear music). In this way they produce habituation. When they have achieved this they suddenly

cancel it. In this way they produce a sort of syndrome of abstinence. They can also use this as a punishment. They can use this technique in a contradictory way: gratify when the prisoner does not merit it, punish when the prisoner has given information. In this way they provoke a confusion, a disorientation that impedes logical reasoning – the capacity to interpret why they are behaving like that.

All these specific techniques were used during the first three years of the military dictatorship. A review of the cases from 1980 to 1981 permits the conclusion that the predominant techniques at the moment are psychological. They can be accompanied by bodily aggressions: blows and electricity are those most frequently used.

Sexual torture

The use of sexuality in the breaking down of the detainee has been widespread. It has, to us, been one of the most astonishing features of the repressive strategies. During the interviews, we found it difficult to ask about this. However, one female psychiatrist who had herself been tortured told us the following:

Rape was very frequent in the first phases of the military regime. I got to know a lot about it, while I was in the women's prison. Many political prisoners arrived from the National Stadium and there they had raped nearly all of them, indiscriminately. This was more or less known, you knew it but … it was understood, but not something we talked about. There were also frequent demands for gynaecological consultations in the prison. Practically all of us went to the gynaecologist – it could be because of injuries from the electrical torture, because of menstrual disorder, pregnancies. In the prison, I knew about two cases of pregnancy after rape during torture.

So there were rapes of this indiscriminate type, and then there were selective rapes of young attractive comrades, 16- or 17-year-old virgins. Then there was also a third type which, for example, was carried out in 'La Venda Sexy' ['The Sexy Blindfold']. This was a name that we gave to a particular torture house in which there were large-scale rapes during the weekends, when the guards were drunk. These were rapes that were not performed as a part of torture and interrogation.

In the last phase of the dictatorship, the rape of women increased – during the repression of the large-scale protest demonstrations. And now, in democracy, it also happens. One month ago, we had a total of twenty-six cases of torture during democracy which had been carried out at the 'Third Police Station', and of these cases, five of the women had been raped by the policemen … and this is after Aylwin. It has been denounced, and a charge has been made.

The Vicarage of Solidarity lists a whole range of sexual torture methods (Orellana, 1989, p. 163): rape by a man, a woman or an animal; oral or anal rape; individual or collective rapes; rape in private or in public; introduction of objects or animals into the vagina; obligation to perform sexual acts in private or in public; isolation together with lesbians or homosexuals; pawing and other types of sexual humiliation.

The use of sexuality seems to be an intrinsic part of psychological warfare – one of the effective means of tampering with the soul, because of the special feeling of *complicity* which this type of torture can provoke: the detainee is forced to participate in the aggression towards him- or herself (Agger, 1994; Weinstein et al., 1987). The traumatizing effects of this type of moral torture are presumably only surpassed by the moral and psychological breakdown of a detainee, who is forced to collaborate with the repressive apparatus in one way or another.

PRIMARY REPRESSIVE EXPERIENCES

The Detainee

In the following pages, we will continue to use excerpts from the document written by Paz Rojas about how to resist torture (Rojas, 1981, pp. 3–14). The passages from this teaching material reveal how the opponent – *the resistor* – must accommodate and attempt to counteract the rationality of the repressive apparatus. In this way, Rojas describes the building up of a new rationality, a new normality in which the opponent attempts to maintain his or her sanity in the midst of an insane reality in which it is regarded as normal to violate universally adopted concepts of human rights:

> On account of the development of the techniques of torture and interrogation, every organization must know that the repressive instruments of dictatorships have the necessary means (psychological drugs) for obtaining – within 48 hours – information, and that it is preferable to assume that the prisoner 'can talk' – although ex-prisoners have been able to resist countless combinations of torture techniques. Therefore, the party or the organization must have a quick, fast structure which permits it within few hours to counteract the arrest of a resistor and the possible delivery of information. To take precautions before the arrest of a resistor does not imply any doubt in him. On the contrary, it is a way of protecting him and of strengthening his organization....
>
> The secret resistor must prepare himself for not talking, not giving information. He must, therefore, have a coherent story, a double life, another life....

During the most recent arrests, it has been a matter of routine that a doctor was there to examine the prisoners before a specific torture, and to evaluate the effects and indicate if the torture could continue or not.

The resistor must seek out and get to know an illness which he can explain that he suffers from. This must be something which is difficult to diagnose, and he should not, for example, say that he has a heart disease if it is not true, because this can be proved quite easily by measuring blood pressure or by listening with a stethoscope; instead, he says:

— that he faints easily;

— that as a child he suffered from epileptic fits, which he now experiences every two or three years. That his father died from an attack...

— that he is a diabetic, and that he also frequently has attacks of hypoglycemia with fainting;

— that he has a tendency to bleed easily;

— that he has a stomach ulcer;

— that as a child he had a kidney disease and that he easily gets blood in the urine....

— that he suffers from migraines, especially if he gets into some crisis which upsets his equilibrium....

He must, moreover, try to 'humiliate' the doctors who participate in this, comparing them with the idea that he usually has of this profession....

Detention: When he has been detained, the resistor must evaluate in which way the detention has been carried out: in public, in a group or alone, in his house with his family or alone; an abduction in front of others gives him, in the beginning, greater space for action and security. There are witnesses, he is not alone. The person who is abducted must always shout his personal data, his name, the name of his family, the name of those who are to be notified.

The detainee must keep calm, quiet, and must try to get information right from the beginning: how many are there, who are they, how do they behave, which service is detaining him. This is counter-intelligence work which the resistor must start from his first contact with the officials of the repressive apparatus. It is his job, it is an obligation. This will not only be a help for himself, but he will also later, when he is free again, be able to give detailed and objective information to his comrades and his organization. He must every day attempt to evaluate and get to know about their manners, their acts, their language, their usual way of behaving. He must also try to evaluate the way they react to his answers, his behaviour. Identify them from the beginning by their voice....

He must remember that no matter how kind they seem, how much they assure him that they will respect him as a person, or how much they assure his family that 'nothing will happen', this is not true. Everyone who is detained by the CNI is taken to secret places for interrogation and torture. There they might not suffer physical aggression, but all prisoners suffer psychological torture from the moment they arrive....

Interrogation: If he has been detained by the CNI he will always be interrogated blindfolded....

The resistor must be prepared to 'forget' in a voluntary way that information which he must not give.... He must never say *anything* about it. Not one single fact, or sign. If he tells just a little bit believing that this will pacify them and diminish the torture, then *he is wrong.* When they find out that he knows 'something', this will urge them to go on, they will soon want to know more, and he will begin to unwind a thread that he afterwards will not be able to cut....

He must never show them his 'weak points' – that he is afraid of something – that he has special feelings for a certain person, that he is trying to protect somebody; that he is afraid that they will torture his children (from now on, he must never carry pictures of his 'loved ones'). If they threaten to torture his children, the experiences of other prisoners have shown us that aggressive answers such as the following are more useful – and have even prevented the torture – than begging them, pleading with them not to do it:

– 'It doesn't matter, then they will get to know the tormentors of their people from when they are little.'

– 'Then they will get to know what you are capable of and they will learn to hate you.'

The Case-Story of 'Julia'

From the above-cited 'teaching-material', we have learned about the rationalities developed during the reign of terror, in the secret detention centres, between the torturer who carries out his job as an official of those in power and the opponent who attempts to survive – maybe resist – the efforts at breaking him or her down. In the following, we will use excerpts of our interview with 'Julia' – a female psychiatrist – who describes her own experience of arrest, detention, torture and interrogation. Both before and after her detention, she has worked as a researcher and clinician in the field of human rights violations. Therefore, she is able to tell the story of her repressive experience with the meta-perspective she has gained from her professional experience.

As mentioned previously, 'to obtain information for a trial (investigation)' is the primary objective of interrogation/torture. There are, therefore, some similarities between the process of collecting information during fieldwork and the process of interrogation/torture: 'The ethnographic investigation will always in some ways violate the others

... the ethnographer must maintain a certain pressure to get the necessary information from people' (Hastrup, 1992, pp. 67–8). These similarities constitute a special ethical challenge for researchers as well as for therapists who work in the field of human rights violations, although the overall aims of interrogation/torture and science/therapy, hopefully, should be completely different. During the long and moving interview with Julia, we were constantly aware of this ethical challenge – which places the therapist/researcher in a position which is halfway between that of a perpetrator and that of a victim.

The meeting

Julia receives us in her office. She is prepared. They talked about us before we came – she is the fourth professional we have interviewed from this institution, and she is the second tortured psychiatrist. 'My director told me to tell you everything,' she says with a slight tremble. There is a good contact between us – she is warm and serious – wants to explain to us how it is. Seventy-five interviews later we realize that it was Julia who gave us the most detailed and eye-opening description of the world of torture, although during our hours together with her, and afterwards, we felt ourselves balancing the advantages of silence against those of speech.

In the meeting with Julia, we enter a world in which silence and speech take on new qualities. To be silent or to speak may constitute the difference between life and death. The life that comes from speaking, the life that comes from being silent; the death that comes from speaking, the death that comes from being silent. We are into the world of torture, where your 'right to life' is threatened as well as your 'right to physical and psychological integrity'. In the world of torture they are tampering with your soul, and maybe you are – or maybe you are not – able to resist.

The arrest

It was about ten in the morning when they called me over the loudspeakers of the hospital. I was told to go to the office of the head of the department. When I arrived at the office, I found four officers in civilian clothes from the DINA waiting for me. They told me that they had orders to bring me to the Ministry of the Interior to make a statement and that it was a short proceeding, but first they had to check the office. They checked everything, they searched. We had a lot of photocopies of articles in English, German and French. To them, they were all evidence. At last we left the office and they locked the door.

We must have been there for about an hour and a half. They did not let me answer the phone. At last they decided that we should supposedly go to the Ministry of the Interior. When we went down the stairs a fifth man joined us. 'We are ready, let's go,' he said. 'Let's go to her house.' We went to my apartment, and they searched everything there. I had a surgical emergency kit, because at any time I could be called to attend to a wounded comrade. While I studied medicine, I also studied philosophy. During the first and second years of medicine I had taken classes in historical materialism and social psychology. Therefore, I had a large collection of Marxist literature. They confiscated all the books and the surgical kit.

At about four o'clock in the afternoon they said: 'Well, let's go...' and they locked the apartment, took the keys and took me to the Ministry of the Interior. They left me, however, in the station-wagon outside together with two of them, while the three others went into the Ministry and returned fifteen minutes later. I imagine that they went by to notify that they had brought me there. Then they put Scotch tape across my eyes and sun-glasses, and they gave me a newspaper which I had to pretend to be reading while we drove along.

The detention

They went for a tour around with me, which for me was... I don't know if you are familiar with some of the names of DINA's secret centres: 38 Londres, the house of José Domingo Cañas, Grimaldi, yes, this was afterwards....

My first impression of the route is that we are going through the bypass which is under the Alameda near the church of San Francisco to Londres Street. My first feeling was that this was the place they had brought me to. I also heard the bells of the church. But later, in the group of survivors – those of us who have given testimony about the disappeared – I have met comrades who also were in Londres and we did not meet each other. Moreover, they were sure that they had also been in José Domingo Cañas. It seems to me that I was in both places: in Londres Street and in José Domingo Cañas. I have only been able to find one explanation for it: in one of the periods of unconsciousness that I had, they transferred me to the other place, so that is why I don't remember it.

I was there for fifteen days. The interrogation was basically ... in the beginning I did not know from where their information came, and how they found out about me ... there was maybe some infiltration of the Committee for Peace ... but because I had to attend to urgent cases I also had a comrade, my superior, who had my telephone number both at my apartment and at the hospital. These were the two possibilities: it could be the Committee for Peace or the party.

The reflections of Julia here demonstrate one of the first and most important questions in the mind of the detainee. How did they get my name? Who has told them about me? To realize that the informant is one of the admired leaders or a close comrade can to a severe degree weaken one's moral power of resistance.

The interrogation

In the beginning, at the interrogation I became aware of – it must have been the third day ... they brought me to a room with a wooden floor – there must have been fourteen, fifteen people with a guard. When you arrive ... they took the Scotch off my eyes and instead they blindfolded me. They took out the books and everything. And my luck, and this was really luck – the good fortune I had was that they took apart the four surgical kits and gathered the four needles, the four scalpels, the four ... they counted the pieces without realizing that they were surgical equipment and that they could be used as they were – instead they listed them as different material.

The torture

From there, the interrogation the third day ... during those days that I was there, the first days ... I heard, well you hear ... you know what it is, you have already heard all this in the stories of the patients – the screams, everything. They fetched you ... at intervals, there was someone who was fetched. The sexual harassments were continuous. For example, when they brought you from the cell to the interrogation room, you had to walk blindfolded. So they told you how to walk, how to go down the stairs, but at the same time they touched you with their hands, they put their fingers into your vagina, or they took your hand and made you touch their genitals. They took your clothes off, you were naked. This was always so. But this is all part of the morbidness, you get used to this mechanism, to this external humiliation. It is not like a rape, an intercourse, a real sexual relation. It becomes part of the environment of terror, of the general, global morbidness with which they damage you, weaken you, make you helpless. And you get used to it, you develop a mechanism – at least I did – to ... just as you do with the radio, with the screams ... the screams of torture ... they turned on the radio, so that we would know that they were torturing ... as if they were saying: 'We turn on the radio real loud so that they will not hear the screams when we torture the others.' But in reality, when we heard the radio, we knew that they were torturing somebody. The noise from the radio, the humiliation, the swearing, the jokes ... you urinated, you defecated – it is usual when you get electrical torture that you lose control of the sphincter. In the beginning you feel ashamed, especially the men, because they dirty their pants. So these types of jokes ... they took you to the toilet from the cell once every day, and you had to sit down on the toilet with the guard in front of you. During the twelve days I was in the torture house, for example, I did not defecate, I only urinated. Twelve days without ... I couldn't.

Neither did I, for example, menstruate. For three months I didn't. It must have been a biological defence mechanism, because there were not the conditions for it. When later we were in isolation cells, we took the filling out of the mattresses, because we didn't have any napkins, nothing to use when we menstruated.

A well-known collaborator was also there, she was a former militant from the MIR who had been turned into a collaborator. She was there, in the same room as I was, in the same cell. And on the third day of the interrogation, Miguel Krashnoff, who was the head of my interrogation and torture team, said: 'Bring Carlos.' I was blindfolded; Carlos said my name, and they began to ask him: 'Who is she? Whom does she know?' He answered: 'She is the person who can bring us to Julio and Franco.' They were two comrades from the leadership of the party. One was from military logistics, the other was from health.

I said that I did not know him, that they should first show me this Carlos, because I did not know who he was. They did not let me see him, and I said that I did not know any Julio or Franco. My father's name was Julio. I said that if I had known someone called Julio, I would not have forgotten it, because it was the same name as my father's. So I said that I did not know anyone of ... then they put both me and him on the 'grill' ... it is a metallic bed where they give you electric shocks. They made him give more and more details which they forced me to confirm ... and to my luck I lost consciousness; I say to my luck, because what saved me then was my unconsciousness.

I also had an advantage because when we had a course in behaviourism during our psychiatric training, I served as a volunteer in the experiments with electrical currents in the psychiatric clinic at the University of Chile. At this time, there had already been a military coup in Uruguay. So when I was asked to be a volunteer, I said: 'I want to find out how much I can take, how much I can resist.' And I found out that I could take 120 volts; for women the average was 80 or less, and for men 60. So I had endured as much as I could to know how much: 120. The machine could produce 150 volts, and the one that the DINA used could produce the same level of voltage. So I used this knowledge: when I felt a rather light tickling sensation, I screamed as if it was too much.

This helped me a lot. It gave me time to think and to orientate myself ... because one of the few things I had learnt from the ex-tortured that I had examined was the importance of not panicking. Panic prevents you from thinking rationally. The fear and the pain that you have is the same, but when it reaches the level of panic....

From then on everything is in a mist. I don't know if I was transferred to José Domingo Cañas or not. Afterwards, I continued ... I maintained that I was a psychiatrist from the Committee for Peace and that I attended to the people who were sent to me from the Committee for Peace or to anyone who asked me, because I was a doctor, and, therefore, I could not deny giving attention to someone who asked me for medical help. Then they stopped interrogating me, and after twelve days they transferred me to another place.

The camp

It was to Cuatro Alamos, a section in Tres Alamos. Tres Alamos was a sort of concentration camp with free communication among the prisoners. This was basically a place for recovery. When you arrived there, they gave you food, you could have a shower every day. The food was not good, it was beans, lentils, but you could have second helpings and sufficient bread. You could have milk and anti-inflammatory medicine to get rid of the bruises, and chlordiazepoxide (Librium), a minor tranquillizer.

There they put you in a cell which was locked from the outside. It contained two bunks – that is, four beds – and through this cell people passed, they came and they went. In the beginning you didn't talk with anyone, because you did not know who the others were. Luckily they gave me my money back, and with this we could buy some things. You could give the guards some money and they would bring you things the following day. So we bought soap, toothpaste, toothbrushes – because you didn't have anything. I was there for one and a half months.

The process

During all of this period they denied having detained me, that is, my *habeas corpus* was rejected. Nowhere did they recognize that I had been detained, although all the people at the hospital were witnesses. So my family, especially my sister together with an uncle (because my father was very ill), searched for me in all the hospitals, in the detention centres and in the morgue. The same as all the relatives of the disappeared have done, but in this case you could say that I was a disappeared who had survived, and I didn't end up like the others.

At the end of October they brought me before the Military Prosecutor [*Fiscalia Militar*]. The prosecutor who interrogated me had a declaration that I had signed while I was blindfolded. In it were listed all the things they had registered when I was arrested. He had good eyes, because on the list of surgical equipment he noticed a sponge which is used to stop bleeding. So he asked me why I had this – you didn't need that for psychiatric treatments. I explained that I was sometimes called to homes where depressives or hysterics had cut their veins. But he said: 'This sponge isn't for that.' It was then that he became convinced that my activities as a doctor were not that clean.

The prison

He sent me to prison. I could receive visitors, it was a public place, a women's penitentiary, where the criminal prisoners are kept. Here there was a section which was called 'The Blue Patio', where they kept the women political prisoners. At that time, we numbered around 150.

However, before letting me into this section they kept me in solitary confinement for five days in a cell. This was the worst part of it, because all the rest of the time I was always in a group. This was the only time that I was alone, isolated, without knowing if it was day or night, what time it was, without food, without nothing. There were rats, and the hygiene was ... the other things were nothing in comparison with those five days of solitary confinement, all alone – and I didn't know where I was or where I was going.

So after those five days they transferred me to the group of political prisoners, and from there I could inform my family about where I was, and they could visit me. They also assigned me an attorney from the Committee for Peace, and he started the defence.... In May they ordered me to be expelled from the country because I was a danger to the internal security of the state.

Julia tells her story, and afterwards we smoke a cigarette with her. She gives us some material about a famous female collaborator, who has now decided to give testimony to the Commission of Truth and Reconciliation about what she did, and what she saw in the secret centres of the DINA and the CNI.

Together with Julia, we have been in the world of torture – the world in which silence and speech take on new meanings, and you are caught in the impossible choice between physical life and psychological death. It is a choice which 'the others' force upon you, and it leaves you in a soul-trap, in a double-bind, in a world with no exits. It is in this moral trap that the real trauma is born; it is in this impossible choice between unbearable pain and 'betrayal' that the opponent is broken down.

Maybe you were lucky enough to pass out at the critical moment – as Julia did – but even then you were wounded. The horror of meeting a world in which the usual concepts of rationality and normality are reversed leaves you with something which can barely be spoken of.

THE PROBLEM OF THE WOUNDED HEALER

To use a metaphorical expression, therapists who have themselves survived severe trauma have been called 'wounded healers', and Julia was one of the many wounded healers we met in Chile. We have borrowed this concept from the works of Jung (1983), Kleinman (1988), Maeder (1989) and Comas-Diaz and Padilla (1990). The problem of the wounded healer has been discussed from two different perspectives. On the one hand, wounded healers are expected through their own traumatic experiences to have a greater empathy with the suffering of their patients. They can transform their own wounds into healing power and hope, as seen, for example, in certain types of shamanism (Comas-Diaz and Padilla, 1990). Many Christian saints have also used their own weaknesses and sufferings as a means of becoming more compassionate and strong (Maeder, 1989). On the other hand, some wounded healers are found to have a compelling *need* to help others (Kleinman, 1988). They are unconsciously attracted to the psychotherapeutic profession in order to gain emotional release through their relationships with patients. This relationship also becomes a way of avoiding their own trauma, which becomes isolated and encapsulated (Maeder, 1989). From this point of view, it would be difficult for wounded healers to maintain 'sustained empathic inquiry' (Wilson and Lindy, 1994).

However, Carl Jung discusses this issue in *Memories, Dreams, Reflections* (1983), in which he, at over 80 years old, writes that 'only the wounded physician heals' (p. 155). The patient must mean something to the therapist. If the therapist is not affected by the patient's message, he will not be able to help the patient. Evidently, Jung finds that the therapist's own wounds are a condition for a genuine empathic stance. From his own experience of a life-long search for self-realization, Jung, however, also emphasizes the necessity for the therapist to understand himself, because 'the patient's treatment begins with the doctor, so to speak. Only if the doctor knows how to cope with himself and his own problems will he be able to teach the patient to do the same' (p. 154). And he continues:

> It often happens that the patient is exactly the right plaster for the doctor's sore spot. Because this is so, difficult situations can arise for the doctor too – or rather, especially for the doctor. Every therapist ought to have a control by some third person, so that he remains open to another point of view. Even the Pope has a confessor. (p. 156)

In essence, the problem of the wounded healer is the problem of how therapists manage their subjective counter-transference reactions to patients. This problem is common in all psychotherapeutic contexts, not only in the space of terror under state terrorism.

NOTES

1. In the beginning the team worked on a voluntary basis, but from 1982 it obtained financial support from the United Nations. In 1984 the team became an independent unit of CODEPU.

2. The DINA existed until 1977, when the CNI was created. For further details consult Chapter 4.

3. Part of her investigation was already published in 1987 by FASIC in the book *Trauma, Duelo y Reparación: Una Experiencia de Trabajo Psicosocial en Chile* (Trauma, Mourning and Reparation: An Experience of Psycho-Social Work in Chile) (Weinstein et al., 1987).

6

Trauma and Healing on the Individual Level

'Because of the tortured bodies…'

We now leave the physical space of terror, the place where the traumatic event took place, and venture further into the psychological world of the survivor – the person who has been lucky enough to survive physically the effort at breaking him or her down. We will attempt to understand the dynamics of the trauma following torture with special attention to the concepts of dissociation and victimization, and we will draw our map of how the therapists in the human rights movement developed their concepts of trauma and healing. As it is our map, we have also referred to general theories of post-traumatic research, primarily of North American origin.

As we described in the previous chapter, in order to understand the dynamics of this trauma, it is necessary to know *what* the repressive system wants to do to people, *how* it wants to do it, and *why* it wants to do it. Such an understanding is the core element of the development of counter-strategies for survival and therapeutic strategies of healing.

THE DYNAMICS OF THE TRAUMA

The experience of torture involves a variety of dimensions: physical, social, political and psychological. In the following, we will examine some important dynamics of torture as a psychological event.

Torture is a *multiple-stressor* event which includes threats to life and exposure to physical, social, political and psychological injury. Moreover, this traumatic event is highly *complex* as it contains a number of conflicting – even impossible – choices of which the most important is the *moral dilemma* of protecting oneself in order to survive or 'giving information' and, thus, possibly sacrificing one's comrades. Lastly, the experience of deliberate, man-made violence directed towards oneself during torture may profoundly change ideological perspectives and beliefs about human nature and life (Wilson, 1989, p. 10). This last dimension may lead to a severe *existential crisis*.

We will discuss these different psychological dynamics from two perspectives: dissociation and victimization. *Dissociation* refers mainly to the victim's relationship to him- or herself, that is, to the mechanisms of defence which are employed in the confrontation with the multiple stressors of torture – the threat to life and the exposure to injury. *Victimization* refers mainly to the victim's relationship to others, and this process describes the reactions of the victim to the complex structure of the torture situation, especially in confrontation with the moral dilemmas and impossible choices to which he or she is exposed. The victimization implies profound changes of ideological perspectives and relates to the victim's relationship to the world and to his or her life-project. Naturally, both dimensions interact with each other in the psychological dynamics of the trauma of torture, but for reasons of clarification we will examine them separately.

DISSOCIATION

'So you turn yourself off, you dissociate,' the psychiatrist, Julia, tells us about her psychological state during torture. 'What I lived through during my own experience of torture was something inconceivable which I could not contain,' she continues.

This process of 'turning yourself off', of dissociating, has an emotional and a cognitive dimension. It is an ego-defence process which involves splitting and repression (Lifton, 1988; Wilson, 1989). Lira (1983) describes the traumatic experience as something which becomes split off and encapsulated in the psychological world of the victim. The magnitude of *damage* spreading from this encapsulated experience will depend on external and internal factors: the degree of continued persecution by the dictatorship after release from prison, and the emotional significance attached to the torture by the victim and his or her primary social group – family, colleagues and political comrades.

Weinstein and Lira (1987) emphasize that the process of dissociation is central to the understanding of a person's experience during torture, and that a dissociative process is also an essential part of the subsequent reactions to the trauma. Dissociation is a means of psychological survival during torture, they claim: by dissociating, the victim establishes a partial disintegration of his or her ego in order to avoid an overwhelming anxiety which would lead to total disintegration. '*This happens to me as an object, not as a subject*' (Weinstein and Lira, 1987, p. 49).

This defence mechanism has also been described as extreme *psychic numbing* by Lifton (1988, p. 10). Julia illustrates how this process works as a protective shield, but she also hints at some of the consequences of it:

> Rape is not a difficult problem – at least for me. I place sexual violation on the same level as physical and psychological aggression – that is, as one more technique. We were all considered to be objects, and the persons who did one thing or another to us were also on the same level. Of course, there have been some cases of frigidity – with women comrades when they met their men afterwards, or others who did not want to establish an emotional relationship because of the sexuality that they imagined would follow.

By seeing the others as objects, not as humans, and, strangely enough, by seeing yourself as an object through the torturers' eyes, a distance is created which helps separate feelings and body. Rape was just a 'technique' used against the body. This numbing helped normalize a highly abnormal situation – making it, thereby, less threatening. But the cost of such normalization is also indicative of the perverse human relationship which torture creates: both the torturer and the victim become 'things', objects, and cease being human.

By dissociating as a mode of psychological survival confronted with the impossible choice between bodily or emotional integrity, the victim creates a *split* (Weinstein and Lira, 1987, p. 49) inside herself, and in this way she participates in her own disintegration. This is a general psychological mechanism in the dynamics of torture and the subsequent trauma. Later, we will go further into this *problem of complicity* which springs from the impossible choices inherent in the situation of torture: keep your subjectivity and disintegrate (totally); or renounce it, and you will also disintegrate (partially).

McCann and Pearlman (1990, p. 41) define dissociation as a cognitive disturbance that is characterized by 'an alteration of consciousness in which experiences and affects are not integrated into memory and awareness'. Depersonalization, derealization and fragmentation are symptoms of dissociation in connection with severe childhood abuse, they add, and the split-off memory fragments can exist as 'a hidden self that remembers the abuse and may be continuing to protect the adult self through the dissociative process' (ibid., p. 286).

Apparently, there are a number of similarities between the dynamics of traumata after incest and torture. Weinstein and Lira (1987, p. 49) use the terms 'indifference' (I felt like an object) and 'unreality' (it was as a nightmare) about the emotional state of the victim both during and after the torture. They also emphasize the fragmentation of the self which happens during torture, and the subsequent projection of the dissociated parts in the victim's intimate relationships.

The inner split will, naturally, also affect the *self-image* of the victim: 'I have changed', 'I am another person now' (ibid., p. 53). The victim cannot join the split parts together, cannot establish a connection between the person he or she was before and after the torture. Likewise, the feelings of derealization, unreality, create a general *confusion* in relation to reality. The boundaries between fantasy and reality are changed when reality has proven to be worse than any fantasy imaginable. It therefore becomes difficult later on to discriminate between the inner and the outer worlds, a state which often leads to paranoid symptoms (ibid., p. 54).

Lifton (1988, p. 10) emphasizes that dissociation interrupts and distorts the symbolizing process: 'The mind needs the nourishment provided by the continuous process of creating images and forms in order to function well.' The distortion of the symbolizing process is described by Weinstein and Lira (1987, p. 56) as a formation of new symbols through which the outer world, the body, the feelings and the words take on new meanings associated with the situation of torture.

Referring to survivors of the Second World War, Lifton (1988, p. 24) adds that 'in order to dissociate itself from grotesque death, the mind must itself cease to live, become itself deadened. The dissociation becomes intrapsychic in the sense that the feeling is severed from knowledge or awareness of what is happening.' This state is accompanied by feelings which are equivalents of death: 'it's like everything is destroyed,' Lifton quotes one survivor (p. 25). For the survivor of political torture these feelings of death also have to do with another aspect which we will now go into in some detail: the relationship between politics and feelings.

Victimization

How does the trauma relate to the victim's relationship to others and to the world – and especially to 'the political project'? During torture a certain power relationship is established between torturer and victim in which the dignity of the tortured person is attacked – he or she is placed in an inferior position. After release from prison, this inferior role may be re-enacted, consciously or unconsciously, in the victim's relationship to him- or herself and in the relationship to significant others – members of the political group or the family. This process of *victimization* is associated with the reactions of the victim during torture – especially to the meanings that the person has attached to 'giving information', 'talking' or 'betraying'. Victimization could also be described as a 'moral trauma', because it changes the person's feelings of dignity and moral integrity.

To understand the significance of these reactions, we must again return to the question of *what* the victim wanted to accomplish, that is, the political rationality of the person. Moreover, we must also return to *what* those in power wanted to accomplish by means of torture, that is, the political rationality attached to this activity. How are politics and psychology related?

To be involved in a political project had for many Chileans, both before and after the coup, an emotional significance which could be compared with the intense emotional attachment of a love relationship. The struggle for better social conditions and freedom was one of the most central themes of life. Thus, political commitment could be understood 'as a particular sort of object relation' (Lira, 1983, p. 1). If this object is lost, it will be felt by the person as if there is no longer any meaning to life. 'The crushing of a life-project' had a tremendous significance (ibid.). However, how could a life-project be crushed during torture? What happens during torture which can lead to a loss of the object, to a failure of the political project?

The problem of complicity and guilt

Let us cite some passages from the educational document by Rojas (1981). Although the attitude reflected herein seems harsh, it also does, however, reflect a general ideology of many resistance movements. In very direct words, the document expresses the principal elements in the fear of any person who is taken to the torture chamber for political reasons – the terrible choice between two different qualities of pain:

> The resistor who is active against the dictatorship – that is, the person who is a militant in opposing parties which have been declared to be outside 'of the law', or in organizations that act against the regime – must have a thorough knowledge of the role he has in these organizations. Fundamentally, there are three different roles: the public opponent, the secret opponent and the mixed opponent.
>
> The resistor must be absolutely sure of the direction and the role he has chosen. His level of participation must be chosen after a careful and profound analysis of his true ideals and interests, his life-project, his objectives as a

human being who is an inseparable part of the society in which he lives. He must attempt to gain knowledge as objectively as possible of his true motivation and to evaluate through a careful introspection his realistic capacities and qualities. This will permit him to assume the role of active resistor without over- or underestimating himself. He should not accept tasks for which he is not qualified, and if he accepts them because there is no one else to do it, he must prepare himself, study, train himself in a responsible way in order: *not to fail....*

Whatever type of torture is applied to the prisoner, it will *damage* him. This *damage* will not only cause a physical, bodily pain − a physiological disorder − but it will also stimulate a psychological pain which has to do with morals, feelings, ideology, *if the prisoner is not able to resist.* (pp. 2−3).

Every resistor must know that the physical pain passes and passes very rapidly as soon as the stimulus that has provoked it has stopped. On the contrary, to 'have given information', 'to have betrayed', leaves an indelible mark which will decisively change the life of the resistor. (p. 18)

Although it is often told by survivors of torture that the torturers appeared already to have the information which they asked for, the act of *giving* information to them will, in the world of the victim − and in his or her social group − be experienced as a personal betrayal and as an act of political failing. From now on, you are no longer worthy to be a member of the political group. The giving to them of something they want (although they maybe already have it) is accompanied by strong feelings of complicity: 'Feelings of loss and defeat result from the failure of the political project, and the loss of the object is accompanied by a sense of responsibility for such a failure' (Lira, 1983, p. 1). The psychological − moral − pain, and 'the indelible mark' in the eyes of the comrades, leave the political opponent in the position which the tortures attempted to bring him or her to.

We will now turn our attention towards them − towards the repressive system and the torturers that represent it. What is the relationship between politics and psychology in their world?

To collaborate?

DITT-CODEPU (Pesutic, 1989, p. 92) notes that the principal objective of torture is to turn the political prisoner into a collaborator with the repressive system, and that this is attempted towards the majority of prisoners. According to Rojas (1981, p. 27), the degree of collaboration can be divided into the following categories:

1. Transformation of the resistor into a collaborator with the repressive apparatus.

2. To give information. The betrayal can be total or partial.
3. A definitive isolation from the resistance.
4. A degree of physical or psychological damage that prevents any useful activities.

To reach one or several of these aims, a whole spectrum of torture methods are used, as described in the preceding chapter. Thus, torturer and victim are placed in a position of mutual psychological warfare in which the torturer has an arsenal of physical and psychological weapons at hand while the victim only has his or her political commitment, life-project or ideology as protection:

Numerous prisoners have told about positive acts that helped them resist the torture:

– To have felt as an indispensable part of a group, to have had a complete certainty about the role that he has chosen in the resistance, always to have felt convinced of the justice of his fight, to have known about comrades who had died in combat or during torture without having given information.
– To have been together with other prisoners who with a gesture, a word reminded him of resisting, to have always known that in all circumstances the official of the repressive apparatus was an enemy that he must not give in to. (Rojas, 1981, pp. 28–9)

This is a very great demand to place on anyone – a demand which, however, is common in many types of resistance movements. Ten years later, one female psychologist added the following comment to this claim:

There was an ideology about torture – that the people resisted and were brave, and that they did not give names, and that they stood a lot of things. This aspect shows the dimensions of humiliation in its most cruel way. It is my experience that this is very difficult for people to speak about. But if you cannot work with this aspect, people never really improve.

To understand the dimensions of this dilemma is a precondition for understanding the dynamics of the trauma following this forced choice between two unbearable possibilities which both threaten psychological or physical survival. As observed by Weinstein and Lira (1987, pp. 41–2), this choice leaves the victim in a 'double-bind' situation or a 'trap with no exits': either you have to suffer intolerable pain or even death, or you 'betray' your comrades, which in fact means that you transform yourself into *their* torturer by delivering them to torture or maybe death. You have to choose between your physical and your moral integrity;

between yourself and your comrades; between the integrity of your family and the integrity of your organization. If you choose to fight for physical survival and relinquish your political beliefs and human values, then this will be another way of dying: a moral death. However, it is virtually impossible not to 'talk' – at least to some degree. As one female psychologist told us:

> I was very impressed by an old militant socialist who had been imprisoned and tortured three times. You know, the myth here in Chile is that the disappeared people are all those who did not talk during torture. So this man told me something which I thought was very strong: 'Look, I think that all the disappeared people, the living and the dead people – we have all talked to some degree during torture. What happens is that very few admit it. Also I talked. Because in those circumstances you cannot...'
>
> But I have met only a limited number of patients who openly said this to me: 'Yes, I talked', or 'I gave them names' or 'I denounced other comrades'. I have never used the word 'betray' and I don't like using it. Because to me, someone who betrays does it intentionally and decides it voluntarily. So to me, someone who talked – they just talked, they gave information, and I always try to give this back to my patients. Moreover, they have never given *all* the information that they have. I think it is very important to show them that although they gave some of the information, they did not give all of it. This is clearly evidence of the fact that the giving of information was not voluntary. They have not decided: 'I am going to talk to stop the suffering or to save my skin.' No, there comes a moment when they cannot bear any more, and some have more resistance, others less, and that is all.
>
> But it is quite a difficult problem, because the environment is tremendously punitive. I have discussed this a lot with some of my comrades who are militants in the political parties. They always talk about betrayers, informers. In our team we do not do that. No one knows, when it comes to the point, how they will react to torture. None of us can say that we would not talk, if the moment came.

Both during torture and afterwards, the only way of psychological survival is to realize that the choices which the torturers confront you with are *false*. It is a trap created by those in power, comment Weinstein and Lira (1987, p. 42). Moreover, the boundaries between breaking down and resisting are very difficult to draw. As Julia told us:

> It has interested me very much to find out about resistance to torture. The subject who experiences political repression can be described from different perspectives: psychological, biological, biographical, historical, family, social, political, ideological – as a whole system containing all these elements in some sort of equilibrium. How come he or she, confronted with an aggression,

had a weak point or a fragile nucleus which could not be compensated by the rest of the system?

In the prison, I was the only psychiatrist, so I had to attend to two different types of problems: the tortured who had problems from the torture as such, and the others who had problems of a more serious type – they were comrades who had given information. I had problems with this last category for two reasons: I was a militant, and at that time no one broke, no one gave information. For example, the party did a lot of investigations to find out if it was true that you had not given information about anything or anybody. And they only allowed you to continue as a militant if it was true, the others were not allowed to.

This distinction was made in the prison and it was exactly the same afterwards, in exile. The secret party consisted only of militants who had been recognized as people who had not broken during torture. But I had to attend to the comrades who had broken. This was a very positive experience for me, because I came out of prison with a much more flexible attitude. Because I understood, I saw the process of the collaborator, I knew why.... Several times when they were torturing me, I only wanted them to kill me – to die during torture. When I thought about it later I could see that basically this was also a break-down. If I wanted to die it was because I had been broken, with the only difference that the question or the interrogation at that moment was not directed towards the information which I could have given, and, therefore, I did not give it. But in another situation, I would also have done it. Just as everyone could become a torturer, I think everyone could break down. If they manage to break the nucleus of the person, to find the weak point, everyone will break down. So this made me realize that I could also have broken down, and it gave me a more flexible attitude when I was in exile – for example, to understand the people who had sought asylum, our leaders, the people you had admired, our leaders who had gotten into the embassies and left the country, had run off three days after the coup.

Psychology and politics

To therapists working in democratic countries with a history of many years of peace, the importance of the relationship between politics and psychology is difficult to grasp. Under state terrorism this relationship is taken for granted – this was one of the cultural positions from which people from the human rights movement talked during our interviews. It did not seem necessary to explain it; neither did we ask very much about it. Only afterwards did we appreciate the impact of this dimension for the understanding of the trauma of torture. Therefore, we must again emphasize the words of the Chilean psychologist who said that 'if you cannot work with this aspect, people never really improve'.

The problem of complicity and shame

The trap of impossible 'political' choices which we have described above is enforced by different methods, which we have reviewed in the previous chapter. These methods also involve conflicting choices but they are, however, subordinate to the central, political trap. The most victimizing of these methods is the use of sexuality as a means of breaking down the resistance of the prisoner. 'In general, men and women perceive this as the most humiliating experience', one psychologist told us. Thus, sexual torture also involves impossible choices; but while the central, political trap mainly creates strong feelings of guilt, the sexual trap creates deep-seated feelings of *shame*. Not only does the victim feel responsible for the abuse; he or she also feels unclean and contaminated (Agger and Jensen, 1993a; Agger, 1994).

The potential of this method is described indirectly in these instructions for how to prepare yourself for sexual torture:

It is common to be naked during the interrogation.

Before being detained: learn to accept your own naked body, with pride, as it is. It's yours. Do not feel shameful about it. Reject the idea of nakedness as a sin, as something ridiculous, as a humiliation. Use it as an instrument of resistance: take care of it, make it strong, do exercises, learn to relax, get to know your capacities and limitations. Take care of it in all ways, with all of its functions.

When you get detained: When they order you to take your clothes off, or they brusquely take your clothes off, you must resist it, or if you already have an 'idea of them', you must attack them in a natural way.

Never show them that it does not molest you to be naked. Behave as if you are shameful, humiliated – try to cover yourself to make them think that your nakedness is a good technique for breaking you psychologically.

The humiliations: *Nothing* that comes from *them* can humiliate the resistor – on the contrary, you must feel pride at being clean in front of their attacks. Inside ourselves we must feel contempt, disgust, hatred – but do not show it. (Rojas, 1981, pp. 20–21)

In this preparation, the person attempts to change culturally engraved feelings about the body and sexuality. That which he or she has learned to be ashamed of, for example being naked in public, shall become an 'as if' feeling – and in this way turned into a sophisticated weapon of defence against shame. This impossible choice between becoming shameless 'inside' and shameful 'outside' is in itself an alteration of normal feelings about the body and sexuality. Feelings of shame and humiliation may be avoided, but instead a dissociation between body and feelings is created. The psychiatrist Julia gave us this illustration of the problem:

> In the prison where I was, there were two cases of pregnancies after rape. Fortunately, in one of the cases she had a spontaneous abortion – fortunately, because she didn't want to have the child. The other wanted to have the child. She said: 'Basically it is a part of me, the rest doesn't matter.' Moreover, she did not see who it was; who, of all those, it was. So for her the person who placed the sperm did not have any value. She also had a very beautiful attitude, because she said: 'Basically, it is the fruit of my resistance.' Anyway, that was the explanation that made her have it. I haven't seen her again; the child must be big now – 15–16 years old.

The capacity to solve the problem of keeping 'clean' in front of the attacks of the torturers is related to the attitudes towards sexuality which have been encoded by the cultural context and the messages received from parents, church and social environment during childhood. Important also are factors such as: the types of sexual methods that were used, and their duration and intensity; possible sexual problems before imprisonment; the stage of sexual life reached before imprisonment (whether the victim had initiated a sexual relationship); the physical consequences, for example, pregnancies, infections, damage to sexual organs (Weinstein and Lira, 1987, p. 47).

'In general, women who were in jail were raped, but it is very difficult for them to testify about this experience', says one psychologist. It is maybe even more difficult for the men. As Julia told us:

> I know several cases of sexually tortured men. For example two cases of genital torture – with electricity, with blows – physical aggression which was always accompanied (this is a Brazilian technique) with them saying: 'You will be impotent for a long time, if not for the rest of your life.' And this is really a very strong suggestive element. In many cases there were comrades – also those in the concentration camps – who started masturbating to find out if it was true or not. And they were not able to. So this confirmed for them that it was true that the electricity had made them impotent. And those who have been through homosexual anal rape, I think that they will be traumatized by this forever – really, this was the worst. There were others who had also been violated sexually, who had water tubes or different instruments put into their anus – but this was not associated with feelings of being raped, but rather with feelings of humiliation. Of course, symbolically it was rape, but it was not on the level of a real rape. I would say that the worst sequels we find in men who have been raped homosexually.

In the sexual trap of torture the person participates – although against his or her will – in a human relationship which is utterly degrading. She or he is 'forced to relate to his or her own inner objects' (Becker et al., 1989, p. 87). In the mind of the victim and the others, the question will always be lurking about the degree of responsibility: did he ask for it himself, could she have been more careful? In both the political and the sexual trap of torture the victim has to *make* him- or herself powerless. This self-induced passivity and impotency is a mode of survival, of protecting oneself against unbearable pain or death. However, in this process the victim also destroys his or her own *identity* (Weinstein and Lira, 1987, pp. 50–53).

Later, this process may be turned into self-destruction as the only way to handle the feelings of guilt and shame. Guilt because of not having lived up to that which was expected by oneself or by the political group; shame because of the contamination from the sexual abuse – the shame of being tainted. Lifton (1988, p. 25) describes how survivors of death camps become 'tainted by death'; they become parts of the destruction which was brought upon them. They carry the psychic stigma of the annihilated. Similar symptoms of victimization are also mentioned by Ochberg (1988).

Likewise, Chilean psychologists describe how certain parts of the victim's self become identified with the aggressor and with the aggression he or she has been submitted to. They mention self-destructive symptoms such as self-loathing, suicidal attempts, feelings of loss, sexual impotency, incapacity to work, destruction of intimate relationships. On the psychosomatic level, gastric, respiratory and cardiovascular symptoms are mentioned (Weinstein and Lira, 1987, pp. 50–52).

'Feelings of death emerge in the person's conscience' (Lira, 1983, p. 1). Such feelings of death also invade the survivor's relationships to other close objects. The victimization may unconsciously be re-enacted in destructive or self-destructive relationships with partners or children. Ultimately, the choice of suicide may be felt by the person to be the only symbolic resolution of the problem of complicity, as explained by Wilson and Lindy (1994) in the case of *Sophie's Choice*.[1]

Thus, a capital problem which confronts the survivor is how to bring the hidden self out of its shelter and handle the affective distress following the reduction of psychic numbing. When the hidden self no longer protects the survivor by staying in its shelter, she or he is also faced with the task of finding a bearable solution to the problem of complicity. In other words, how is the split-off memory fragment integrated, and how is a connection to life re-established?

THERAPEUTIC STRATEGIES

Counter-Strategies during Torture

There are different ways of managing the states of psychic overload during torture: different coping responses to the excessive demands of the situation. Dissociation is one such response.

Several therapists from the human rights movement have attempted to prevent this type of coping by suggesting the adoption of other attitudes during torture:

> In order to survive this situation in the most adequate way, it is essential that you see that the choices to which the aggressors submit you are false, and that they place you in a trap with no exits. This meta-comprehension permits you to *consciously* reduce your stimulus field, to *voluntarily* create fantasies that this is happening to another person and, in this way, to reduce the intensity of your emotions and perceptions. (Weinstein and Lira, 1987, p. 42; our emphasis)

The strategy suggested here intends to avoid psychic overload by reducing information. The above-mentioned proposal by Rojas (1981) to 'behave *as if* you are shameful, humiliated' (our emphasis) during sexual torture is also a means of reducing the risk of psychic overload by creating psychological distance from the situation. Moreover, it is a means of cognitive restructuring by changing the meaning of the torture. This complex attitude can, however, also be interpreted as a distortion of reality: the torturers are, in fact, violating your bodily and psychic integrity.

Rojas (1981, p. 32), furthermore, suggests the following strategies for diminishing emotional distress:

> During torture/interrogation the feeling of fear can only be defeated by the resistor if he opposes it with *other feelings, which are*:
>
> — the certainty of his belief, his decision to resist, not to betray;
> — the pride in the role that he has chosen;
> — the feeling of not being alone, of being part of a whole in a historically determined moment.
>
> Your only weapon in front of the most brutal aggression will be: your contempt, your disgust and anger towards the officials who in this moment reveal who they really are.

Although this may be a means of restructuring feelings of distress in a positive way, it is also a strategy which leaves the person in the trap of impossible choices. It is inferred that you are able to 'resist', and if it is not possible to live up to this demand (which very few are), expressive coping strategies such as dissociation and splitting are likely to be employed as defence mechanisms, as described above.

Rojas (1981, pp. 9–10) proposes other strategies for positive cognitive restructuring such as those cited earlier:

> The detainee must try to get information right from the beginning: how many are there, who are they, how do they behave, which service is detaining him. This is counter-intelligence work which the resistor must start from his first contact with the officials of the repressive apparatus. *It is his job, it is an obligation....* He must every day attempt to evaluate and get to know about their manners, their acts, their language, their usual way of behaving. (our emphasis)

Seeing the situation of torture as a job of evaluation, of counter-intelligence, changes the meaning of an extremely negative event into something of potential value. The traumatic event is positively reframed. However, most likely, the victim is caught in a trap with no exits, even though he or she is able to manage some cognitive restructuring.

As Julia told us:

> So all this becomes part of daily life. It becomes part of the environment. You see it all as something planned, organized. So it is something you also become part of ... the torturing environment.

Counter-Strategies after Torture

Most survivors will probably not have an opportunity to get professional therapeutic help. They will have to find ways of self-healing. An important means of counteracting the consequences of having been 'part of the torturing environment' is the participation in the movement's human rights groups. In the following chapters, we will describe the organization and working methods of such groups. For the former prisoner, the Association of Ex-Political Prisoners is relevant as well as the groups of 'witnesses' from the different torture houses (see Chapter 4). As stressed by Wilson (1989), pro-social actions and self-disclosure in such groups facilitate the healing process. Bearing witness to what happened helps alleviate psychic numbing. Likewise, the act of helping other survivors who have suffered the same trauma counteracts victimization. In many cases, however, this type of self-help work is not sufficient. If the trauma is associated with having 'talked' during torture, such groups may also become counter-therapeutic, because the survivor will have to hide guilt and shame, or else he or she will be condemned by the others. That is, the traumatized person will not be able to receive help for his or her most serious problem: the hidden self which remembers that which the remaining part of the self cannot contain.

Professional Healing Strategies

During the first years after the coup a new theory and practice had to be built up by the mental health professionals who gave assistance to the victims of the regime. It was in every way a new experience for the therapists, who had to build up a practice relying completely on their own resources in an attempt to confront the realities of the dictatorship. As one psychologist told us:

> I was at the same level as the other psychologists and psychiatrists, who were very familiar with some types of psychotherapy, but they had the same level of ignorance that I had about the problems that were presented by the people affected by violations of human rights. I think this allowed us to work with less prejudice when looking for methods to work with these types of problems. I had a lot of prejudice about current diagnoses with the labels 'psychotic', 'neurotic', and so on. This type of diagnosis did not tell us anything. I think that the composition of the team with psychiatrists and psychologists with different experiences and theoretical perspectives contributed to connect this approach. We were able to search for different ways to work, but at the same time I think that this influenced the emphasis put on the body as the real support of the psychological problems. It was as if we forgot that people had a body. This was very strange. We spoke, all the time, about the meaning of somatic problems but not as if they were real somatic problems. People needed somatic *and* psychological treatment, and there were injuries to the body – also to the brain, possibly. I, now, consider this to be the main error of our early work. We discussed it with the Uruguayan medical doctors. They said: 'Why do you Chilean psychologists and psychiatrists forget about the body in torture?' I do not have any explanation for this, but that was our experience. During the first years, all the institutions only had medical doctors related to emergencies, or for people who were really sick because of somatic problems. It was not an ordinary way of treating people. Today, I consider this to be very important, because people need to know about themselves, to know that they are physically OK.
>
> There were also very important limitations on treating the somatic problems of people. We had no money in the institution for sending people for private treatment, and treatment was impossible through the national health

service. I think that maybe this was the explanation. It was probably a way of not feeling impotent when we faced problems which we had no possibility of solving. And the body-problems were really beyond our capabilities. When we later organized another institution we decided to give the same amount of attention to the medical problems of people as to the psychiatric or psychological problems. I think that this was a very good decision, because in the majority of cases today, people readily consult for somatic problems, while it is very difficult to gear up to a psychological consultation. It is difficult because it entails a lot of suffering. It is easier to formulate the problem in somatic terms and say: 'I have a headache.' We must accept that people, at first, only recognize the somatic problems, they avoid speaking about suffering. If you can follow them in this, they will probably identify the relationship between the somatic and the suffering. I think it is a mistake to differentiate torture into physical and mental torture. What is the difference? Also, I think it is very difficult to see the difference between psychological and somatic suffering.

During the early years after the coup, important theories and methods of psychotherapy were gradually built up. The therapeutic frame of reference was founded on the Chilean reality, but theories from the outside were also an inspiration. Most significant were the experiences of therapists working with victims of the Holocaust (for example, Bruno Bettelheim), philosophers such as Frantz Fanon and Jean-Paul Sartre, but there were also references to the psychoanalytic school (Freud and Fenichel) as well as to the system-oriented approach of Paul Watzlawick, for example. The objectives of psychotherapy are described by Weinstein and Lira (1987, p. 62) as follows: to re-establish the relationship to reality in a process where the person regains his or her history and the capacity to relate to other people, and where the person again has a vision of a meaningful future with a commitment to his or her 'task'. This also includes a consciousness-raising process in which the traumatic experiences during torture are now seen from a broader, political perspective, that is, a de-privatization process.

The testimony method

One of the early and most important methods of de-privatization was the use of testimonies as a part of therapy. In the beginning, testimonies were used for recording and denouncing extreme examples of torture. The survivor's story was taped, transcribed and sent to international organizations as evidence against the dictatorship. Little by little the therapeutic value of the method also became evident and started a series of reflections on the possibilities and limitations of the method for the healing of the emotional conseuqences of torture (Weinstein and Lira, 1987, p. 65).

> The practical procedure of testimony is quite simple. You propose that the affected people record on a tape-recorder what has happened to them in order to make a documentary proof of the illegal acts and the violence which have been perpetrated against them. You point out to them that this detailed reconstruction can be painful but that it will permit them to understand the emotions, contradictions and ambivalence associated with this traumatic experience. Thereafter, a sequence of sessions is started with the aim of tap-ing in detail everything which has happened to the person in relation to detention and torture. You also include the complete life-story from early childhood, because this contributes to the integration of the traumatic expe-rience into the entire life of the subject. In this way, the testimony registers everything which has to do with the core of the trauma as well as previous events and the social factors from the past and present which explain the type of participation and motivation of the subject.
>
> An alternative way of working that was developed was to achieve a final, written version of the story which expressed all of the work that the therapist and the subject had done together on the basis of the transcriptions of the tape-recordings. (ibid., pp. 65–6)

Weinstein and Lira (ibid.) discuss the different therapeutic aspects of this method. They have observed that it alleviates symptoms, that it transforms something painful into a document which can be useful to other people. It is not only cathartic but is also a political and legal weapon against the aggressors. In this way, some of the aggression which the torture has created in the survivor can be channelled and elabo-rated in a socially constructive manner, thus changing the self-destruc-tive spiral.

> It is a paradox that the testimony in some ways is a complete confession – that which they tried to extract by means of torture and which the subject protected at the cost of his or her pain. But now it is an act which is in-scribed in the original existential project. The information will not be used against the comrades, but, rather, against the torturers. (ibid., p. 67)

At a meeting in Santiago in 1980 on 'Political Crisis and Psycho-logical Damage', therapists from FASIC first presented their – now famous – paper on this method: 'The Testimony of Political Repression as a Therapeutic Instrument'. The paper was later published in Spanish (1983) and in English (Cienfuegos and Monelli, 1983). One of the origi-nators of this method, a psychologist, told us about the development of the method, and her thoughts about it now – more than ten years later:

The testimony is inspired by a study of poverty in Mexico by the anthropologist Oscar Lewis. In the fifties he recorded stories of poor families in order to give the scientific community knowledge about poverty. We also thought about how we could give our community knowledge about torture, about the suffering of people and the political context, and how we got them to accept different political ideas. In general, the Chilean population justified the repression of certain political ideas. They said: 'These people are communists, and that is why they suffered torture.' No, they suffered torture because we have a terrorist state, and this state made the laws against the communists and the leftists in general. The communists had their ideas, and if these ideas are criminal, they should be brought to trial. One should not kill them or make them disappear or something like that. It was very important, not only for the patients but also for society, to understand why people behaved as they did. In this sense, I think that the testimony was very valuable. If you receive information through the interpretation of other people, you have the possibility of denying it. But if you receive this same information correctly, in the words of the people who were affected by this or suffered that, it is different.

Another source of inspiration for the testimony were the stories of the saints, the Christian martyrs. The Catholic church used to teach people by giving them examples of the lives of holy people who lived in the past and suffered martyrdom, and all of us in the team had received this kind of teaching. I remember that we discussed how the Christian church puts a lot of emphasis on the example. So we thought that this was a very important legacy of humanity's knowledge about how you teach others about something: by telling stories. I think these are the main assets of the testimony. But for us who work with therapy now, it is not as necessary to use this tool as it was in 1983. If eight or ten years ago it was important to confirm the experience, today it is important to confirm the feelings. This is a great shift, because at that time to confirm the experience was the basic need of the person. Now, the whole country agrees that this experience was true, that what the Rettig Report said is true – that people were really tortured in this country. We must discuss therapy in this new context. I think that we have perceived the new and different needs of the people, and we have changed. In some ways we have gradually approached the more common methods of psychotherapy, because in all psychotherapy you need to work with feelings, but in 'ordinary' psychotherapy you don't need to confirm reality.

It is possible that in this country, now, the testimony is useful for some people who have never talked about their experiences and consult a therapist for the first time. But in general, this method was useful when you needed to confirm reality as a reality lived and experienced by a lot of people, and you needed also to communicate feelings, facts and a lot of things, and to give it into the hands of the people, of the person, as an instrument that could be used, if he or she needed it. Because in the cases where we used the testimony, we gave a copy of it to the people, and they sent it to the United

Nations, the High Commissioner for Human Rights Affairs, and the special court reporters in charge of Chile.

To me, the most important thing was to confirm the reality and also to avoid people having to tell the same story again and again. People had the story in their hands, and they could photocopy it and send it, and so on. It was very destructive to have to repeat their story time and again because they were denouncing it – but in a dissociated way, without linking emotions with facts. We decided to correct this, because I think that this only produces a deeper dissociation. People don't cry every time they tell their story, and they can tell the story without any feeling, without any emotion, and this is the worst. I think that if they could keep the paper and say 'this is my story', they would not be forced to dissociate. They would only tell it on one or two occasions. We discovered this with the relatives of the disappeared, because they had to tell their story again and again, and today it is very hard to work on this type of dissociation with them. It appears now as a characteristic of their personality, a feature. Over sixteen or seventeen years, the person has worked with these feelings by dissociating when he made denouncements, when he was an activist. It is a great risk, and the psychologists have the same risk – to speak about this without any personal engagement.

I think it is very interesting to hear from you about the testimony's transcultural value, because we also discovered that this method was important for the poor people, in general. Now, this method does not have the same importance, because we have no cultural differences, and we know, in general, that we have the same interpretation of things. But if you have to work with these cultural differences, it is very important – this is an application of the testimony that I have not thought about.

When you ask about the testimony, I begin to think that we need to reflect more about it. Because we used this method in a certain historical situation, and we lost it. Later we tried to understand things in another way.

It is our experience in therapeutic work with refugees in Denmark that the testimony method has proved valuable as a transcultural therapeutic tool (Agger and Jensen, 1990a). The Chilean experiences with this method also seem to be useful in other countries suffering state terrorism.

The psychotherapeutic process

In all the insurgent institutions that grew up after the coup, *denunciation, investigation* and *treatment* were the three pillars of the healing work. The testimony method is an example of the unification of these three principles: the testimony denounces the human rights violations, it supplies new knowledge about the repressive system, and it has a healing effect on the person who bears witness. The testimony was, however, not the only way of carrying out psychotherapy. As observed by Pesutic (1989, p. 238), the tortured person has always been wounded in the area of *basic trust* in others, so maybe therapy will have to begin by re-establishing trust.

Disturbed schemes

Following the theoretical framework of McCann and Pearlman (1990), the tortured person has suffered a disruption in a number of vital cognitive *self-schemes*. The concept of self-schemes can be 'broadly defined as assumptions, beliefs, and expectations about self and the world' (ibid., p. 57). Such schemes may be largely unconscious. McCann and Pearlman focus especially on schemes that are closely related to central human needs prior to victimization. Thus, 'trauma disrupts one's central needs and alters, disrupts, or disconfirm one's beliefs, assumptions and expectations in those central need areas' (ibid., p. 61). The most important schemes are those related to one's frame of reference, and those related to the psychological needs for safety, trust, esteem, independence, power and intimacy (ibid., p. 79).

The trauma of torture disrupts all the above-mentioned schemes, and from this perspective the aim of therapy is gently to challenge disturbed schemes in the above-mentioned seven areas of need. The outcome of therapy may be an alteration of schemes in a positive, growth-producing direction.

The steps of psychotherapy

Chilean psychotherapists have themselves developed new models for their work under state terrorism. Weinstein and Lira (1987, p. 65) describe the steps of psychotherapy as follows:

1. Catharsis and reconstruction of the traumatic experience.
2. Alleviation of symptoms.
3. Emotional elaboration of the traumatic experience.
4. Linking the traumatic experience to the existential meanings of the subject's life.
5. Recovery of his or her social role.
6. Reframing of the traumatic experience in the context of the subject's life experiences.
7. Reorganization of the existential project: continuity between the past, present and the future.

8. Recovery of collective links.

9. Confrontation of marital problems and problems in relationships with other family members because of the torture experience.

Although Chileans are themselves rather sceptical towards post-traumatic theory in general (see Becker, forthcoming), it is interesting to notice that their actual way of work encompasses many of the very same elements, although in a different language, as in the work of McCann and Pearlman (1990) referred to above and John P. Wilson's important book about post-traumatic therapy (1989).

The hidden self: a clinical case study

In the following we will use a clinical illustration related to us by a female psychologist. This is a case of psychotherapy with a woman who had a very strong dissociative defence against her 'hidden self', which was so ashamed about the sexual torture to which she had been subjected that she was unable to express herself in words.

> If you suspect that the patient has been sexually tortured – and that is very probable – and you avoid creating conditions that facilitate him or her being able to speak about it, you are, in some ways, an accessory. People know that you, in some ways, help them to let the problem appear – they have difficulties speaking by themselves about it. I had a patient for three years. The first year, she told me about a lot of very important problems, but far removed from the problem of rape. In general, I was captured by the importance of the other problems, but her somatic problems continued. I began thinking that rape was the main issue in her life, but she was very active in limiting my possibilities for putting the problem forth. She erected very strong walls, signalling: 'don't go into this problem!'
>
> One day, I said: 'I suspect that you were raped,' and she answered: 'What?' I continued: 'It is probable because all women in this country who were in the hands of the secret police were raped. I never heard of a woman who was not raped.' In this way, by introducing to her the fact that it had occurred to a lot of people, I allowed her to say something about it. She said: 'Yes, but I have decided not to speak about it.' This was a very important step, because she accepted it, and we both accepted as a part of the therapy that this type of thing can occur in the life of a person who has suffered the things she had.
>
> Some time later, she said to me: 'One day I will say something about my experience but on one condition: that you have an entire day for me only.' The next time we met, I said to her: 'It is impossible. We can have an hour and a half or two hours, but not a whole day.' This was the result of a discussion with our supervisor. I had said to the supervisor: 'If she needs to speak for a whole day, wouldn't that be OK?', but the supervisor answered:

'No, this is a trap. She is using it to capture your attention and give you conditions. The problem is that *she* needs to speak. *You* don't need to hear this. That is the difference.'

This difference is very important. When I had the opportunity to transmit my feelings about it to the patient, I said: 'I think it is very difficult for you to speak about this, but I can wait.' Then, a strange thing happened. When I said: 'I can wait,' she left her normal state of consciousness. She fixed her eyes on a certain point. She did not say anything, but she moved as if she was living through something awful. She tried to vomit, and she had a terrified expression on her face.

I was very afraid, because I had never seen this before. She was not a hysterical person. I was really afraid, because I was in another city without any colleagues nearby. I tried to describe in words to her what I was seeing. I said: 'I think that you feel very threatened, you feel very bad,' or something like that. I did not know what would happen in the next seconds. For some time, I spoke slowly. I did not touch her, because I thought that this was very strange, and I preferred to speak and not to do anything else. Suddenly she said: 'I am very tired. I need to sleep,' and she lay down. She did not sleep, but it was like a sleep for a few minutes. She woke up and asked me: 'What happened?' and I told her and said: 'You moved in a strange way. I think that you were threatened by something, and I think that it was related to torture.' 'It is sufficient for today,' she answered.

Later on, this sequence was repeated – she replaced words with this type of movement, but I was more calm the next times, because I knew that it was possible for her to recover consciousness by herself. I discovered that it was impossible for her to put this experience into words, but because she had heard my words three or four sessions before, she could say something about it. Only very slowly was it possible to go into her experience. I had supervision twice a week on this case. It was very interesting for me, because it was the first time I received a person who did not have words. In general, people found words – some symbolic expressions – but in this case, it was impossible for her. She was a person with a very strong degree of repression, especially in the area of sexuality. For this reason, it was very difficult for her to put it into words. She did not have words, and when I discussed it with my supervisor, she said to me: 'Possibly, this sexual repression is the reason that her rape-experience remains as a black hole, but I also think that it is important that she was able to put part of the experience into words.' She improved a lot, but I think that the damage was very profound.

THERAPEUTIC RELATIONSHIPS

The dictatorship defined the possible target-objects as 'enemies of the fatherland'. 'This threatening situation produced a great closeness between helpers and victims' (Lira, forthcoming). In a very polarized political situation this implicitly or explicitly suggested that 'we belong to the same side', Lira continues.

Thus, the situation of the patients was not much different from the situation of the therapists. Those therapists who began giving assistance to the victims of the dictatorship were all committed to this work for ethical, social or political reasons:

> We all had some level of participation in the government of Popular Unity[2] either as sympathizers or as active members of one of the parties of that coalition. This produced a significant concern for the destiny of the victims. (ibid.)

As noted by Wilson and Lindy (1994), empathy is based on counter-identification, and it is this process that permits empathy to be therapeutically useful. The political and institutional context we have described could be an obstacle to the process of counter-identification, which implies that the therapist can *also* view the patient's conflict with objectivity. The political consciousness of the therapists and the link to a human rights movement may, however, have been an aid in maintaining only partial identification with the conflict of patients. The connection between the personal and the political could act as a defence against over-involvement with the patient.

Some of the therapists we interviewed stated that it was often hard for them to find anyone to help them with their own trauma. As one male psychiatrist told us:

> I was on one of those lists.... I did not dare to present myself to the police immediately. So I went into hiding for a week, and then I presented myself. The person who received me was a major. He made very threatening remarks about the bad records he had of me. He told me that I was a dangerous extremist, a terrorist, things like that ... they didn't have anything to do with my reality.
>
> But after that came periods of solitary confinement, torture ... my personal experience ... from then there were moments that were very difficult for me, moments of fear. I was very afraid because they told me that they were going to shoot me, or that they would give me a very long sentence, or that they would take my wife prisoner. Well, afterwards I was in a prison in a small cell together with twelve other prisoners. The treatment was rough, bitter, intimidating ... the comrades from the cell were taken out to be questioned. They returned with marks from torture, and then they came to me because I was a doctor, and because I was also a psychiatrist they asked me for advice about how to ease the anguish, depression and panic which they had ... and I also had my own feelings. I am a man with depressive

tendencies and at times I was feeling quite bad. Unfortunately, psychiatrists many times don't have anyone to talk to about their pain. We have to carry our pain ourselves, take care of ourselves.

The Bond of Commitment

The fact that therapists and patients belonged to the same side created a sense of trust between them. This 'bond of commitment' and of 'ethical non-neutrality' (Weinstein et al., 1987) was a necessity under the conditions of state terrorism. A so-called 'neutral' position was not possible, but this did not imply that the therapist could not view the conflicts of patients objectively. The bond of solidarity gave patients the necessary confidence to consult and the ethical commitment permitted 'the translation of meanings between the different levels of contexts involved in the patient's suffering' (Lira, forthcoming). There is, thus, both an emotional bond between therapist and patient and a common discourse which allows them to interpret − translate − the individual symptoms into the language of human rights violations.

Elizabeth Lira (ibid.) illustrates this perspective in the following description of the first session with an old man who consulted her in 1986:

> *Therapist*: ... Why have you come? ... What has happened to you?
>
> *Patient*: Nothing. I had a little problem. I was arrested 12 or 13 days. I resisted well there ... but now, every night I dream of the jail. I don't feel like doing anything ... I was also taken prisoner in 1974. Afterwards things were catastrophic. A lot of searches. In the nightmares, I go back to the chains, to the tortures ... I want to get out of this jail ... of this enormous fall on the scale of human dignity....

In her comments on this dialogue, Elizabeth Lira underlines the following aspects: the patient associates his suffering and symptoms directly with the repressive experience. Also, the repressive experience appears 'to be a threatening, repetitive and never-ending situation, in spite of his efforts to minimize it'. Lastly, his depressive final comment 'could be understood as a metaphor either of his personal situation or that of Chilean society'.

It is, thus, a clear and fundamental ideological objective of the human rights and mental health work to link patients' personal symptoms to the social and political context. By the understanding of symptoms in this framework, the first step in the therapeutic process has already been taken. It is important to note that Lira *confirms* the experience of the patient: also she links his symptoms to the repression. One of the important elements in the testimony method was also to confirm reality. The dictatorship continuously denied that human rights violations had taken place.

The bond of commitment also had some difficulties. Mario Vidal (1990) from CINTRAS mentions the risk of mutual idealization and seduction. In the context of threat in which both patient and therapist lived, it became difficult for the patient to express aggressive feelings towards the therapist who risked so much to help him or her. Likewise, it was difficult for the therapist to allow him- or herself to experience anger towards the patient, who had suffered so much. This could imply that forbidden reactions on both sides induce a reverse 'conspiracy of silence'.

The Problem of the Wounded Healers

Julia discussed her feelings on returning to work:

> When I returned from exile, I knew that I could not start working as a psychiatrist at once. First of all, because I was not feeling well. After a while, however, my colleagues asked me to return to work, and so a year ago I started working here. I was very afraid, afraid of not knowing the medicaments, the names, the doses, of how to do psychotherapy, afraid of failing, that the patients would not progress, that they would not get well. I was very insecure. But my colleagues helped me a lot, and now I feel at ease being a psychiatrist again.
>
> In the beginning, it was very difficult for me to ask patients about their experiences of torture. I was afraid that I would not know what to do with them when they had told it. I did not know if it was worse for them to tell it, if it was better to leave it hidden. This was in the beginning. But later, we recognized the importance of telling everything, so at least I knew that.

However, the professional teams struggled with many difficult issues, especially concerning the management of aggressive feelings. According to Lira (forthcoming) and other therapists we interviewed, feelings in the team could vacillate between narcissistic omnipotence and impotence. This pattern implies maybe a regressive reaction towards the external threat. Therapists could feel isolated with their own pain in the team:

> We, as therapists, were subjects and objects of the same situation. We were dealing with the aggression and destruction of the patients. We were affected both by the patients' suffering and by the political threat, because we belonged to the same society. We had ambivalent feelings which ranged from total omnipotence to total impotence which circulated between us without

a real holding, in the sense that Winnicot gave to this concept. One of the characteristics of the team functioning was that personal isolation was hidden under very sensitive and vulnerable collective ties. We had great difficulty tolerating differences and facing conflicts. We also had difficulty with aggressive feelings, as if they were the legacy of the dictatorship inside the group. (Lira, forthcoming)

It is only now, after the emergency situation of the dictatorship has ended, that therapists have allowed themselves to look at their own situation. 'We were not able to be conscious of those perceptions and feelings or to go beyond them under military rule,' Lira continues. Only when a hope of liberation from the dictatorship became more realistic did therapists get the energy to turn their attention towards their own traumatization. In the present-day situation, where Chile is in a democratic process, supervision is an important resource for the safe 'holding'[3] of therapists (ibid.).

We can conclude that many therapists did find that their work had helped them overcome their own trauma. It was especially their political commitment and participation in the human rights movement that had helped them manage their subjective counter-transference reactions. The experiences from Chile seem, then, to demonstrate that the problem of the wounded healer cannot only be discussed from the perspective of the inner psychic dynamics of the therapist. In a context of human rights violations, this problem must also be related to the political context. To be on a survivor's mission in Chile was not only a question of surviving oneself but also of the survival of democracy and human dignity.

Some therapists did, however, describe difficult subjective counter-transference reactions on both the cognitive and emotional levels. On the cognitive level, they mentioned the risk of over-identification with patients and of becoming overly committed to helping. The context seemed to facilitate an excessive belief in personal responsibility for the therapeutic process. An ideological and clinical disillusionment could develop – enhanced by the listening to a continuous stream of trauma stories. This disillusionment could shift towards an omnipotent perception of self as a rescuer. As we have explained above, a number of these reactions were also felt by us, the researchers, during fieldwork in a traumatized society.

They also mentioned the difficulty of handling aggression in the therapeutic relationship. Emotional counter-transference reactions of anger towards patients had to be repressed or denied. Likewise, aggressive feelings in the team towards other therapists seemed to have been difficult to manage. How to contain their own aggression and that of the patients seems, then, to be a problem which is difficult to solve in the context of state terrorism.

The need expressed by therapists to have a safe holding environment in the team should, then, also include a forum where such aggressive feelings can be expressed. The safe holding should, however, also include supervision with special focus on the dynamics of empathic enmeshment.

NOTES

1. This choice refers to the movie *Sophie's Choice*, in which Sophie on her arrival at the Nazi death-camp was forced to choose which of her two children should be sent to the gas-chamber.

2. The coalition of political parties which was the basis of Salvador Allende's government.

3. A concept developed by Winnicot. See Wilson and Lindy, 1994.

7

Repressive Political Experiences on the Family Level

'Because of the flowers that were torn up...'

The psychological warfare of state terrorism is directed against dangerous individuals and social relationships between them that threaten those in power. Maybe the most important social group is the family, which may be persecuted directly or indirectly by the dictatorship. Thus, in this and the following chapter we will focus on the family in a repressive society.

THE CHILEAN FAMILY AND THE REPRESSION

Chileans present the traditional and extended family as a cornerstone of their society. The family group is defined as a group bound by kinship ties, the members of which have continuous social contacts with one another, whether or not they live under the same roof, and whether or not they depend on each other economically. This group can include one or more couples, not all necessarily with children. In a study by CODEPU (1989, p. 736) the Chilean family is described as follows:

> The family cohesion is very strong and embraces the extended family. Family members help each other with financial and legal assistance during emergencies and in time of crisis. Families also have an influence in marriages, in the selection of place of residence, in educational norms for the young and even in more personal spheres, such as the political orientation of the members, party membership and religion.

In the CODEPU study, sociological and psychological characteristics of families before, during and after the experience of direct repression are analysed.

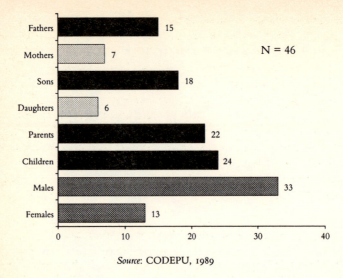

Source: CODEPU, 1989

Figure 7.1 Tortured family members

The characteristics of the families seen in their mental health service (DITT-CODEPU), however, *did not* conform to the traditional nuclear structure of Chilean extended families, as described above. The structure of the families had been disrupted and various family members had regrouped themselves in 'sub-groups' after having experienced different types of repressive experiences.

Repressive Experiences

Individuals, families, groups and collective structures can experience repression either directly or indirectly. *Direct repression* refers to the following: assassination, kidnapping, disappearance, detention, torture, exile, internal exile (relegation), home searches without warrant, imprisonment and intimidation (threats, surveillance, continuous harassment). *Indirect repression* refers to: dismissal from work (exoneration); deprivation of housing, health and food; severance from social, political and labour organizations; censorship, distortion of facts and systematic manipulation of information; the limitations and loss of the right to due process; total or partial loss of individual and collective freedom of expression, imposed at times under the pretence of legal principles, at other times by self-censorship provoked by fear (CODEPU, 1989, p. 736).

In the 24 families of the CODEPU study, 46 out of the total group of 140 individuals (33%) had suffered one or more forms of direct repression, and all 46 had been tortured. In relation to the family system, 15 of the 46 were fathers (33%), 7 were mothers (15%), 17 were sons (37%), 6 were daughters (13%) and one was a grandson (2%) (see Figure 7.1). Described from another angle, 48% of the directly persecuted persons were parents, 49% were unmarried children of 18 years or more. The majority of the fathers were young adults, while mothers tended to be of middle age and older.

Social and Individual Marginalization

The consequences for the families of direct and indirect repressive experiences must also be understood in relation to their surrounding social context. The CODEPU study, therefore, also operates with the concepts of social and individual marginalization. The left-wing ideology of the majority of the human rights movement becomes visible in the concepts used to express social realities. In the CODEPU study, the families are divided into five *social classes*. The North American editor of the scientific journal that published the study found it necessary to comment that the stratification 'differs somewhat from the conventional definition of social classes' (ibid., p. 736):

- *Petty bourgeoisie* Middle- and low-level public employees, professionals and small merchants.
- *Proletariat* Urban and rural families with wage earners, or skilled workers who do not own any means of production.
- *Under-proletariat* Urban and rural families, which are not part of the productive process and live in extreme poverty, such as the chronically unemployed or the young rural migrants in the city.
- *Lumpenproletariat* As the previous category, with the exception that people of this class exhibit delinquent behaviour.
- *Peasants* Rural families that own small pieces of land or share-croppers.

In fact, this stratification was useful in recording a significant deterioration in the social status of the persecuted families. Before 1973 all families but one had good possibilities of upward mobility.

Afterwards, the under-proletariat became the major group, and the families in general took a step downwards in social class.

Social marginalization, then, is defined, by CODEPU as:

> The process that leads individuals and family groups to be excluded from economic production, from the enjoyment of social benefits and services (such as retirement plans, health and educational services), from participating in social, labor and neighborhood associations, and as a result, from having an influence on decision making. In other words they are persons deprived of political and social power. (ibid., p. 736)

Individual marginalization is defined as:

> The process by which individuals experience a loss from non-use of skills and/or the decline of knowledge acquisition and cultural interests and a progressive erosion of self esteem. In many instances individual marginalization develops into psychological disturbances. (ibid., p. 736)

These concepts clearly connect different types of repressive experiences which families may suffer to the individual and collective reactions to state terrorism. In other words, this understanding establishes a link between individual, private pain and social, political suffering. The definitions are, in fact, also in accordance with the content of several articles of the UN Declaration of Human Rights (1948), especially Articles 22–7, which deal with social and economic rights. However, this connection is not obvious from the specific formulations in the study, but is rather, we assume, an implicit ideological framework on which both CODEPU and the other mental health organizations of the human rights movement build their conceptualizations.

Family Responses to Repression

The responses to repressive experiences suffered by members of a family can, according to CODEPU (ibid. p. 736), be divided into:

- *The united family*   All family members either support the political stand of the individual exposed to direct repression and/or help their imprisoned or persecuted member.
- *The divided family*   One or various persons show solidarity, while others are passive or explicitly reject the persecuted family member.
- *The rejecting family*   Family members do not provide assistance or support of any kind.

In the CODEPU study of 24 families (140 individuals), 17 families (71%) were united in support of the persecuted family member, although their usual family pattern had been disrupted. Some 5 families (21%) were divided with respect to their political stand, and no significant information was available about two families.

In the following section we will examine different types of repressive experiences which couples and families may have.

If a couple or several other members of a family are imprisoned and tortured together, they suffer *primary traumatization*. In this type of *family torture* two or more members of a family are either tortured in each other's presence or are tortured in different places of detention. According to Becker et al. (1987), in many instances a couple or, for example, a father and his sons have been tortured simultaneously. Also, children have been forced to witness the torture of their father or mother. On other occasions, one member of a family knows that other family members are also detained and are probably being tortured, but does know exactly what is happening to them.

Family torture exploits the emotional relationships within the family and places the victims in the trap of impossible choices which we have described in the preceding chapter. It utilizes feelings of loyalty, caring and also conflicts between family members before the detention. It is an altogether humiliating and destructive experience for the family. Instead of leading to a feeling of mutual suffering, the tortured family members, afterwards, mostly isolate and separate themselves from each other because of the 'double-bind' character of family torture (for example, the choice between giving information or the continued torture of a wife).

In individual torture, the double-bind is primarily expressed in the relationship between the victim and the torturer, and the victim's internal object relations. In family torture this double-bind is extended to the whole family system and to the victim's real relationships. For example, as expressed by a husband: 'How can I make love with my wife, when I have seen her be raped? Why didn't she defend herself more? Can she love me and understand that I couldn't help her?' Or a wife may ask: 'When my husband asked me to give information, did he do it to protect us or because he betrayed his ideals? Can I respect him after this?' Or a father may ask: 'Can my son respect me after he has seen me like that?' (Becker et al., 1987, pp. 95–7).

Thus, after family torture there is a destruction or a confusion of the ordinary family roles of father, mother and children. There are feelings of guilt towards each other, and family members retract into themselves in an effort to protect the relationship. This, however, may readily result in the opposite: the mutual isolation leads, in fact, to the relationship being broken off. Altogether, this results in a severe state of confusion in the family (ibid.).

The couple and the family structure can also experience *secondary traumatization* through the primary traumatization of one of the spouses, of one or several members of the nuclear family (children, siblings, parents) or of members of the extended family:

- A family member disappears *forever* from the family because she or he is murdered/executed or is detained and disappears.

- A family member leaves the family *temporarily* because of imprisonment, exile or relegation, often with uncertainty about *when* or even *if* she or he will return.

- A primary traumatized family member lives *within* the family with sequels of the trauma which affect the whole family system, be it in families of ex-political prisoners, in families in exile or in families that have returned from exile (or internal relegation), or in families of the exonerated (those who have been dismissed from work for political reasons).

The same family may experience one or more of these different secondary types of traumatization. In fact, the secondary traumatization of family members becomes *their* main trauma. More than one family member may be primary traumatized, which will increase the stress of each family member and the sum of stressors in the family. The repressive strategies against the group and social network as well as collective repression and fear may further contribute to the stress experienced by each individual in the family structure and in the family group. It must be emphasized, however, that *the categorization of primary or secondary traumatic experiences still tells us nothing about the degree of traumatization*. As noted by Summmerfield (1992, p. 2):

> There is no easy predicting how an individual orders traumatic experience. I have met survivors of torture in London ... for whom the impact of these experiences was exceeded by others: the ominous disappearance of a younger brother, witnessing the gruesome death of a close friend or the defeat of political ideals. (p. 2)

FAMILIES OF DETAINED AND DISAPPEARED PEOPLE

Close to one thousand people were detained and disappeared during the dictatorship. The effects of this direct gruesome strategy of repression have, however, spread to all of society, and have had a severe impact on the families of the disappeared. Its effects have been felt heavily by therapists in the human rights movement who, for example, have had to accompany family members to the identification of the corpses which have been found. On the collective level, the desperation of the family members of the disappeared has affected both therapists and the rest of society – no one could ever feel safe: people just disappeared – who would be next?

The consequences for the mental and physical health of the family members are still uncertain, as are the consequences for the succeeding generations in these families. The healing counter-strategies developed by many of these families have, however, been significant for the development of the collective consciousness and the moral community of the human rights movement. The disappeared, themselves, were the primary target-objects of repression, but their husbands, wives and children became pioneers of the organized resistance against state terrorism.

We have chosen to give a detailed description of this specific group of families since, in the strange hierarchy of 'who has suffered the worst trauma?', they seem to be given priority among the different groups of victims. This hierarchy, which astonished us when we first arrived in the culture of the human rights movement, is itself a symptom of traumatization, as one psychologist explained to us.

The Photo

'Excuse me for a moment,' says Estér, and opens her handbag. We have just finished our interview in one of the small and ice-cold windowless rooms at the Vicarage. She is on the steering committee of the Association of Family Members of the Disappeared, the tape-recorder has just been switched off, and we have asked her permission to take a photo. 'I always have this on when my picture is taken,' she continues and pins onto her breast the old black-and-white photo of her husband, who has been missing for eighteen years. 'We will always be together, I will always be his wife and could never engage with another man. Now the group here is my family and my psychologist,' she adds on our way out.

Visit to Hades?

Outside it is close to 40 degrees and the sun is burning. We are knocking at a door in the lazy suburban area of a provincial town. The face of a woman in her forties appears with an expression which seems a mixture of fear, expectation and mistrust. 'We come from Mireya,' we say, and she lets us enter a small, dark room.

She tells her story about the younger brother, who was a high-school student back in 1973 when he was detained. He was accused of hiding weapons for the revolution. He was an active participant in political discussions at his school, but the very thought of her younger brother as a dangerous revolutionary seems far-fetched to her. He never returned from the prison.

She mentions some of the severe reactions among other relatives of the disappeared. The mother of a disappeared son dressed herself for several days in her son's clothes, acted like him, talked with his voice and ended up in a state of massive psychological deterioration and alcoholism.

She gives another example of a mother who has been searching for her son for seventeen years, who constantly watches hospital forensic medicine departments to find out if her son's body or just his bones and skeleton have been brought in. She returns to her own experience: 'My brother has become a central person in my life. I always think about him, how he was, and all the things we did together. Often I talk with him and share important things in life with him.' Her husband and a friend are working in the back of the room, totally unaffected by her emotional outpouring and story. They are packing things into big wooden boxes.

The story takes a new turn. 'My brother was in the grave at Pisagua, where they found the bodies of the disappeared.' Although the official authorities denied the disappearances, the discovery of graves such as the one at the former prison camp of Pisagua confirmed the suspicion that the disappeared had in reality been murdered by the military. This reality, which was continuously denied by the military, was verified by the discovery of well-conserved bodies in the desert sand. A group of identifiable disappeared people were placed in a grave just outside the churchyard close to the concentration camp. Even in 1990 the local forensic authorities tried to deny the facts: 'They are old corpses of native Indian inhabitants,' they said on television.

'We identified him and received the bones.' She tells how relieved she had felt by this and how she had kissed his cranium several times before the funeral. (Afterwards, we found that we both had written words like 'Hamlet', 'Orpheus and Eurydice' and 'Hades' on our writing pads.) 'Now', she adds, 'it is our plan in the Association to build a mausoleum in honour of the disappeared and murdered.' Later, we learn that the Association of Ex-Political Prisoners from Pisagua also want to build their own mausoleum.

The mausoleums are one of their important tasks in the rehabilitation process. We understand their symbolic and memorial tasks, although part of us also feels 'they are the living dead'. It is as if we have become enmeshed and invaded by a strange experience of being visitors to the land of the dead.

The door is closed behind us, and we walk up again – into the sun. It is somewhat astonishing to notice how life up here seems to be just as before – a few hours and an age ago. In a small café we try to get back to reality. We share what turned out to be a mutual fantasy experienced during the interview: all the detailed talk about bones, combined with the sounds of something being packed into the wooden boxes in the back of the room, had awakened the same fear in both of us: in a moment they will unpack one of the boxes and show us the bones. The psychotic structures of the terrorist society had such a 'power of madness' that we too, as researchers, have been invaded by a transitory reality disturbance.

The Grave at Pisagua

The old churchyard is situated outside the idyllic fisherman's village of Pisagua. Wooden crosses in the sand are the last memorials of ancient epidemics of cholera, wrecks of English sailing ships and a few of the local inhabitants. No sounds, no people, no dogs, the conspiracy of silence surrounds us. They lead us through the churchyard, and behind the last wooden crosses we reach the grave of the disappeared. It is a large, rectangular hole in the sand.

The bodies were wrapped in brown sacks and mummified so that recognition was still possible seventeen years later, they tell us. Our companions, a man and a woman, are former prisoners of Pisagua, and they tell their story to us and to the tape-recorder: In 1990, a group of volunteers worked by themselves for a long time to locate the burial grounds, despite constant threats. Since 1974 there had been persistent rumours that executed prisoners were buried here. One night, a former prisoner of the camp who knew where the grave was but did not dare say so openly, had placed a flower on the exact location and had written 1973 in the sand. Shortly after he fled the country from fear of retaliation. Under the sand he had demarcated, they found the first dead bodies.

Later on, they show us a video that proves how a forensic doctor – with a military degree? – tried to deny or nullify the importance of the discovery of the bodies. The process of digging out the bodies was video-taped, and the film tells its own truth in accordance with the testimonies we have already heard from many different informants.

Back there in the Atacama desert, one year later, there are still, halfway hidden in the sand, a few old pieces of the sacks in which the bodies were wrapped. At the bottom of the grave pit, a small memorial stone has been placed together with some flowers and a sheet of paper with a poem by Pablo Neruda:

> Aunque los pasos toquen
> mil años este sitio,
> no borrarán la sangre
> de los que aqui cayeron.
> > Recuerdo de la Agrupación de Presos
> > Politicos 1973-1974, Pisagua 28.10.90.[1]

FAMILIES OF EXECUTED OR MURDERED PEOPLE

The Video

My husband came back illegally from exile. I had very sparse contact with him during his clandestine life. It was risky for him, for me and for our children. He was killed in an armed confrontation, they said. The pictures were shown in the media. He and his companions were lying on the ground, dead, and with a gun at their side. We investigated the information we got in detail: something was wrong. Later we learned that the bodies had been arranged to look as if a fight had taken place. It was cool and intentional murder, nothing else – except one thing maybe. We learned that they had recorded a video about how they arranged everything in this scenario. An educational film for hopeful young members of the secret police?

'To Believe in Chile'

To Believe in Chile, the Report from the Commission of Truth and Reconciliation (the Rettig Report), recognizes the death of 2,279 victims from 1973 to 1990. Furthermore, 641 persons who have been killed or have disappeared are declared cases 'without conviction' due to lack of time, lack of witnesses during the moment of detention, and lack of information among human rights organizations. Other deaths cannot be verified because of the burning of documents, the disappearance of bodies, the death or disappearance of witnesses and the dispersion of relatives of the victims in countries of exile. The names of these 641 persons and the recognized 2,279 people (in total, 2,920 persons) are written at the end of the report.

Among the 2,279 recognized persons, 1,322 are recorded as dead

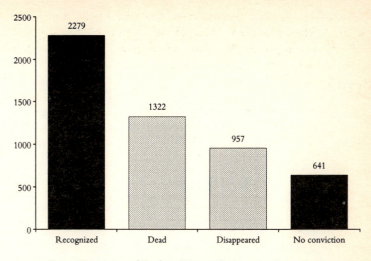

Source: Commission of Truth and Reconciliation, 1992 (pp. 123–67).

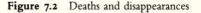

Figure 7.2 Deaths and disappearances

(58%) and 957 as disappeared (42%). The period from September to December 1973 resulted in deaths due to political reasons of 1,261 persons (55% of all recognized deaths in the Commission Report) (see Figure 7.2).

The executions were sometimes announced as the result of a court martial, sometimes as a result of a formal, 'legal' process that had been carried out:

> The commission has decided that the deaths resulting from courts martial violated the human rights of the victims, due to their substantive and formal irregularities. In all of the courts martial in 1973, the accused and the sentenced did not enjoy the right to due process. (Commission of Truth and Reconciliation, 1992, p. 48)

Some executions took place without any formal process. Victims were simply shot or knifed to death. Several deaths occurred during torture, and the Commission considers this to be an execution as well.

The initial repressive strategies of executions

The Commission states that, already at the beginning of the dictatorship, the families were ill-treated:

> During this period the denial or concealment of those executed or disappeared was an irrational and anarchic procedure. There was a practice of not handing over the bodies, concealing them in different ways, in clandestine graves or mine shafts, throwing them into the rivers or the sea, or dynamiting them. (ibid., p. 48)

The Commission continues:

> The following practices repeated themselves monotonously:
>
> — Denying to the family that the person was detained.
> — Concealing the death of the prisoner.
> — Destruction or theft of objects during house searches.
> — Extortion of relatives under false promises of freeing the prisoner.
> — Handing over the remains in a sealed casket.
> — Direct order to leave the city or town. (ibid., pp. 48–9)

The DINA period (1974 to August 1977)

During this period most of the executions were concealed as disappearances (see Chapter 4). Apparently, the majority of the disappeared were taken from the secret centres where they were held and executed near the place where they were to be buried. Many executions were preceded by torture and were generally carried out by submachine guns with silencers or by handguns. Other executions were carried out inside the detention centres. Some were shot in the back under the excuse that they were attempting to escape, and some were murdered by, for example, bombs in foreign countries. One type of execution consisted in giving the prisoners sleeping medicine or strong sedatives. Thereafter, the victims were taken sleeping or semi-awake into a helicopter from where they were thrown into the sea after their abdomens had been cut open so that their bodies would not float (Commission of Truth and Reconciliation, 1992, p. 70).

From the same source, it appears that the disposal of bodies was carried out in the following ways:

- clandestine burials;
- throwing the corpses into the sea or a river;
- leaving the corpses in the street;

- taking the corpses to the Legal Medical Institute (the morgue);
- burying the corpses in a cemetery as 'NN' – no name;
- returning the corpses to the relatives.

'On most of the bodies buried clandestinely by the Joint Command the cadavers were mutilated and the faces disfigured to prevent identification' (ibid., p. 71). To conceal the executions several methods were used: the prisoners were hidden from their families by the use of false identities; there were arrests without witnesses; there was denial of the fact of detention to the relatives; and false information was given to national and international authorities as well as to the public.

The CNI period (August 1977 to March 1990)

Three types of execution were recorded by the Commission as having been used during this period:

- In some cases there was an armed confrontation between security forces and those they were going to detain or kill. In several of these cases they killed people who were already captured or wounded.
- In other cases, an ambush was arranged to kill the person and the murder was later characterized as an armed confrontation.
- In a few cases executions were carried out by kidnapping the person and cutting his or her throat or by shooting him or her in the head. In this period, the bodies of people killed in real or simulated confrontations were generally given to their relatives. The bodies of the last category of executions were thrown in the fields or at the side of the road.

Several deaths were also connected with excessive use of force against protesters in collective demonstrations. This especially happened from 1983 to 1985 (124 murdered people). In this period a further 93 persons were killed by private citizens under political pretexts (terrorist acts and political violence). Finally 66 persons were killed by 'Excessive use of force and abuse of power with the tolerance of the authorities':

- *Excessive use of power* was defined as all actions in which there was a lack of proportionality between the force employed by the authorities and the situation they were trying to avoid and that in principle justified its use.
- *Abuse of power* was defined as violations of human rights when the actions of government agents occured for private reasons and therefore

outside their assigned functions and with the acquiescence of the authorities in charge of preventing these events (ibid., p. 85).

The Parents

We are visiting the meeting place of the Association of Family Members of the Executed in a provincial town. They have invited us to sit in the corner while they discuss how and to whom economic compensation will be offered after the publication of the Commission Report. Once more we are confronted with an atmosphere of death. Most of the participants look much older than their age. A social worker tells them about their rights, but there are no questions and no comments. It's like watching a group of shadows. They will receive their compensation, but life will not be restored. Their pain is now recognized by the authorities, but it seems to be too late. If it was not for their extreme poverty the small amount of economic compensation would not be important.

Afterwards, we interview a couple whose daughter was executed. In the small office where we carry out the interview they come alive. Although poor people without any education, they are articulate and precise in telling their story and giving their opinions.

> Our daughter was a student at the university. She was a bright girl and we really worked to save money for her studies. One day we got the message that she was dead, because of the premature explosion of a bomb that she was carrying on her way to commit a terrorist act. The newspapers and the television reported that she was a dangerous criminal. Later, a former member of the secret police went public and said that her death was arranged by them. We will take the compensation – we need the money acutely in our family – but the compensation is not our main purpose. Tell us, why should we forgive her murderers and the criminals who called *her* a criminal? We do not want revenge, this will not bring our daughter back; but her murderers should be taken for trial. We will insist on truth and justice till the day we die.

FAMILIES OF POLITICAL AND EX-POLITICAL PRISONERS

The Unrecognized but Violated Families

Many of the violations of 'the right to life' committed against the disappeared and executed have, thus, been recognized by the Commission Report. The publication of their names in the report and the small amount of economic compensation given to their families have to a certain degree been healing: at least, the truth about the death of their relatives has been recognized by society, although justice has not been fulfilled (and maybe never will be).

Registration of detainments, torture, number of people sent into exile, relegation and exoneration have, however, not been considered in the Commission Report, although they also constitute violations of basic human rights. It is still uncertain exactly how many people suffered these kinds of violations, and the misinformation and concealment carried out by the repressive system have undermined the strength of the available information.

Some data exist, however, and we will here base our information on data from the Vicarage of Solidarity. Since this organization started in 1976, it has only recorded the number of violations of the 'right to personal liberty', that is, the number of detainments from 1976 to 1989 (see Figure 7.3). In its comments it quotes Colonel Jorge Espinoza, head of SENDE (Servicio Nacional de Detenidos[2]), for the information that 42,486 individuals had been detained *before* February 1976. According to the Vicarage, these are minimum figures since several groups of those detained are not included. From 1976 to 1989 the Vicarage records 40,043 more imprisonments.

Since the figures we present here are only imprisonments recorded by the SENDE (1973–75) and the Vicarage in Santiago (1976–89), it is reasonable to expect that the total number of detained Chileans due to political reasons by far exceeds 100,000 individuals. All these people belong to extended families, which implies that a large number of Chilean families have been affected by the detention of at least one of their relatives.

Information about the number of severely tortured people is even more uncertain. Since 1978, the Vicarage in Santiago has denounced 1,312 cases before the tribunals. But these figures do not contain the number of people tortured during the first five years of the dictatorship when most of the torture was carried out.

Vignettes

Temuco

November 1989 in front of the prison. At 8.30 a.m. the line starts to grow. The wives of the prisoners are arriving from out of nowhere to form a line outside the wall. A single guard with a submachine gun watches us from the other side, while we join the line. Most of the

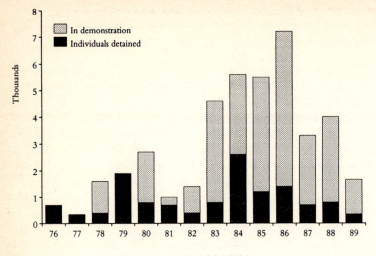

Source: Vicaría de la Solidaridad (1990).

Figure 7.3   Detentions, 1976–89

women carry baskets with bread, fruit and maybe toothpaste. We still have an hour to wait. The camera is in the bag; the temptation to take a photo of the scenario is obvious, but *la compañera* (our friend), who accompanies us and will help us to get to visit the political prisoners, has advised us to let it stay in the bag.

At 9.30 the line begins to move slowly. One by one the women pass a small desk where their baskets are searched. Today they seem to have decided that apples are not to be allowed in. The wives are sent one by one into the area in front of the prison. No, they are not allowed to place the forbidden apples on this side of the street. Place them across the street and then go back in the line and try again, they are told. The wives and some of the comrades from the Association of Ex-Political Prisoners and the Association of Family Members of Political Prisoners are common visitors here. They know about the harassments, which have become an integral part of daily life. They are resigned: this is not the time or place to make trouble or shout.

Iquique

May 1991. Meeting with the Association of Ex-Political Prisoners from Pisagua. Together with us are three men in leather jackets with eyes that flash with anger: the steering committee of the association. They tell us about life in Pisagua in 1973 and life in Iquique now. The former prisoners are still stigmatized and without employment. Everyone in the small provincial town knows that they were in Pisagua. They are still classified as criminals in their legal records, which they have to show in order to get a job – a silent *Berufsverbot*. They meet some of their torturers in the street or in the supermarket; *they* are still employed, some are even promoted.

The theme of the meeting of the Association tonight is the planning of a mausoleum. The scenario reminds us of the play *Les jeux sont fait* by Sartre, where the dead walk invisibly around among the living.

PUNTA ARENAS

February 1992. In a small house in Punta Arenas, a windy suburb close to the Magellan Straits, a middle-aged man brings his evidence: the censored letters he wrote to his wife from the prisoners' camp on Dawson Island and a copy of the transcript of the sentence he was given by the 'Honourable War Tribunal'. He was tortured and sentenced to ten years in prison for being a 'militant socialist'. Now he is unemployed and severely traumatized, while his wife earns the money for survival. His daughter and wife sit down to listen, while he gives his testimony to the tape-recorder and to us.

FAMILIES RETURNED FROM EXILE

The Father (48 years old)

While we lived in exile, we always had a lot of fantasies about the good life in Chile, 'La Cordillera', my family and friends and how happy we would be when the day came for our return. When it was time to go, the children did not want to go back. They spoke the foreign language, they had accustomed themselves to the new country, and I even had to insist that we spoke Spanish in my own home. My wife also wanted us to stay, I think. She was afraid of what would happen to our family and especially to the children when we returned. I think that her hope was that the children would go back with us when they had finished their education. She never said this directly, she knew how important it was to me to go back.

The Son (20 years old)

I came back to Chile when I was 17 years old. My parents had always talked about Chile, the wonderland. To be honest I wanted to stay over there. I had lived there nearly all of my life, I had my friends and my school there. To me, the return was like going into a new exile.

The Mother (46 years old)

To my husband, his country meant everything. He was committed politically, and at that time we had no choice, the party asked us to leave Chile, and I think that was our survival. The worst was when we came back. When we returned we expected to be received warmly by our friends, 'the prodigal son returns to his father's house', but times had changed. We had saved a little money in exile and could open a small shop for ourselves. That was our new survival. My husband had no chance of getting work. Because of his imprisonment in 1973, he was still in the criminal records and his former organization would not let him in. We were still 'suspects'. In fact, we experience that we are even more outside of everything now. Many of our former friends have left this town and even some of our old comrades from the party are different. We sense that they look at us as cowards, as those who ran away when it really came to the crunch. *They* are the unrecognized heroes, those who stayed here. They envy us. You lived there in exile in safety and with economic support, they say, while we were suffering here. And then afterwards you come back with your money, while we are still poor, unemployed and without any compensation. I understand them; they are the group who got nothing but pain. But to me all of us have suffered; we still need to unite and not to fight each other.

The Daughter (15 years old)

My only wish is to go back. I do not want to stay here. I'm not a Chilean, I was born in France and I belong there. I want to study, I want to live as in Europe, where girls' prospects are totally different.

These stories illustrate some of the dilemmas of the families returned from exile. The family is divided according to generations: the parents want to return, but are disappointed by the reality they are confronted with, while the children feel that they are in exile in their parents' country.

Programmes have been introduced to facilitate the return. Therapeutic assistance is offered, especially to the children, by PIDEE, which now nearly exclusively takes care of children returned from exile. But the reality for many returnees is a new marginalization. In some cases the difficulties are too many, and they may choose to go into exile once again.

The family dynamics of the returned families are, therefore, often dominated by severe inter-generational conflicts. To be back home also constitutes a confrontation with the traumatic experiences of the past. Some of the family members may have had psychotherapy while in exile, but most have not. The encounter with the home country and with trauma-symbolizing situations can result in psychological symptoms from the encapsulated trauma. Moreover, the unresolved process of 'truth and justice' will constantly remind them of their old pervasive fear. Some of the elements in the situation of the former political prisoners can also repeat themselves in these families of returnees.

The challenge for these families is the integration into their new Chilean life of the 'dual vision' which they have developed from life in exile. They do not need to perform like real Chileans did seventeen years ago. They now have the chance to create a 'third culture', in which they can find a new life-style and cultural position. In that case, the crisis of exile and return can start a process of transformation and healing.

CONCLUSION

We have presented some of the repressive strategies directed against relationships on the family level. In retrospect, we wonder how intentional the secondary traumatization was. It is obvious that the destruction of opponents through direct and primary repression is a 'man-made' abuse of power. The severe consequences of this repression on the indirect or secondary/tertiary level against the family group has, however, played a significant role in the generation of collective fear and traumatization.

Nevertheless, important counter-strategies against the repression and also some of the professional healing strategies took their point of departure in the resistance developed in the associations of family members. In these groups, families that had been exposed to repressive political experiences could confirm and reframe these traumatic events. They could create new supportive structures, a new family of fellow survivors and a new group identity which helped them connect their private pain to the political context. The power of resistance acquired a new dimension, when they were not just 'dancing alone':

They Dance Alone (Gueca Solo)

Why are these women here dancing on their own?
Why is there this sadness in their eyes?
Why are the soldiers here
Their faces fixed like stone?
I can't see what it is that they despise
They're dancing with the missing
They're dancing with the dead
They dance with the invisible ones
Their anguish is unsaid
They're dancing with their fathers
They're dancing with their sons
They're dancing with their husbands
They dance alone:

Its the only form of protest they are allowed
I have seen their silent faces scream so loud
If they were to speak these words
They'd go missing too
Another woman on the torture table
What else can they do...

One day we will dance on their graves
One day we will sing our freedom
One day we will laugh in our joy
And we will dance...[3]

NOTES

1. 'Although steps will touch this place for a thousand years, they will never erase the blood of those who fell here.' Memorial from the Association of Political Prisoners 1973–1974, Pisagua, 28 October 1990.

2. The National Service for the Detained, an organization connected to the military.

3. Lyrics by Sting from the album *Nothing Like the Sun* (A & M Records, 1987).

8

Trauma and Healing on the Family Level

'Because of the trees that were pruned...'

THE TRAUMA

Families of the Disappeared: A Disturbance of Reality?

The discovery of the Pisagua grave and other secret burial grounds has been an important step in the psychological regaining of reality for the families of the disappeared. The mere act of making opponents disappear, the constant denial and distortion of these acts, was, in fact, a psychosis-inducing procedure. You watch the arrest of your husband whereafter you never see him again. All authorities deny that he is dead or that they even know where he is, and they confront you with *your* possible disturbance of reality ('He has probably run off to Argentina with another woman'). If you insist on an experience which the surroundings deny, then the message you receive is that your experience is a delusion. When you insist that you saw it happen, you are confronted with the possibility that you have had an uncommon experience, that you have seen, heard and felt something which never happened – a hallucinatory experience.

This experience can lead to a disturbed sense of reality, to feelings of having delusions and hallucinations. In fact, this feeling of unreality was connected to the massive exposure to a psychotic world. Therefore, it became tremendously important to form groups in which people with similar traumatic experiences could join and testify to what had really happened. The formation of the Association of Family Members of the Disappeared and the constant denunciation and outcry: 'Donde estan?' ('Where are they?') were important healing counter-strategies in this psychotic world. It *did* really happen and it did not only happen to *our* family.

This has been an important strategy on both the individual, family, group and collective levels for counteracting the continued psychotic threat induced by repression. The question is, however, whether those strategies have been sufficient. Several of the stories of the families of the disappeared that we have listened to, heard and read about leave us with the impression that these families have suffered continuous traumatic stress to such a degree that it goes beyond any human capacity for resistance.

We found dissociative survival strategies and threats to the mental health of even the most resourceful individuals, with a risk of transitory or even permanent psychotic manifestations. The impact of the extreme and continued stress can probably be further substantiated. Several reports and testimonies from both the associations of survivors' groups and mental health professionals (see Madariaga, 1990), as well as from our informants, describe a high frequency of severe illnesses among survivors – especially cancers and deaths as late consequences of their repressive political experiences.

The frantic search for the body of the disappeared becomes an important symbolic task in many of these families. The finding of the corpse is perceived as the only way to escape from the unbearable situation. The disappeared person becomes a phantasm in the home. He or she does not exist and is not present in reality, neither is he or she dead. The fact is that none of the disappeared has ever returned alive. Most of the families know that.

On the other hand, to declare him or her dead signifies both the giving up of hope and the giving up of political resistance – the acceptance of the reality of the repressive power. To insist on finding him or her dead or alive, however, also constitutes a social disaster for the family since the spouse cannot take over the legal rights of a person who has not been declared dead. Thus, the discovery of the corpse releases the family somewhat from the painful situation. The funeral ritual enables a mourning process to begin, and sanity can be restored through the confirmation of reality. The change from the status of relatives of one who has disappeared to the status of relatives of one who has been executed is important, but it is no guarantee of an improvement in the family's mental health. The damage is still there and is manifested as deep wounds in the family structure, and in its individual members.

The wives

To disappear means to be neither alive nor dead. There are no explanations, no legal process. It is the same as to be and not to be. It means to be permanently present for the family and close friends, and not to exist for society. Also the uncertainty and the pain is permanent for the families. (Traverso, 1989, p. 1)

In a paper from ILAS, Traverso (1989) discusses the mourning process of wives whose husbands have disappeared during imprisonment. The paper is based on the theoretical concepts of Bowlby (1980, pp. 112–25), who delineates the following general sequence in a mourning process:

- a phase of emotional numbing;
- a phase of longing and search for the lost figure;
- a phase of reorganization (in various degrees).

Traverso studied in detail ten women, wives of prisoners, who had disappeared between 1974 and 1976. They all had children, and they were aged between 20 and 40 when the loss occurred. In the *first phase* of confrontation with the loss, the women had multiple reactions: fear, helplessness, shock, stupor, rage and anger, paralysis or numbness, dejection, death wishes and guilt – with fear and helplessness as the predominant feelings.

In the *phase of longing and search*, Traverso states that most of the women had reactions which 'extended beyond the foreseeable time, which led us to wonder if it is the mourning that is being evolved, or rather, if we are faced with an aborted or stopped mourning process'. She describes how the most outstanding elements in this phase are: fury; the permanent presence of the missing person in the wives' life because of their identification with him; daytime hallucinations about his presence; dreams in which he is present; as well as bad physical health. Feelings of loneliness and despair predominate.

In the *phase of reorganization*, Traverso (ibid., p. 4) finds that the wives have been able to reorganize their lives with respect to motherhood and work. However, the wives still have severe emotional problems. Only one woman, ten to twelve years after the disappearance of her husband, has a new, stable relationship and new children. The rest of the women still consider themselves to be married to the disappeared husband.

In the discussion of her findings, Traverso finds that the social context seems to be crucial for the wives to be able to undergo a mourning process. A new social reality is required in which the human rights violations are acknowledged by the victimizers. Also, the wives need their pain to become visible to those who did not want to acknowledge it.

The application of a terminology of mourning gives one theoretical perspective on the suffering of these women. The mourning process may have been arrested for years or maybe it never developed. However, it seems obvious to us that the problems we are facing in these families cannot only be described as an incomplete mourning process. We find the concept of *traumatic stress* useful here.

The trauma is of human origin, it is inflicted deliberately and is of an extreme character. The stressors in these types of repressive political experiences are characterized by a societal context which is unsafe (without any safe holding environment) (Agger and Jensen, 1994). The stress is, therefore, continuous, because the repression is still a reality after the traumatic event has happened. We would therefore consider the trauma of disappeared relatives to be associated with *extreme and continued traumatic stress.*

The survivors' pattern of reactions includes the core symptoms of traumatic stress:

The traumatic event is persistently reexperienced in recurrent nightmares, sudden acting or feeling as if the traumatic event were recurring (includes a sense of reliving the experience, illusions, hallucinations, and dissociative (flashback) episodes) – intense psychological distress at exposure to events that symbolize or resemble an aspect of the traumatic event.

Persistent avoidance of stimuli associated with the trauma or numbing of general responsiveness – like efforts to avoid thoughts or feelings associated with the trauma – like efforts to avoid activities or situations that arouse recollections of the trauma – inability to recall an important aspect of the trauma – diminished interest in significant activities – feeling of detachment from others – restricted range of affect and a sense of foreshortened future.

Persistent symptoms of increased arousal like difficulties falling or staying asleep, irritability, difficulty of concentrating, hyper-vigilance and an exaggerated startle reflex response. (Ochberg 1988, pp. 8–9)

The continued and unresolved situation in a repressive context means that a constant re-traumatization is a constant risk; the traumatized becomes 'trapped in the trauma' (ibid., p. 310) and may experience recurrent flashes of symptom revival with accompanying anxiety.

The children

In Traverso's (1990) study, all wives of disappeared prisoners had observed changes in the personalities of their children. In general, they were observed to be introverted, sad, cried easily, and they had formed anxious attachments. The children said that they were afraid of losing their mother and siblings, on whom they lavished exaggerated care. Many had disturbed sleep patterns and refused to talk about their fathers. In one out of the twenty-four children in the study, psychotic reactions were found. Also, a high frequency of psychosomatic illnesses was found, as was a case of Hodgkin's disease (cancer in the lymph nodes).

Most of the children had only been told about the disappearance of their fathers after a considerable lapse of time. Some were deluded by their mothers as a way of protecting them (but maybe as an unconscious identification with the aggressor – the mother also tried to distort reality). The family had, in this way, introduced an important 'secret' into their dynamics; they had become 'a family with a phantom' (Minuchin et al., 1978):

> In the families, a phantom-like atmosphere develops. Although daily life continues, the home of the disappeared is a place of dreadfulness and darkness. To live with the dreadful as part of daily life generates in the family a process of endless misty feelings such as: the shameful feeling of accepting the non-acceptable, the necessity of making the impossible possible for simple daily survival. When neither life nor death are possible – neither happiness nor suffering are acceptable feelings. The family, therefore, becomes silent: everybody knows, nobody speaks out. (Faúndez et al., 1991, p. 7)

Faúndez and his collaborators note that:

> in these cases, the condition of the shared secret is the most serious in the ethical order of moral conditions. It is not only a consensus about the forbidden, but also about which questions not to ask. The silence, then, is more than a strategy for preventing threats against the family. The silence is also a direct expression of the fear of facing a pain without any meaning. The expression of joy is forbidden, the mourning is suspended and the expression of pain has no meaning. This installation of silence is the main experience in the families living with the unspoken. (ibid. pp. 7–8)

The survival strategies of the children encompass denial, silence and concealment through lies or pretensions of knowing. The isolation of the family, the installation of silence, the denial and the pretending lead to a rigid, although vulnerable, family organization. A homeostasis is developed through – often inappropriate – strategies of survival and attempts to keep the family together.

The children in these families often experience difficulties in the internalization of the idealized parental figure. To separate from the missing father is a difficult process when the forbidden anger against him is unspoken and unspeakable. The mere thought of such anger creates feelings of guilt. The disturbances in the psychological development of such children and the rigidity of the family structure can make the children feel obliged to behave nicely – not to make any trouble – to behave 'as if' nothing in reality has happened.

Faúndez and his collaborators (1991) introduce the metaphor 'When the phantom is a totem' to illustrate how these unsolved parental conflicts can influence the future marriages of the young adults in these families. For example, the daughter's 'non-living/non-dead' father becomes idealized and an ideal not to be challenged, especially not by her husband. Although she knows how the reality was, she keeps silent. It is still impossible to speak about the unspeakable: that would imply a violation of a strong, latent moral rule. She thus adds to the conspiracy of silence and brings the phantom into her new home as part of her dowry. In a therapeutic setting the intention is to help her break the silence, to let her recognize her right to share the secret (including the anger against the father).

Families of the Executed or Murdered

The execution of a member of the family group will, of course, be a severe traumatic experience for each of the individual members, and it will have an impact on the family dynamics in general. The families of the executed share with the families of the disappeared the knowledge that their loss has now been recognized by the Commission of Truth and Reconciliation (1992). This means that *society has now recognized the deaths as a direct consequence of human rights violations*. In 1992 these families also received a minor economic compensation.

In both types of family, the individual exposed to the primary repressive experiences left the family forever. Most often the husband/father of the family was the target of this primary repression, but also grown-up children and other members of the family group were among the executed. A marked difference between the two groups of families, however, is that while the disappeared person is 'not alive/not dead', there is no such doubt in the families of the executed. Their family member *is dead* as the result of execution or murder. They have no hope of his revival; they have a recognized position as 'widow' and as children whose father is 'dead'. However, in the families of the executed or murdered, the mourning process is also often severely disturbed.

The execution or murder was often accompanied by misinformation, concealment and covering up by the authorities. The executed or murdered was not allowed to die as a 'hero' or an 'honest defender of human rights'. The husbands and fathers in these families were 'dangerous elements, terrorists, criminals and lawless'. Although the public, little by little, learned to read between the lines, the direct announcements in the newspapers and on television, nevertheless, were very diligent in their use of labelling words.

Half of the population believed the misinformation and were thereby confirmed in their support for governmental activities against the terrorists, Marxists and criminal elements. In consequence, the family is often left alone with the grief and the loss of their dead relative. They also experience a public outcry which blames the dead person and shames the family – a social disaster and a repressive political experience at the same time.

Some of these families have turned their grief and rage into energetic political resistance and a committed motivation to fight against repression. They demand truth and justice – and some also want revenge. Others feel victimized by the event and the fear of what can happen next. 'If they can kill innocent people, my husband or my children, why not also me? When will they come back and kill my son?'

This constant threat to life induces an extreme level of stress in the families. In consequence, we find traumatic stress symptoms as nightmares, flash-backs and intrusive thoughts related to the executed, as well as severe stress symptoms of a psychosomatic nature. The constant threats of new repressive experiences maintain the condition, and any trauma-symbolizing event can induce a reliving of the painful feelings.

Besides the traumatic experiences of the individuals in the family, which in turn have an impact on the family dynamics, specific changes in family interaction and behaviour can be observed. The families withdraw and isolate themselves to eliminate, or at least reduce, the risks of new violations. Inside the family group unhealthy changes can be introduced by the development of uncertain generational boundaries, a process in which children have to take over the responsibility for the family and act as adults. There is also a tendency to develop homeostatic and rigid family patterns. This pattern is maintained by the efforts of the family not to 'speak about the unspeakable' and, on the surface, to keep things going. In fact, a side-effect of this strategy of survival is that the families participate in 'the conspiracy of silence' – a conspiracy that is in complete agreement with the psychological warfare of the dictatorship.

The children in the families have problems with the integration of the executed or murdered father in their developmental process. Although mother says that father was a hero, they say something else in school or in the newspaper: 'No matter whether my father was a hero or a criminal, he is the main reason for a lot of our pain.' There is forbidden rage against him for not being there: 'Why did he not keep out of politics and stay here as my father?' The problems of children of the disappeared and the executed were the direct cause of the establishment of the PIDEE centre in 1979 to offer psychological assistance to these children.

While the major group of executed were husbands and fathers, some families have had to face the murder or execution of their adolescent or adult child. These families have been exposed to the same threats from the environment, but within the family the dynamics are often less disturbed because both parents are still there. The strong emotions of rage, injustice, sorrow and fear are, of course, still a reality in these families. The basic structures of the family, however, have not been destroyed. Several of these parents have become committed members of the Association of Family Members of the Executed.

Families of Political or Ex-Political Prisoners

Among the families of political or ex-political prisoners, family dynamics have also been observed to change in the direction of withdrawal, isolation and marginalization. This process has been most evident in the families of the disappeared or murdered, but a break-down in communication is also seen in the families of political prisoners. Through the defence mechanisms of denial and avoidance, the fathers of these families especially have developed a pattern of silence. Almost all political prisoners have been subjected to torture – of one type or another. These traumatic experiences are, usually, not a topic about which the entire family can communicate and reflect.

Although many have been unable to speak about their pain with the family, many ex-political prisoners have been supported by the fact of their belonging to the Association of Ex-Political Prisoners or other human rights groups. According to CODEPU (1989), the traumatic experiences of torture and imprisonment have remained unintegrated longer for men than for women, and longer for older men than for the younger. Generally men were able to lead a functional family life while the children were small. After the children reached adolescence, however, fathers were often unable to cope with the generational confrontation and the family structure disintegrated. The typical traits observed in these fathers were introversion, withdrawal, aloofness, isolation, anger and stubbornness. They also maintained authoritarian rule as a means to regain status and to resolve differences of opinion among family members.

Their position can be understood from a feeling of loss and defeat which may result from the failure of the political project and the loss of the object [the political commitment]. This is accompanied by a sense of responsibly for such a failure. (Lira, 1983)

The repressive experiences, then, have brought the former opponents of the authoritarian dictatorship into an existential position where within the family group they reproduce the archaic model of the authoritarian patriarchy which they have been fighting against outside of the family in the social context.

In this way, some traumatized fathers have *identified with the aggressor* by becoming dictators or violators in the family. The members of the families can adapt to this by resignation – or start their own 'liberation movement' within the family. In a revolt against their fathers, some youngsters take a right-wing political position (whereby they, in fact, also identify with the outer aggressor), or they choose to abstain from any political commitment.

The choice of non-involvement in politics can be taken either from the position of pain and resignation ('We have got enough of that stuff in the family, it will do nobody any good'), or from an active anti-political attitude, which can end up in an anarchist position ('I just hate everything about politics and meetings'). Some of the aims of torture can, therefore, be fulfilled in the reactions of the next generation.

These positions aggravate the inter-generational conflicts, and they reduce the self-esteem and increase the self-blame of the fathers even further. Likewise, the social conditions of unemployment and the drop in social status of many of these families leave them vulnerable. The fathers of these families will often be the key persons in therapeutic assistance to the family, although they are often the last family member who will accept this. To enter therapy is interpreted by many of these fathers as an acceptance of their defeat – and it can also be experienced as a threat to their political position.

In other families, according to CODEPU (1989), the young men assumed and practised a political commitment, although their parents had become politically passive. In such families, sons tended to drag their parents into political concerns, though they were more successful in influencing their mothers than their fathers. The political behaviour of the daughters was determined by male family models (brothers, fathers and boyfriends). Among middle-aged and older people, males tended to become more politically passive, even in the case of those who had an active political past. Middle-aged mothers, on the other hand, were inclined to assume greater political commitment, regardless of their political past. For example, more mothers than fathers were active in the different survivors' groups. Thus, in some families the opponents gave up their struggle, while other families were radicalized as a response to the human rights violations.

THERAPEUTIC STRATEGIES

Therapeutic Strategies on the Private Level

The most important therapeutic strategies for the healing of family wounds were already developed in the early phases of the dictatorship. At that time, in 1974, the first survivors' groups were created (the Association of Family Members of the Disappeared).

The participants left the privacy of their individual families and joined in street demonstrations. Although scared and with a high risk of being exposed to even more violence, the first steps were taken towards the connection of the private and the political pain. The strategy of making people disappear was directed against individuals, but, as we have described earlier, it became a serious trauma for the family members also.

The creation of the survivors' groups enables families, at least in part, to de-privatize their pain. They can thereby see that a disappearance is not only suffering inflicted on their specific family, but that it is also an event that is part of a politically intended, collective repression from those in power.

The survivors' groups have a double function: to serve as a new family and social network for the violated families and to function as a platform for political commitment and work.

The development of the survivors' groups was closely connected to the development of the NGOs within the human rights movement. This interaction played a major role in the establishment of professional assistance to those survivors who were most severely affected by their repressive experiences. Initially the individual approach in psychotherapy was most common, but, little by little, family and group therapy were introduced.

Therapeutic Strategies on the Professional Level

In the following we will discuss and illustrate some of the work developed by the professionals in the treatment of survivor families. Although the centres have developed different therapeutic strategies during the last decade, it seems to us that they share some basic elements in their understanding of trauma and in their basic approach to clinical work. First, we will briefly recall some of these basics. Thereafter, we will illustrate the clinical work with some cases based on professional reports and on our own observations during fieldwork.

Some general aspects

The understanding of those reactions which call for psychotherapy can be summarized as follows:

> We view the psychopathology of our patients as a consequence of extreme traumatization produced by political repression and structural violence, leaving them ensnared in an experience that initially succeeds in breaking down their psychic structure. Social and political disaster become psychological damage, manifested in diverse symptoms whose main characteristic, however, is chaos, despair, and a repetition of the traumatic experience, that originally external, now becomes intrapsychic and subjective. (Becker et al., 1989, p. 85)

This therapeutic model was developed as a counter-strategy to the psychological warfare of the dictatorship. As we described in Chapter 6, a core element in what we have called 'the Chilean model' is the concept of '*the bond of commitment*' ('el vinculo comprometido') and the attitude of '*ethical non-neutrality*'.

To establish any kind of therapy, the therapists need a working alliance (a transference alliance). In the Chilean model this alliance is called 'the bond of commitment'. This concept recognizes explicitly that a political, social and psychological alliance must be established between the patient and the therapist. This also implies an *ethical, non-neutral attitude* towards the patient's pain. The symptoms originate in repressive political experiences; they are results of traumata which were purposely inflicted. They were inflicted for political reasons and they were a violation of the patient's human rights.

The therapist thus assumes an active and definite position of solidarity with the patient. The committed bond establishes the minimal conditions for the creation of a space for recovery and healing. This active position functions as a support for the survivor which enables him or her to elaborate the traumatic experience. The bond of commitment is seen as a bridge between the traumatic experience encapsulated by the patient − or the family − and their resources. In a therapeutic process based on this relationship,

> The therapist must ask everything about the traumatic situation. His or her silence will appear like complicity with the repressor's threats against the patient if he or she tells what happened. How can a patient have the courage to tell what he or she has experienced if he or she perceives in the therapist's

silence a reflection of his or her own fears and anxieties? A therapist who remains neutral, without 'ideology', generates in the torture victim considerable anxiety and resistance, which makes it impossible for the latter to 'trust' in him or her. (Becker et al., 1989, pp. 87–8)

Assimilation of the contradictions

The different traumatic experiences have in common an attempt on the part of the survivor to 'forget' the destruction and return to an integral and unhurt stage through a process of dissociation, as we have described in Chapter 6. In the family context, an alteration of the roles of the family members will always occur after a severe traumatic experience. It is not possible just to go back to previous ways of relating.

Families of the disappeared have to live through a real experience of the object loss. The family is, however, confronted with impossible choices: either to endure the absence of the disappeared while they offer relief and protection to the remaining family members, or to restructure the family while they keep the role of the disappeared untouched. Survivors are forced to make unilateral choices to solve the contradictions. The therapeutic process thus aims at facilitating an assimilation of the contradictions: it is possible to be both weak and strong, both to mourn and to fight. Unilateral choices are perceived as a continued repetition of the damage: I am either weak or strong, I either mourn or fight.

Confrontation with the trauma

It is a core element of the therapeutic work to elaborate the traumatic experience through the reconstruction of the events and the accompanying emotions (the testimonial element). This is part of the investigation and documentation of reality. In the therapeutic space the unspeakable can be spoken, and the secrets can be brought out into daylight. In this process, the family members share their pain.

Counteracting the privatization of the damage

Survivors of repressive political experiences often live with their traumata as if they were private problems separated from the social-political context. The survivors thus need to link their traumatic experiences with the social and political context in order to reframe the events. If the damage involves the whole society, a new societal context is, then, an important element in the healing process.

The commitment of the families and the advocacy of the professionals in the human rights movement for 'truth and justice' has, thus, become a logical response pattern. Collective rituals of purification such as mass meetings at the National Stadium or the Stadium of Chile have been important also for the healing of the survivor families. The recognition by the report from the Commission of Truth and Reconciliation of the families of the disappeared and murdered persons has had a similar healing effect. In consequence, the lack of recognition of the former political prisoners and their families, and of the families exposed to exile, internal relegation or exoneration, has contributed to their continued psychological suffering.

CLINICAL CASES

In the Mirror

The setting

We visit a centre where the therapists work with systemic family therapy. We observe one session of a therapy in which the family and two therapists work in the therapy room while we and the supervisors watch through a two-way mirror. Contact between therapists and supervisors is established through: (1) a telephone by which the supervisors can call the therapists, and (2) a direct microphone through which the supervisor can speak directly into the room. (The nickname of the microphone-voice was 'God'.) There is a break in the middle of the session in which the therapists and the supervisors consult.

The time schedule consists of fifteen minutes of briefing (therapists and supervisors), one hour of therapeutic work, a twenty-minute break for consultation, twenty to thirty minutes of continued therapy, and a few minutes (five to ten) for follow-up after the last session. The family is informed about the observers sitting behind the mirror. We are presented to them prior to the session and they have accepted our presence in advance.

The family

To us the family constellation is rather uncommon. The mother is in her mid-thirties; her husband has disappeared, but he has not been recognized by the Commission Report, since nobody witnessed his detainment. Also present are two children – a son, 12 years old, and a daughter, 6 years old – and their maternal grandmother, in her sixties.

The main issue

The mother is a hero of everyday life. She is the first to get up in the morning and the last to go to bed in the evening. Although poor, she is nicely and very formally dressed. It is important to her that the family looks as if nothing is wrong. The daughter has been the primary symptom-carrier in the family, overly energetic and troublesome, while the son is shy and introverted. Grandmother is severely worried about what is going to happen to the family.

Earlier in the therapy it has been a main theme to reconstitute the inter-generational boundaries by letting the mother regain the power in the family, and not let the scene be totally dominated by either the grandmother or the children, especially the daughter. The mother has now begun to be the one in charge, but she is overly responsible and never cares for herself. 'Who takes care of the caretaker in the family?' is a question for the discussion.

Since we observed only one session in a long sequence of therapy, we will primarily illustrate the process by a brief scenario.

The puppet theater in the rear-view mirror

Several glove-puppets and toys are dispersed in the therapy room. When the therapy starts, the daughter constantly knocks 'the wolf' against us, the invisible, behind the mirror. After a few minutes, 'the wolf' is placed on the mother's knees. When the mother starts to talk about her pain, she still has 'the wolf', while the daughter takes a conch and listens to it. The female therapist, who is identifying with the mother, has a big baby puppet in her arms, which the daughter just gave her. The son is stroking a small white cat puppet, while the grandmother nervously turns a bundle of plastic keys which were also given to her by the daughter.

The counter-transference

The mother tells how happy they were in exile, maybe inspired by our presence (the family was in exile in Europe). She cries and feels pity for herself. The female therapist, who has also returned from exile, cries too.

'How could he bring us back into this? He knew it could be dangerous, to him, to our family. Why did we not stay?', the mother cries. The female therapist has disappeared into her own world and her intrusive memories. The male therapist, a returnee himself, takes over and asks the mother about her anger, the forbidden anger against the disappeared husband.

The mother continues crying and denies any feelings of anger towards him. She misses him – nothing else. The daughter races back and forth among all of them – even out on the balcony – in an attempt to steal the scene. No one reacts. The son looks totally scared. The male therapist puts a supporting arm around him. Grandmother works on a solution, but ends up by quietly throwing the bunch of plastic keys on the table. The mother stops crying, wipes her tears away and folds her arms across her chest. The daughter comes back and is placed on her chair by the grandmother. The son says nothing, and the female therapist comes back from her own world. The mother starts to talk practical business, about a lawyer, new information in her case. She has regained her composure and re-established control of the situation.

After the break

During the break, the counter-transference of the female therapist is pointed out and discussed. A new strategy is worked out in which the female therapist is now more aware of her own vulnerable points and becomes a more central person with the possibility of using the identification with the mother in a caring way. The strategy is also to respect the duty and responsibility of the mother and at the same time give her some practical exercises which permit her to have some spare time and take care of herself. The grandmother can assist at one level, and the children can take on some duties appropriate to their ages. The session finally ends up rather undramatic and even with a small optimistic smile from the mother because of the new plans which leave her a little more space for self-care.

Discussion

The systemic family approach seemed very appropriate and comprehensive to us. The model with the two-way mirror allows for both supervision and training of the involved therapists – and on the other side of the mirror it is a fine educational model for training therapists through direct observation and supervision. The model is cheap and can be modified according to many different settings. Since the disappearance of a father from the family has a massive impact on the family dynamics, it seems obvious to include the children – and also the grandmother, who belonged to this family group.

Children in these families may also need special assistance from child psychologists/psychiatrists as the repressive experiences in these families are severe. As described earlier, such experiences can also contain psychosis-inducing elements. So at different levels these families will need assistance from different sources. Family therapy constitutes one level of assistance. Child therapy in individual or group sessions constitutes a second level. Participation in a survivors' group with families that are in a similar situation constitutes a third level. The pain of the mother may also in certain situations call for an individual approach.

A Boy Was Killed in the Street

The following case is abbreviated from a report by Becker et al. (1989, pp. 93–7).

Background

Manuel, 13 years old, was killed in 1984, on a day of national protest against the military regime. He was shot through the head with a bullet in a settlement in the outskirts of Santiago. The family came for psychotherapeutic aid on the fourth day after his death.

After the death of Manuel, the family consists of the mother and her younger daughter. The father has left home and lives in the provinces; an older daughter is married and lives by herself.

The presentation symptoms of the mother and Manuel's sister are: anxiety, uncontrollable weeping, nausea, insomnia, difficulties in walking, self-destructive behaviour (striking the head), and repetitive and monotonous verbalization – in brief, a feeling of disaster accompanied by psychic disorganization.

First session

The beginning of the session is chaotic: screams, tears, confusion, helplessness, despair and pain. Two interventions by the therapists constituted the focal points:

- The boy was not killed by them, but by members of the security forces – it was not the family's fault.
- The daughter had assumed the role as key patient as a defence against the danger of disturbance of the family equilibrium.

At the end of the session, the therapists gave the patients something to eat; the family had eaten nothing for three days and were reluctant to do so. The therapists begged them and gave assurances that it would do them no harm. This symbolic intervention showed that the therapists cared for them, and an emotional bond began to be established. The mother and daughter gave their accounts of Manuel's death. The mother said:

> He was lying in the street with a bullet-wound in his eye. The bullet had come out at the back of his head; I asked them to help me take him to the hospital. He was alive, and no one helped us; the guardsmen laughed and I was screaming, begging for help. Twenty minutes later we took him there, but they had already said that he was dead. I did not want to hear it; it was not right. Manolito could not be dead.... When I touched him, I knew he was alive. It could not be my despair that made me imagine that he was alive because I touched him and he was warm. When I touched his hands, his heart was beating slowly inside him. I begged on my knees for them to please help me take him to the hospital. No one, not even the guardsmen, wanted to help me. They laughed, and said that Manuel and the others were thieves.

The first phase

After the establishment of a committed bond with the family, the principal topics were loss and death. By the active participation of the therapists, the family was helped to verbalize the events. Death and destruction could be transformed into elements in a 'bond of life' between the patients and the therapists. In this context, the family could start to look at what had happened. The bond became a therapeutic tool for the family, because it enabled them to face their pain and loss. For the therapists, this bond helped them examine their own feelings about the grief.

The second phase

This phase lasted one year with weekly sessions. The mother had to work with her contradictory feelings towards her children. Aggression towards Manuel before his death now became feelings of guilt and persecution that she could not accept. The therapists worked to put the mother 'in charge' in relation to the daughter. This allowed the daughter to stop producing symptoms.

The mother began to participate in a committee concerned with political assassinations and started to denounce the death of her son to the newspapers, although she was an almost illiterate person with few educational resources. Therapy helped her discover the reality she was living in. Part of the therapy consisted of working with dreams, which was an easier way for her to communicate her feelings, wishes and fantasies. Towards the end of the therapy, a separation phase was included, a necessity for both the patients and the therapists.

The group space

The purpose of giving this woman a group space was related to her need to re-establish a social network. The group is a place in which time and space is shared; it is a place where one takes a look at oneself and sees the gestures of the others, where people perceive one another and fulfil a task. Through this task, a transformation takes place which creates a structure of mutual bonding.

In this process the 'we' emerges. The mother was able to learn from the group how to reconstruct her internal world and acquire a group identity that implied her continuous participation in a group of her peers. She gained an awareness of social belonging and social participation. This enabled her to feel that she was loved and wanted, and to live in an atmosphere of protection and kindness with the possibility of a predictable future.

In the therapeutic process this means that one can gradually overcome sadness, come to terms with the social and political reality and understand the dialectics between social and political events and one's own private grief (Becker et al., 1989).

Comment

This case is of course special: the murder by the authorities of a 13-year-old boy – an abuse of power, a meaningless execution. The primary intervention is aimed at the acute overwhelming crisis, where the turning point is the establishment of the bond of commitment. The family therapy works as a support for the mother, on her road towards greater consciousness of her life situation.

In a way, the death of her son, with all the mourning and pain, also becomes a process of transformation which allows her to find a new sense of social belonging, which could have been meaningful even before the tragedy occurred. The therapeutic interventions combined with the group strategies seem to be an appropriate way of working in general, and contain a structure which can also be useful in less dramatic situations.

Children in Exile in their Parents' Homeland

The workshop

A circle of fifteen teenagers and two adult group leaders, a psychologist and a teacher, are leading a workshop in one of the NGO mental health centres. Usually, the participants attend the workshop six or seven times in weekly sessions of two hours. The focus of the workshop is more pedagogically than therapeutically oriented, although therapeutic techniques are used in the work.

All of the teenagers are returnees; most of them have arrived recently from all over the world. The aim of the group is to facilitate their return to their parents' homeland. The adolescents themselves were nearly all born in exile. Several of our interviewees among the therapists have pointed out that these youngsters belong to a high-risk group. The development of emotional disturbances and psychotic episodes especially have been reported in this group of survivors.

Some of the group members, as we saw them

The session starts with a presentation, both because of our presence, and because of the arrival of three new members in the group. Every time new members arrive, the youngsters must present themselves to the new members as well as to the old group. The group leaders have observed how the presentation gradually changes during the course of the workshop. The youngsters give a more solid picture of themselves, and at different times some will come forth when they are ready to express more of themselves.

Ana arrived from North America a few weeks ago after fifteen years of exile. She is participating in the workshop for the first time. She is, of course, fluent in English, a useful skill in Chilean society, and this resource is pointed out to her by the group leaders after her presentation. 'You can be the interpreter for the Danes,' they say. The leaders want to stress that having two cultures is a resource rather than a problem.

André has been in exile in France. His parents were divorced because 'they loved and destroyed each other,' he says. His Spanish has a very pronounced French accent. You can almost guess in which country they have been in exile from their clothes, attitudes and, of course, their accents. Two 'Russians' do not speak any Spanish and understand only a little of what is going on.

A future intellectual who reads Kafka brings up the topic of religion. He always ends up discussing bitterly with people about this topic, he tells the group. The leaders grasp the theme and apply it to discussions with parents and others. How do you manage anger without getting unfriendly with everybody? On the other hand, you have the right to your own opinion. They ask for comments and experiences from the group members and give their own good and caring comments.

A girl from exile in Cuba – there is no doubt about that – is in constant motion; her movements are Caribbean. A guy from exile in Brazil talks in a cocktail of voodoo and communist ideals. Some of the participants do not say much, but seem to listen carefully.

The tools

The group leaders use simple group techniques in their work. They facilitate the sharing of experiences by asking questions directly, calling for similar or different experiences among the group members, ideas for solutions to problems brought up by individual members. They also intervene themselves by sharing their thoughts with the group.

They have developed the use of collages in which the participants make a picture of their family situation by combining drawings with pictures and texts they take from magazines and newspapers. Afterwards the collages are shared with the group and the youngsters tell the others about themselves on the basis of this.

Many of these teenagers know very little about present-day Chilean society. A long time has passed since their parents lived here. They share information on how to use the buses and where the cinemas and the sports clubs are. They arrange parties and invite people from the group and maybe also their new class-mates. Some of them live in the same areas and become friends.

So the workshop facilitates the development of a network. Usually the youngsters find out themselves when it is time to leave the group – when they feel ready to move on independently. Through observation in the workshop, adolescents who need more specific therapeutical assistance can be referred to other settings.

Comment

We find this combination of education and basic therapeutic strategy very useful and in some ways unique. The model can be used by competent teachers with some special training. This is important in countries where there are few psychologists and psychiatrists. The model could also be useful in exile countries.

9

Repressive Experiences on the Territorial Level

'Because of the fish in its bowl...'

In Chile, there is a long history of poverty and exploitation, which did not start with the military dictatorship. There have been tensions for years between the sectors of society that attempted to improve the conditions for the majority of people, and the sectors which supported the landowners, the establishment, the military and multinational interests.

So even before the dictatorship, the social conditions of the country provided the basis for the development of structural violence on the individual, family and 'territorial' level. Symptoms such as alcoholism, family violence, suicides and behavioural disorders in children were common in the poor sectors or territories. Therefore the reality for most poor people during the dictatorship was to be exposed both to repressive political experiences and to the consequences of structural violence.

In the following, we will visit some of the territories of structural and political repression. The first part of our journey will bring us through the prisons, the concentration camps and the 'tortured town', while in the second part we will pass through territories of combined social marginalization and repression – the psychiatric hospital, the Mapuche territory and the shanty towns.

THE REPRESSION

'Behind Bars': The Political Prison as a Microcosm of Society

The political prison is a territory in which general aspects of psychological warfare are expressed in a concentrated form – it is a symbolic microcosm of the repressive society. The traditional purpose of the prison is to isolate and punish criminals. Under state terrorism, the prison territory was extended so that it could also encompass political prisoners – the opponents of those in power. Political prisoners were either placed in separate units of the prisons or were mixed with traditional criminals.

When those in power insisted that their intervention was not a 'coup' but a 'war', a consequence of this label was the right to take 'prisoners of war' and later to justify the presence of 'political prisoners'.

Usually, systematic interrogation and torture were carried out in special centres, whereafter the detainee was brought to a prison, as described in the case of Julia in Chapter 5. Torture could, however, also be continued in prison in some form or another. In fact, one can see prison life as an extended form of torture.

The torture houses

The Commission Report names fourteen different places of detention and torture in the period from 1974 to 1977. They were all administered by the DINA, the secret police (Commission of Truth and Reconciliation, 1992). Some examples are as follows:

(1) *Tejas Verdes* This was located in San Antonio, in the prison camp of the School of Military Engineers. It was used by the DINA to detain and interrogate persons who came from different centres in Santiago.

(2) *Villa Grimaldi* This was the DINA's most important location for its detention and torture activities. The place, also known as 'Cuartel Terranova', was operating already in 1974 as the headquarters of the Metropolitan Intelligence Brigade. It was located in Santiago (José Arrieta Avenue, La Reina). Prisoners were taken in here for their first interrogation after detention. Objects for all kinds of torture were kept there. Torture in Villa Grimaldi was practised continuously. The 'operation teams' went in and out twenty-four hours a day, and prisoners were brought in at any moment and tortured at any time. In addition to torture during interrogations, the officers as well as their aides continuously battered and abused their prisoners

(3) *The Discothèque or 'la Venda Sexy'* Many of the DINA prisoners who later disappeared were held in this house. It was located in Santiago (No. 3037 Irán Street, Quilin). The installation had permanent music. Sexual torture methods were commonly included. Frequent

episodes of torture alternated with periods of relaxation and kindness ('the good and the bad torturer').

(4) *The Dignidad Colony* A connection between the DINA and the German, Nazi-like, colony of 'Dignidad' has, as we have stated, been proven. DINA prisoners were taken to this place and some of them subjected to torture with the participation of the DINA and local inhabitants of the colony.

Many of the torture centres were located behind the walls of the existing military installations. Others such as Villa Grimaldi and 'La Venda Sexy' were created with the specific purpose of torture. In the brief comments on each location, the typical last sentence written in the Commission Report is: 'Torture was practised throughout the day.' But no numbers are given, since torture was outside the mandate of the Commission. Whenever the DINA was accused of human rights abuse, the head of the organization, Manuel Contreras, blamed either the CIA or the extreme leftists.

The CNI, which continued the activities of the DINA, also had several centres for torture. The best known of the CNI facilities in Santiago were at *No. 517 República Street*, where the general headquarters was also based, at *No. 1470 Borgoño Street* and in the *Villa Grimaldi*, where the former activities continued. The DICOCOMCAR had a torture centre known as '*La Firma*' ('The Signature') in 18th Street, Santiago, at their headquarters.

The prisons

When the detainee arrived in one of the prisons, she or he might have come from days or weeks of torture in one of the specialized centres. Life changed a great deal after this transferral. From now on, the prisoners could communicate with the world outside; and in the 'communicative space' between the world inside of the prison and the outside world an exchange took place in which the prisoners could deliver some of their pain to the outside, while some types of emergency aid on the healing level could pass from the outside into the prison world. Doctors, psychologists and social workers from the human rights movement were allowed to visit the political prisoners and give them some assistance.

From an outsider's perspective, it is astonishing that this type of communication was permitted. However, as was explained to us by one of our interviewees, the prison authorities recognized that this communication actually helped them keep the political prisoners calm.

So, the entrance of professionals from the human rights movement was an aid both to the prisoners and to those who kept them behind bars.

A circle behind the bars, 1989

There is a heavy metallic sound of the wrought-iron gate when it closes behind us. We have been waiting for two hours in front of the prison office. The former political prisoner who accompanies us often visits his old comrades in the public prison. He has told the prison authorities that we are from a foreign country and that it would be unwise to risk bad international press one month before the presidential election.

They collect our passports and later we notice that they also take a photo of us through a window. To our surprise, we are at last invited in for half an hour, and a guard armed with a submachine gun escorts us into a rather large visiting room.

Two electric bulbs hang from the ceiling; there are no windows. The room contains about eighty people – the prisoners and their families. Most of these prisoners are ordinary criminals. In the meeting room, criminals and political prisoners are mixed. Small groups of family members gather around the prisoners with their fruit (except apples, which were not allowed in that day), biscuits and tea. In the back of the room, maybe one and a half metres above the floor, there is a box made out of bulletproof glass with small hatchways to open. In the box there are two guards in military battle-dress armed with submachine guns and a microphone that enables them to talk directly out into the room. (Maybe they call the voice 'God' here, like in the family therapy setting, but we do not ask.)

The eight political prisoners arrive from their special unit. We are greeted cordially and they form an intimate circle which also includes us. In this way, the accompanying guard is left out, one step behind the circle. The guard seems rather bored; he is chewing gum and is looking at everything and nothing.

The leader of the group of political prisoners moves out into the circle and gives a political speech. He talks about amnesty. Only some prisoners – those who are not designated 'prisoners of blood' – will receive amnesty according to the plans of the forthcoming democratic government. Those who were involved in armed confrontations with the security forces will not. They are designated 'terrorists'; to grant them amnesty would be dangerous for democratic transition, it is said.

'It is absurd,' he says. 'The security forces are the repressive agents. If it were not for them, there would be no blood. They are the ones who have blood on their hands.' The guard remains impassive. The leader tells us how the prisoners have organized themselves to keep up their spirits and political commitment. Most of them have not been sentenced yet, although some have already been imprisoned for years. Hence they do not know how long they are going to stay here. They live in the same unit and do not mix with the criminal prisoners. Their sense of community is important for the effort to resist the constant stress of being here without any time limit.

'We have a psychiatrist who visits us here. Sometimes he works with the group; he assists us in resolving conflicts between the comrades. Sometimes he talks with a single person and the group shelters them and gives them space for a confidential talk here in this room.' He finishes his speech: 'Now we want to hear what you have to say to us.'

We were not prepared for this, but have to improvise a brief talk on international solidarity in the fight for human rights. We exchange cigarettes and coffee, and seconds later the guard commands: 'Vamos' – time to go. His keys enable our escape back to freedom. The sound of the wrought-iron gate is now heard from the outside, the passports are returned, and the guards are duly thanked.

The women's political prison in Santiago, 1991

On the corner opposite the women's prison, an old woman makes a little money by taking care of visitors' bags. Bags are not allowed into this prison, which only contains women political prisoners. On the outer walls of the prison, someone has painted a large piece of graffiti which calls for the liberation of all political prisoners. In the middle of this wall there is a heavy door with a hatchway through which a shadow of a guard's face can be glimpsed.

Our passports are exchanged for a wooden brick with a number, and after a body search we are led into the prison yard. The sun is sharp; autumn is already in the air, though it is May; and against the blue sky we see the outline of a guard with his submachine gun pointing in our direction.

Female guards in green uniforms lead us to a table in the sun and agree to call the coordinator of the prisoners. Right now, the atmosphere resembles an ordinary Sunday afternoon. The visiting children are playing, the husbands play football, and at the tables there are coffee and cigarettes.

She arrives, Valentina, their coordinator. We learn that at this moment there are twelve women political prisoners in this jail. They estimate that close to 275 political prisoners are still in prison throughout the country. All the women prisoners have given their written testimony. Some of them have been detained since the democratic government was elected in March 1990 and at least one of them reports having been exposed to torture (including electrical torture and rape).

The wall in the yard is covered by a massive mural: a bird in a cage, a totally red map of Chile and a submachine gun. A text is written on the painting: 'Juicio y Castigo. Libertad a todos los p.p. Brigada Erich Silva' (Judgement and punishment. Freedom for all political prisoners of the Erich Silva Brigade). There is also a poem:

Tu risa	Your smile
me hace libre	makes me free
me pone alas	gives me wings
soledades me quita	takes my loneliness away
Carcel me arranca	takes me out of prison
	Miguel Hernandéz

Some of the women have been here for more than five years, while others have arrived recently. Most of them have not been sentenced; their cases are dragged out by formalistic procedures. Why are these twelve women still here when most of the other political prisoners have been set free? 'Because we are militants and they know that we will continue to fight once we are outside again,' Valentina answers in the sun, while another cup of coffee is served and one more cigarette is lit. International action to set them free is planned.

Concepción, 1992: the last political prisoners – or terrorists?

The lawyer from the Vicarage is on one of her visits to the two remaining political prisoners in the jail of Concepción. We accompany her into their room. Formerly, close to thirty political prisoners were packed together here. Now, only two political prisoners remain. The room is 6 by 4 metres and there is a small kitchen and a television.

They are locked into this room from 8 in the evening until the next morning. During the day, they participate in different activities and workshops along with the criminal prisoners. Eight other prisoners in the same prison are on a hunger strike because they are not recognized as political prisoners but have been placed together with the ordinary criminals.

The official number of political prisoners has been reduced during recent years. Participants in armed confrontations are now designated 'criminals', and this, to some extent, explains the reduction. From the point of view of the new government, it is impossible to accept the arrival of new political prisoners in the midst of a democratic process.

On the other hand, the lawyers, the prisoners and the professionals in the human rights movement all confirm that torture has been carried out even after March 1990, although it is no longer a systematic procedure. For some of the policemen, it is not easy to forget old skills. Who is responsible for this, and is it still possible to torture with impunity under the shelter of the law? The reported cases of torture have been denounced by the human rights movement, but nothing has really been done to punish those responsible.

It is obvious that the situation for political prisoners has considerably improved since 1989. We also find it interesting that elements observed outside of the prisons in the organization of human rights work are repeated behind the prison bars.

The use of *basic groups* is one example: political prisoners are members of an organized group with special leaders, well-defined internal rules and a mutual aim of keeping up political commitment and emotional resistance. The *interaction between the political prisoners and the professionals* is in line with the three basic principles of the human rights organizations: denunciation, investigation/documentation and treatment. The therapeutic approaches in prison, both in the work with groups and on the individual level, are quite exceptional. Once more, 'the academic rules of psychotherapy' are violated. Purists may insist that this is not 'real psychotherapy', but who can afford this discussion under the conditions of state terrorism? The professionalism of the work within the prison setting is, nevertheless, fairly convincing.

'Behind Barbed Wire': The Concentration Camps

The camps

Immediately after 11 September 1973, concentration camps were set up to contain all the 'prisoners of war'. Based on information from Weinstein et al. (1987, pp. 245–8) the main places were:

In the Atacama desert

1. *Pisagua* in the north, on the coast between Iquique and Arica. It can be reached by a three-hour drive through the Atacama desert. The steering committee of the ex-political prisoners in Pisagua claim that close to 1,500 prisoners (among these, 30 women) were kept here from 1973 to 1974.

2. *Chacabuco*, 110 kilometres from Antofagasta. It was opened in November 1973 and between 600 and 1,000 prisoners were kept here. They were released gradually, during the first six months of 1974.

Near Santiago

3. *Tres Alamos* in Santiago (No. 53 Canada Street). It was opened in June 1974 as a transitional placement for the prisoners who had been kept in the Stadium of Chile. It contained about 300 prisoners and in the interior of this camp there was a special barracks, *Cuatros Alamos*, for those prisoners who were kept in isolation ('incommunicado'). This camp is described by Julia in Chapter 5. The camp was run by the police (*carabiñeros*).

Near Valparaíso

4. *Puchuncavi (Melinka)*, a camp close to a village in the province of Valparaíso. Nearly 250 persons were detained here. This camp was run by the Navy.

5. *Ritoque*, also in the province of Valparaíso. In June 1974 the principal persons of the Allende government were transferred to this place from Dawson Island. It was run by the Air Force.

Near Punta Arenas

6. *Dawson Island*, at the extreme south of the Magellan Straits. Five days after the coup, the leading figures of the former government were placed here. Next to this camp there was another camp which contained more than 300 local political prisoners from Punta Arenas and the Magellan region. The camps were run by the Army.

7. *Punta Arenas*: 'El Palacio de las Sonrisas' ('The Palace of Smiles') started to function on 11 September 1973 in the town's old naval hospital. This place was run by the Navy.

8. *Punta Arenas*: the Bahia Catalina base. It was run by the Air Force.

9. *Punta Arenas*: the Cochrane regiment. This camp was run by the Navy.

Near Concepción and Talcahuano

10. *Talcahuano*, the naval base. It functioned from the first months after the coup in 1973 until 1975. The number detained fluctuated between 20 and 45 individuals.

11. *Talcahuano*, the Borgoño Fortress. It was situated inside the naval base. Here there were usually between 40 and 50 prisoners.

12. *Quiriquina Island*, in the bay outside Talcahuano. Close to a thousand political prisoners were placed here.

In most of these locations the prisoners were kept without any contact with the outside world – in contrast to the conditions in the prisons. The prisoners in the camps were exposed to torture, humiliation and intensive interrogation. Several of the camps functioned mainly during the first one or two years after the coup.

From a testimony: Dawson Island (September 1973)

I was arrested on 12 September 1973 at my office. I was 22 years old at that time. After having been detained on a naval ship [*Destructor Arana*] and in a military camp [Pudeto], we were put on a ship bound for Dawson Island. I was dressed in my usual office clothes. It was winter and there was a snowstorm while we sailed the couple of hours it takes to cross from Punta Arenas to Port Harris on Dawson Island.

We landed close to the former Salesian Mission in the small town which is inhabited by naval staff. We walked the 15 kilometres to the camp, Compingin, which was an already existing military facility. Later, they built the Rio Chico camp specifically for the purpose of a concentration camp.

The first twenty-four hours we got neither food nor sleep, and it was bitterly cold. From 19 September it was prohibited to talk with other prisoners. We each got our prisoner's number. At night we were taken for interrogation and torture. Some of the comrades never returned to our barracks, so we did not know if they had been executed or if they had just been moved to another location. It was an extremely effective method for creating a pervading, collective fear.

We wondered what our crime was and learned through the interrogations that it was 'Plan Z' concerning all the hidden weapons that was the main theme.[1] Some Catholic priests (or where they just in disguise?) participated in the interrogations and tried to make us talk. After a month we were transferred back to Punta Arenas for new interrogations and humiliations.

Two months later we were again sent to Dawson Island. I think it was because the new camp was now ready. We numbered several hundred prisoners now. In between we were taken back to Punta Arenas in order to appear in front of the War Tribunal. I got a sentence of twelve years for terrorism. On Dawson Island, they separated those with and without sentences. I was there for nearly six months more.

We numbered close to 120 prisoners – I guess about 80 communists and 40 socialists. The guards were changed every second week to prevent alliances developing. Most of us were from Punta Arenas, and, due to the historical tradition of the town, a lot of us had family or friends among the military. In consequence, our guards were not local people, but came from other parts of the country.

Each day started with a morning parade at 7.00 a.m. We got our orders and had to sing the national anthem. Little by little, we got into our routines. Our main food was lentils and sometimes berries. We made some alcohol from these too. Among the prisoners there were big discussions about how we should behave. The socialists argued that we should not communicate with our captors, while we, the communists, tried to get involved with them when it was possible, for example by offering to remove garbage from the barracks, or to go to Port Williams, to the post office, with letters. We thought that this was the best way to get information and to keep in contact with the outside world. Another problem was the discussions about who had told them what, and whether somebody had maybe told them too much.

I will try to describe how this camp was. The Rio Chico camp was in a valley along the banks of the river with precipitous slopes on both sides, and it was surrounded by two rows of barbed wires (2–2.5 metres high). Guards were placed with submachine guns in overview positions on both sides of the river, and there were also two cannons to avoid us being 'liberated' – they thought that the Russians would come and attempt to liberate us.

In each barracks there lived close to fifty prisoners. Each barracks contained one big room with bunk beds and a stove in the middle and toilets and showers at the end. The barracks were made of sheet metal.

Today it is still a military location. None of us who stayed there has ever got the chance to go back and see the place. We do not know, in fact, if it still exists. Some of the fishermen have told us that they think so. Some day I would like to go back there, just once, to see it again; somehow I feel that it could be a release for me.

Pisagua: 'To follow the tracks back to where it happened'

'I stood right here on this spot,' says Manuel suddenly. 'This building was the prison in Pisagua and here in the square outside we suffered climate torture. We were forced to stand here in the sun with a lot of clothes on, and in the night in coldness without clothes.' For a moment he is back there; he disappears in silence. We stand beside him and gradually he returns. He wants us to take a photo.

It has taken three hours to drive through the tracks in the sand of the Atacama desert before arrival at this 'natural concentration camp'. The camp was, in a strange way, both part of the village and yet also in its own territory. Manuel has not been back since he was here as a prisoner in 1973. On our drive downwards from the mountains of sand we realize how impossible any flight from here would have been. Any movement and any person would be seen from far off.

In the small fisherman's village on the coast, all windows and doors are closed. There are no people in the streets. 'They have seen too much and are still scared,' says Manuel.

First, the old taxi moves to the churchyard outside the village. We have to appear as if we are visitors to the graves, we are told. The police out here do not like people to sneak around. Manuel does not go to the grave of the disappeared. He walks alone in the periphery of the churchyard. When we meet him again, he talks about some old graves of sailors from an English ship in the nineteenth century. We ask no questions, just accompany him.

We go back to the village. Parts of the camp are destroyed; no barbed wire and no barracks are left – only the old buildings which were part of the village and which also served as prisons and torture centres. The former public prison is empty and locked up. We wonder if the children in this town use the square in front of it for ball games.

We pass on to the old colonial theatre, which – absurdly enough – served as the women's prison. Anita shows us the rambling and rusty building. Now it contains only one big room, and its atmosphere is redolent of the past.

We continue to another old wooden building: the former hospital. A sign on the front of the building still has a painting of a nurse in uniform. 'This was the torture centre,' says Manuel. 'You can go in there. I will wait here in the shade.' We walk up the staircase in the burning sun, open the door and freeze when we suddenly hear voices and barking dogs. A family has moved in, and they look at us with surprise but without any signs of the usual Chilean hospitality.

Back at the square, where there are no restaurants or cafés (the only town in Chile?), we eat our packed lunches, with a beautiful view of the sea. The old tracks from the mines end here. The last two metres of the rusty tracks symbolically cross each other. There is a strange and threatening atmosphere, and all of us want to leave as soon as possible.

On the way back, we pass the old and deserted miners' town near Humberstone and end up in the kitchen of Manuel and his wife. They start to speak. In passing they mention that they had announced our visit to Pisagua to the PRAIS team and some neighbours, just in case.

Later, they want to show us an old video from the Pisagua camp and the camp in Chacabuco. It was a clandestine recording made by a team from East Germany who had said that they were German right-wingers, and hence were invited in by the Pinochet people. The family gives a lively commentary on the happenings on the screen. We join the family and their friends on a journey back to the past.

Manuel does not want therapy. 'It's water under the bridge,' he says. We understand that to him therapy is only for weak people. Some day, maybe, he will go to the doctor in the PRAIS team to have a health check. This evening he decides, however, to join a collective demonstration which will take place in a few weeks' time, arranged by the local Association of Ex-Political Prisoners. He ends the day heavily influenced by alcoholic self-medication, for neither the first nor the last time.

'Quriquina Island' – to document the reality

It is 1992. We visit the small office of CODEPU in Concepción. One of their main tasks right now is to complete a book documenting the concentration camp on Quiriquina Island. We receive a copy of the manuscript (CODEPU, 1992). This book is an important part of the work in this organization.

The island is still under military control. It can be seen from the coast, but no one is allowed to go there. In their book, the authors document all known details about the history of the island, as well as geographical and anthropological data. They document what happened after 1973 through testimonies from former prisoners, data collected from different sources, and they provide a list of names of all the people who were responsible for what happened there. To document what really happened is part of the collective healing process. It is a cry for truth and justice.

The Dignidad Colony

This 'colony' is a community situated close to Parral in the province of Linares. Nearly 15,000 inhabitants of German origin live here in a sort of separate state. It has been confirmed by Amnesty International that the colony had close relationships to the military government and that it functioned as a location for torture and detainment.

The colony has not accepted Chilean law, and it is impossible to enter the heavily guarded area. A newspaper published during our stay in Chile shows a picture of Pinochet's wife visiting the colony. Its territory reaches the Argentinean frontier and it has its own airport.

Testimonies have borne witness to experiments with the prisoners with the aim of finding the limits for survival with different methods of torture. There have been experiments with different kinds of drugs and the use of specific methods, for example the use of specially trained dogs that attack the sexual organs of men and women. A testimony in front of a court in Bonn 1979, recounted in Rojas (1987, p. 53), details the reception in the colony of a prisoner who is destined for death. The testimony is given by a former guard, and it testifies to the participation of a German-speaking individual by the name of 'Professor'. Other testimonies confirm the participation of 'experts' from Brazil.

In the Dignidad Colony, the inhabitants have chosen to stay voluntarily behind barbed wire and keep the world out: 'They have survived four presidents,' says one of our interviewees. 'Right now the only way to break down their walls would be through military action – but some of the military leaders do not need weapons to get inside, so I think they will survive several more presidents.'

Emotionally the camps still exist

To learn about the concentration camps was a source of revelation to us. Maybe we knew too little about what really happened, when we started this project. Anyway, it was astonishing to learn that the Nazi experiences of the Second World War were carried out here nearly thirty years later. (Several times our informants talked about German 'gentlemen' who had been involved as advisors.) The mere existence of the Dignidad Colony is a harsh testimony to this and one of the remaining taboo areas: a territory to which only special guests are invited.

We noticed how these camps, dead or alive, still played an important role in the thoughts of the former prisoners. It was obvious that the military power was still in charge of most of these areas and concealed these places from the public. They say that this is due to military security, although one might well ask: whose security?

From a therapeutical point of view, it serves an important function for the former prisoners to return to these camps, visit those old, traumatic places with a sympathetic witness as part of a healing process. The healing of a trauma can include an external as well as an internal journey. In traditional psychotherapy, too, we revisit the old traumas of childhood with a sympathetic escort, or witness. It is often a long journey. The external journey back to the location of torture or imprisonment with a sympathetic escort may be the first step. To confront all the intrusive experiences of the past with the realities of today can reduce anxiety, although the immediate encounter may temporarily aggravate the painful feelings (as in the case of Manuel, above).

The individual journey also has a documentary aspect. Through the official denial of what happened and the continued marginalization of former prisoners from parts of society, there is a need to confirm reality and the truth of what happened in the past. This becomes both a part of the individual process and a symbol of public rehabilitation and recognition.

The military forces may have removed the barbed wire, but invisible lines still keep the public out in general, and the former prisoners in particular. Through this attitude the military attempts to prevent the truth from being known, and it also prevents the public rehabilitation of the former prisoners.

As in other collective rituals of purification, the former locations of torture and imprisonment need to be opened up for a collective journey back to the scene of crime: 'Let us send a fleet of small ships manned with former prisoners and sympathetic escorts to visit the Dawson and Quriquina Islands so that we can purify ourselves and the places, and let the President speak at the unveiling of a memorial,' one interviewee said.

'Behind the Town Wall': The Tortured Town

Punta Arenas, 1992

On the day of arrival, we are walking down one of the main streets in Punta Arenas. Although it is summer, the temperature is 8 degrees above zero and a strong wind is blowing through the town. In a flash, two men are seen in military battle-dress armed with submachine guns at the staircase in an, apparently, ordinary house. Our immediate thought is to take a step back to verify the sight, and our second impulse is to walk on.

The next morning, before we have made any contacts, the hall porter of the hotel calls to tell us that two gentlemen are waiting for us at the reception disk. Here we meet two men in their forties. They have heard that two Danes are in town to study human rights and they would like to see us. In fact they were friendly and proved to be good contacts, but we never knew how they found us, although in this closed society you soon become visible. 'It is like living on an island,' says the priest, one of our interviewees.

'The red town'

Salvador Allende was elected senator in Punta Arenas, a strong bastion of Popular Unity. At the same time, this town has a strategic position because of its proximity to the oil wells and other natural resources in the Magellan region and Chilean Antarctic. Moreover, the town is close to the old enemy, Argentina. Therefore Punta Arenas is full of military installations from all branches of the armed forces. No accurate numbers are known, but it was said that close to 20,000 out of the 65,000 inhabitants were connected to the military in 1973.

On the day of the coup, the armed forces immediately took total control of the town. The Commission of Truth and Reconciliation (1992) reports only five deaths in this region during the first months of repression. On the other hand, the Commission mentions that 'torture was practised regularly and it is estimated that approximately a thousand persons were detained and subjected to this treatment in 1973.'

Opponents were just too visible and the roads of escape were few and easily controlled. The number of non-military families who were not affected by the repression was limited. The detention centres were numerous.

Punta Arenas, 1973/74

In the following we cite a few extracts of our interviews with former prisoners in Punta Arenas:

> I was 17 years old and was in my last year of school. I was arrested and was at first in Casa Deportista, then in Villa Roblecitos, where I was tortured. I do not like to talk about this now, you know how it is …, there was a psychologist involved in the interrogation, they tried to use hypnosis and the 'good and bad cop' routine. I stayed in 'Ojo Bueno'. There were twenty-one women there at the time in one big room. I was sentenced to thirty years of prison.
>
> (Female interviewee)

> We were taken back to Punta Arenas from Dawson Island. We thought it was over now and were cheering each other up. But we ended up in 'Pudeto', where we were living in something like a big container without toilets. We stayed there for thirty days. Then I was taken to 'The Palace of Smiles' – you know, the nice green house 50 metres from your hotel, next to the telephone company. It is still a military building. In December, most prisoners were taken to Dawson Island, but some of us remained. Once again we thought that we were lucky, but the next stop was the stadium, where the Air Force was in charge. We were beaten and exposed to several kinds of torture methods. I lost 12 kilos during that month. People could see from their windows next to the stadium what was happening. After one more visit to Dawson Island, I was transferred to Cochrane, where we had food and were kept during the 'process' of the War Tribunal. I was sentenced to twelve years for 'terrorism' and was sent back to Dawson Island.
>
> (Male interviewee)

I was 16 years old when they arrested me. They blindfolded me. I was in 'the Palace' – I know because one of my family worked in the telephone company and saw me through the window the night they brought me in. Later I was in the Sports House [Casa Deportista] and then transferred to 'Ojo Bueno'. I was sentenced to ten years for all kinds of alleged offences. I spent four years in the women's prison in town among alcoholics and prostitutes. I learned quite a lot about life during these years.

(Female interviewee)

Punta Arenas, 1992

I think that only about 180 out of all the persecuted people have not left. It is still a military town. The old left-wing bastion has only a few outstanding leaders left and this is still a town of the uniformed. One of the generals once said: 'Here in Punta Arenas the left wing got their very special treatment.' How can we achieve any purification of this town when even a democratic plebiscite would be in favour of repression?

(Male interviewee)

SOCIAL MARGINALIZATION AND REPRESSION

As stated throughout this book, structural and political repression are interwoven. Likewise, social marginalization can be the consequence of both forms of repression. We will illustrate this by the description of three different repressive territories: the psychiatric hospital, the territory of the ethnic minority, and the shanty towns.

'Behind Locked Doors': The Psychiatric Hospital

After the coup official health institutions, such as the psychiatric hospitals, were also affected, although more indirectly. Many of the doctors, psychologists and social workers had been dismissed for political reasons. Most of the remaining staff were, therefore, either supporters of the regime or did not want to get involved in anything political. A reduction in funding to the hospitals, including a cut in staff salaries, further exaggerated the already significant social differences between the public and the private health systems.

On the first floor

'Promise me not to copy our model when you return to your country,' says the medical director of the psychiatric hospital ironically, with a smile. We pass through the only public psychiatric department in the region for a population of 1 million inhabitants. It is located on the first floor. To the left is a ward with twenty-five beds for women, and to the right a ward with twenty-five beds for men. On duty today is a staff consisting of two people on each ward.

Behind the locked door is a common corridor where patients walk back and forth; and four ward rooms, three of them with eight beds and practically nothing else. The patient group is severely chronic. Most of them are schizophrenics or suffer from alcoholic dementia, and a few are oligophrenic. Most of them get neuroleptic medicine, but the budget does not allow for sufficient amounts of medicine, so at the end of the month, ECT (electric shock treatment) is used instead. This treatment is applied without general anaesthetic in the bed on the ward. No patient is offered any psychotherapeutic assistance and there are no opportunities for occupational therapy either inside or outside of the ward.

In the background there is a constant noise. It is the noise of shootings. A military training facility is a neighbour of the hospital. This institution is the only a place for poor people with psychiatric problems. Private clinics offer much better facilities for those who are able to pay. The military hospitals also offer psychiatric facilities for their staff.

Most of the psychiatrists employed in the public system work only part-time here. The salary is currently 85,000 pesos a month half-time (that is, US$300); this equals what a psychiatrist will earn per day in his half-day private practice. In consequence, most psychiatrists will invest their primary energy in their private practices: '80% of the psychiatrists' time in Chile is spent on the 20% of the population who are able to pay,' says one psychiatrist. 'It is expensive for a country to be poor.'

Repressive political experiences and psychiatry

'Traumatic repressive experiences did not exist in the official system,' says the psychiatrist. 'To my knowledge, we have never seen psychotic reactions or severe traumatic consequences after torture or other human rights violations here at the hospital.'

The mental health teams of the human rights movement tried to help psychiatric patients without using the psychiatric hospitals. People were primarily referred to solidary colleagues in private practice or were treated in the NGOs as outpatients. When a referral to the hospital was necessary, nothing was mentioned officially in the records about the patient's repressive political experiences. As one psychiatrist told us:

We talked with colleagues we trusted at the hospital and sometimes they knew the real story. The official psychiatric system today is unable to document any findings about psychotic reactions due to traumatic experiences during state terrorism. The official system has taken no initiatives to develop any programmes of assistance. You might call it one big group denial, because when you look at the general knowledge of psychiatry in this country, I think that our skills are not that different from what is the normal professional standard elsewhere.

Psychosis and repression

'It is an interesting problem, but we do not know much about this,' says one of the psychiatrists in a mental health team of the human rights movement:

> We tried to avoid the psychiatric hospitals when possible; they were of very little help in fact. It is a difficult task to diagnose psychotic manifestations when the societal context also shows psychotic traits. We have seen a lot of our patients suffering from depressive and paranoid reactions, but when all these things happen, it is difficult to draw the specific limits between paranoia and a realistic feeling of being observed or persecuted – or between a realistic fear and an inner anxiety. It is a difficult task to separate the mourning after severe repressive events towards your spouse or children from a reactive psychogenic depressive psychosis, and so on.

It is outside the aim of our study to examine in detail the interrelation between repressive experiences and psychosis. However, seventeen years of psychological warfare could offer an absurd but realistic opportunity to learn more about the interrelation between severe, extreme and continuous stress and psychotic reactions. We must conclude with NGO colleagues that this theme has not been studied well enough to draw any conclusions. What we *have* learned could be abstracted in the following way:

(1) The official psychiatric system has to a great extent denied the existence of the problem; therefore there are no systematic data or investigations about psychosis and human rights violations.

(2) The NGOs have seen some of the patients, but due to the circumstances, no systematic evaluation has taken place. Most data are casuistic and non-systematic, although they do document the existence of psychotic reactions.

Many professionals insist that patients are not ill, but that they 'suffer from the dictatorship'. In consequence, the number of psychotic manifestations may have been underestimated. A diagnosis of psychosis could stigmatize the patient and bring up questions about pre-morbid psychopathology. However, if repressive experiences are so severe that they result in a psychotic reaction, we believe that this does not necessarily disturb the political perspective of the aetiology.

(3) Psychosis is rarely a consequence of human rights violations. Massive repression, such as that experienced in Chile, does not induce a substantial number of psychotic reactions.

(4) Cross-cultural differences in the diagnostic criteria for psychosis, in general, and the use of the concepts of psychogenic psychosis may be different in Chile. We have observed throughout the Chilean literature on this topic that symptom patterns of a depressive and paranoid nature, as well as disturbances in reality-testing and severe disturbances in emotional contact due to repressive strategies, are commonly described without a discussion of whether the condition has any possible psychotic element.

(5) There are difficulties in the discrimination of symptoms of a psychotic and non-psychotic nature in a societal context containing collective psychosis-inducing elements.

(6) The primary target-persons of the repressive strategies may be pre-morbidly more sane than the population in general.

One interesting theoretical question is whether individuals without a pre-psychotic or maybe borderline personality structure can develop psychotic illness if the trauma is sufficiently extreme. Are the defence mechanisms (including the political or religious commitment) of a pre-morbid healthy individual sufficient to resist even the most severe trauma?

Another question is whether the diagnosis of a psychotic manifestation makes any difference for the treatment or preventive strategies to be employed. Current psychiatric knowledge argues that the optimal treatment of a psychogenic psychosis would be a combination of a temporary neuroleptic or antidepressive medication and a psychotherapeutic treatment.

If the psychotic reaction is not recognized, the patients will not receive any medicine. The psychotherapeutic treatment which is offered to nearly all patients who consult the NGO teams could easily be disturbed either by the patient's own use of minor tranquillizers for the reduction of anxiety and for sedation, or by self-medication with alcohol, or simply by needless suffering.

We were told that the following groups had been considered to be at special risk of developing psychosis in relation to repressive experiences: (1) young people returned from exile; (2) family members of the disappeared; and, as a special group, (3) former soldiers who participated in the repression in 1973/74 when they were very young.

'Invisible – Behind Invisible Lines': The Ethnic Minority

The ethnic minority group – the Mapuche – who live in the middle and the south of the country have experienced continuous social deprivation and political repression of their human rights. Their hopes for social change and a more just division of the land initiated under the Allende government were crushed after the coup. As one Mapuche leader told us: 'We have always been exploited, the foreigners [the non-Mapuche] have always wanted to take our land, so to us life during the dictatorship was not much different from before.' After 1973, the Mapuche were forced back into invisibility in reservation-like territories.

Where the women carry out witchcraft and the men talk about the land

Through the door you can watch a team of oxen pulling a load of wood along the tracks. Behind them there is a grey and black sky and the beloved land of the old Mapuche leader Don Eusebio. Inside the *ruca* (traditional Mapuche house) the old man talks and his wife comments while she goes back and forth between the table and the fireplace. Two sons are listening quietly in the background. Their daughter is a student of medicine in Moscow. Next year they expect her to return to the village and work as a doctor.

'I was in the Temuco prison for five months from 1973,' says Don Eusebio. 'Several of my kin have died and one of my sons was in prison and tortured. We have done nothing except to support Allende. He understood that something had to be done about our land.' He starts a very long speech about the land, the injustice and the discrimination against the Mapuche's rights to their land through history.

Some of the first words from an anthropologist about the Mapuche come to mind: 'This is a people where the women carry out witchcraft and the men talk about the land. They can talk for hours about the land in such a way that you will sometimes have difficulty sorting out when they are talking about themselves and when they are talking about the land.'

In the interview we try to go back to Don Eusebio's repressive political experiences. He does not believe that exposure to torture will result in serious psychological damage. 'Those who were resistors against the Pinochistas are people with a strong soul. A disease or weakness will only develop when you lose your soul.' His wife argues from the fireplace something in Mapuche language, but he continues: 'No, I do not believe much in the ability of the *machi* [the female shaman] to solve problems after political repression. She is more like a doctor – and she is expensive. One *machi* who lives near us takes 70,000 pesos ($250) for her assistance.' From the wife's long speech in Mapuche, we feel that she has quite another opinion.

'If an individual has a disease, the *machi* will perform a series of rituals in which she will use the drum and sing her hymns to bring the disappeared soul back through the hole in the roof and let the evil out through the door,' translates our companion from the local human rights movement. The husband takes over again. He knows about the NGOs and the new PRAIS team, but 'it is a long and expensive journey from our villages to the office in the hospital in Temuco, so our people out here will only rarely attend'.

Afterwards there is a long walk along the tracks back to the village of Chol to catch the old, rambling bus to Temuco. We learn that there is quite a distance from this *ruca*, with the chief's symbols painted on the wooden wall at the back of the house, to the psychotherapeutic work in the NGOs and PRAIS teams – in more than one sense.

The Mapuche and the repression

Close to 1 million out of the 12 million Chileans are Mapuche. Most of them live in the area between the river Bío-Bío (at the level of Concepción) and the island of Chiloë (at the level of Puerto Montt). One large group, however, has moved into the suburbs and shanty towns of Santiago, where most of them work in low-class positions as housemaids and unskilled workers – if they are not unemployed. The main town of the Mapuche is the capital of the IX. Region, Temuco, where 40,000–50,000 – close to one third of the inhabitants – define themselves as Mapuche. That is, they have a Mapuche name and belong to a specific Mapuche village community.

Several Mapuche organizations are now working to fight for the rights of the Mapuche people. From the Mapuche perspective, the human rights violations did not start in 1973. Exploitation has been part of life for centuries and has to some extent been integrated into their life as a kind of resignation: 'It has always been so and it will always be like that.'

After the coup, the repressive measures in the region were even more severe against the Mapuche than against the 'Chilean' left wing. The loose infrastructure of the Mapuche communities and the lack of political organization made them more vulnerable to individual and collective violations.

The anthropologist Roberto Morales has published a specific report about the deaths of 137 Mapuche which were reported to the Commission of Truth and Reconciliation as well as a map of the repression in the region (Morales, 1990, 1991a).[2]

We observed that most of the political prisoners in the Temuco prison in 1989 had Mapuche names.

The Mapuche share the general problems of poverty, social marginalization and repression with other underprivileged groups in Chilean society. In addition, they have the problem of being an ethnic minority and are exposed to both discrimination and racism (Morales, 1991b).

The Mapuche do not have much trust in non-Mapuche, and basically it seems as if they expect nothing good to come from the outside world. They have been marginalized in the health system as well, and probably contribute to this marginalization by not using the limited support structures available to them. Thus, the marginalization is connected to the economic, cultural and historical conditions of the Mapuche.

'Outside the Town Wall': The Shanty Town

On the outskirts of all major cities, poor shanty towns are found, another territory of structural and political violence. Three special shanty towns were El Progreso (Progress), La Victoria (Victory) and San Pedro.

El Progreso, 1989

'Welcome, the President is expecting you.' The taxi has stopped a couple of kilometres outside of Temuco. Most of the 'houses' are combinations of tents, cartons, boards and plastic sacks. There are a lot of skinny dogs, a single cow and hundreds of puddles of water in the mud.

The President is sitting in one of the tents. The ground is covered with several carpets, and in the middle a woman in her forties, the

President, welcomes us with dignity. Gradually, an increasing number of people enter the tent: the Secretary General, the Treasurer, members of the steering committee.

Somehow it could have been a very formal meeting, if it were not for the context. Coffee is served and cigarettes are exchanged. They tell about this community. There is only one water pump and no sewerage. They are one out of four shanty towns in this region. Close to four hundred people live here; more than half of them are children.

'We had no place to stay, so we decided to do something about it ourselves. We are trying to organize the people here so that they live in a healthy way. The men who are employed pay a certain amount each week to the community and we cook together so that the children at least will have one good meal a day.

The authorities have unofficially accepted that we stay here by not doing anything, but they told us that our children were only allowed to go to school at the opposite end of Temuco and that they could not offer any school bus. A few days ago we went in a protest march to see the Mayor. We were not allowed to talk to him, the police met us with their batons – a pregnant woman had to go to the hospital, even some of the children were hurt – and all of us have blue marks,' they say and draw up their sweaters while joking comments are made across the tent. 'We are honest people here, we want to work and to raise our families in democracy. Of course, many of us are communists. What choice do you have in the middle of this poverty?'

La Victoria, 1989

'Maybe 15,000 of us live out here,' she says, the impressive guide who leads us through the shanty town of La Victoria on the outskirts of Santiago. 'Here at the borders of our district, you can see this other community a few streets away. There you will find a lot of criminality and each person will primarily take care of his own interests. After several years of work, we are on our way towards a healthy, although poor, society here. We never know exactly how many people live here; several hundred ex-political prisoners are here or have been here.'

The pavement on the main street is decorated with paintings and graffiti demanding peace, Allende, socialism, the MIR and human rights. One of the 'culture houses' is close by: 'Here we have space for the meetings of the survivors' groups and of all the different organizing committees out here.'

The house looks extremely barren with almost no furniture. 'Here you can see the bullet holes from the last time we were visited by the security forces,' she points at several holes in the walls and doors. 'Things are better now, but you never know.'

'We think that our organizational structure and our political commitment have been our best resource in the resistance against poverty and repression. Our main problem today is the deterioration of our health assistance out here, and right now the staff of our small health clinic are expressing their protest in a hunger strike. We need better care for the mothers and the children.

Another health problem is alcoholism. A lot of the men drink too much, they want to forget what they cannot forget, and they often do not want any help. We have opened our own clinic for alcoholism treatment. We think it is necessary if we want to reduce domestic violence against wives and children. In fact, we also need professional assistance to help many of the survivors, but they do not want it; they act tough and drink instead.'

San Pedro, Concepción, 1992

We live in our small rented house on the southern banks of the River Bío-Bío in San Pedro near Concepción. Three times a week, in the morning before the garbage is collected, several people search our garbage to find something useful. Once a week, five women from the Pentecostal movement shout their threats, blessings and hymns on the corner. When we walk along the river, we are constantly confronted with poverty only a few minutes outside the invisible town walls.

Even when the immediate collective fear due to political repression is reduced, the consequences of years of repression and poverty will exist here for generations. These problems will not be overcome even after the installation of a democratic government.

NOTES

1. 'Plan Z' was an intelligence operation started at the time of the coup. It served as an excuse for the repression of left-wing supporters – a psychological warfare strategy.

2. An article based on the report is published in the journal *Nütram* (Morales, 1991a).

10

Trauma and Healing on the Territorial Level

'Because of the grass that was downtrodden...'

We have drawn our maps of different repressive territories: the prison, the concentration camp, the town, the psychiatric hospital, the land of the Mapuche and the shanty town. In these territories, we found different strategies of psychological warfare which, directly or indirectly, destroyed those relationships and networks that were a threat to the regime. No organized resistance is possible without relationships between people, groups and networks. Individuals, no matter how numerous they are, will have no chance against organized violence if they are not connected to others.

Therefore the psychological *counter-strategies* for survival and resistance which are developed both inside the repressive territory and in the surrounding social context are aimed at strengthening relationships between people: groups are developed, social networks are reinforced.

The development of professional *healing strategies* to deal with the consequences of the repressive experiences is primarily possible outside the repressive territory. These strategies work on the individual, family, group and collective levels.

In the borderland between the repressive territory and the surrounding social context an exchange takes place which promotes psychological strategies of resistance. A *communicative space* develops between the groups inside and outside the repressive territory. The intensity of this exchange is limited by the permeability of the boundaries around the repressive territories.

An important element in the counter-strategies inside the repressive territory is to get some kind of access to the outside world. Likewise, an important element in the healing strategies developed outside is to get access to the interior world of the repressive territory.

In the following, we will analyse the strategies of psychological resistance on both sides of the boundary, and in the communicative space which develops in the process of exchange between the two worlds. First we will examine different counter-strategies inside the territories, then we will focus on the exchange which goes on in the borderland between the territories and the outer world, and finally we will describe different healing strategies developed outside the repressive territories.

REPRESSIVE TERRITORIES

The Prison

The interior

Inside the prisons, the separation between political prisoners and criminals is important for the establishment of a group to which the individual political prisoner can belong. We found that the political prisoners organized themselves in a hierarchical structure with a leader/ coordinator and a steering committee. These groups offer a possibility of developing a group identity and a space for keeping the political commitment alive. The group can also become a forum in which emotional distress after torture can be counteracted. Moreover, the group helps the prisoner to break out of the isolation and individualization of his or her problems. Thus, the formation of such groups is an important psychological counter-strategy which helps both survival in and resistance to the destructive atmosphere of the prison.

The boundaries and their permeability

The boundaries marking the outside world are visible and materialized in the walls, the armed guards, the locked doors and the iron bars. The boundaries can be permeated by several types of visitors from the outside:

The family group is allowed in on conditions similar to those that apply to the criminal prisoners. This gives the prisoner the opportunity to have some contact with his or her family, although it also involves a confrontation with his or her restricted life. The families outside of the prison have organized themselves into survivors' groups, the Associations of Family Members of Political Prisoners, in order to reconstruct their social network and to fight for the liberation of their family members.

Members of the Associations continue to visit the political prisoners even though their own family members have been set free. Likewise, members of the Association of Ex-Political Prisoners continue to visit their old comrades inside the prison. This is felt to be an important dimension of the psychological counter-strategy in the survivors' groups, and it is also considered to be a moral obligation. As one female ex-political prisoner told us:

> I will continue to visit the prisoners every Saturday until the last political prisoner has been set free. I can never feel free, myself, before all political prisoners are out. I know what it means that people outside have not forgotten you.

For the ex-political prisoners, these visits can provoke old traumata, but visiting the prison can also have a healing effect if the ex-prisoners can integrate past events. For those who are in prison, the visits offer a network to join when they have been set free.

Members of the NGOs – the professionals – are also allowed in. The professionals are, for example, lawyers from the judicial departments of the NGOs, social workers, psychologists, psychiatrists and other doctors. In the beginning, most of these professionals figured on the visitors' lists as friends or family – later the authorities accepted their visits because it reduced 'trouble' with the prisoners.

During these visits, the professionals have the chance to talk with the prisoners individually, sometimes sheltered by the group, in the large visiting halls. At other times, the mental health professionals talk with the entire group. In these talks, they can work with conflicts in the group, and can help reduce the impact of the 'psychotic' climate in the closed space of the prison. These healing strategies can initiate a process to be continued after liberation in the therapeutic space of an NGO mental health centre (see Becker and Kovalskys, 1990).

International organizations are to some extent given access to monitor the situation of the political prisoners. These visits are very significant for the prisoners, because they allow knowledge of their plight to become known – and condemned – internationally.

The exterior

The creation of survivors' groups, which we have continuously referred to, has been the main psychological counter-strategy developed outside the prison territory. These groups have acted as a support for individual survivors, but they have also had an important function in calling attention to the situation of political prisoners.

Healing strategies at the professional level have mainly been developed in the mental health centres of the human rights movement. These centres have also provided judicial and social support for prisoners. The professionals have worked closely together with the survivors' groups in the campaign for prisoners' freedom.

A special group of opponents, 'the Sebastián Acevedo Movement Against Torture', was active in demonstrations against torture outside the torture houses and prisons, and in the streets. In the following we will give a more detailed description of this important component of the human rights movement. The Sebastián Acevedo Movement was an expression both of psychological counter-strategies at the private and the political level and of healing strategies at the societal level.

The Sebastián Acevedo Movement Against Torture

The movement started in 1983. The members were people who had a special commitment to non-violent struggle against torture and repression, some with and some without prior personal traumatic experiences. According to one of the pioneers, Father José Aldunate, the movement was inspired by the work of the survivors' groups, especially the Association of Family Members of the Disappeared. Other inspirations were the international peace movements and, more specifically, the life of Gandhi, which was well-known in Chile at that time, from the movie about him.

From their first action on 14 September 1983 and through several hundred demonstrations, the movement developed specific strategies for the denunciation of torture. The demonstrations were met by severe repressive actions from the police, who used water cannons, tear gas, beatings with batons and mass detentions.

The movement was named after Sebastián Acevedo, a man from the town of Lota on the Coal Coast south of Concepción. According to Father Aldunate, Sebastián was respected as a straight and honest Christian worker. He and his children were persecuted by the authorities because of their political commitment. Although Sebastián often had to leave the house to live a clandestine life for certain periods, he recommended his children to stay in the house. One day his son and daughter 'disappeared', and he and his wife searched all over to find them, but no authorities had ever heard about them. He asked his priest for permission to crucify himself in public as a protest, but he did not receive it. In desperation he burned himself in front of the cathedral in Concepción. A few hours after his death, his children were set free. In honour of his martyrdom, the movement took his name. The children were later arrested again and tortured.

Concepción 1992

Three representatives from the survivors' group of the ex-political prisoners tell us about their present situation. The small room in the Vicarage is without windows and extremely cold. The group is militant and frustrated. They are still marginalized; they will neither receive any compensation nor get any jobs and they are totally dependent on their family group. All of them feel severely traumatized, in need of medical and psychological attention, and they explain how traumatized their families – including the children – are. One of the interviewees is a woman named Maria.

Coronel, 1992

The smell in Coronel is a heavy mixture of fish and coal industry. In the poor shanty town we find the blue house of Sebastián's widow, Elena. She sits down at a table together with Maria, who turns out to be Sebastián's daughter.

Elena tells us the story once more. Although it affects her to tell it, she recalls the events with dignity. She expresses the hope that the death of her husband has been meaningful in the fight against the dictatorship. However, the price has been high on the private level.

When we are permitted to take a photo she takes a picture from the shelf – their wedding portrait – and places it in front of herself and her daughter. The rest of the family, which seems numerous, listen silently to her story from every corner of the small house.

The Sebastián Acevedo Movement, Concepción, 1992

They are expecting us in the house of the Chilean Commission for Human Rights – seven members of the local Sebastián Acevedo Movement. The meeting has been arranged by their grand old mentor, Jorge Barudy Senior. They have planned a round in which each of them will give his or her perspective on their work. They are well prepared and structured in their presentation. Each one adds a new dimension.

We learn how the widow and the children of Sebastián Acevedo often participate in their demonstrations. The atmosphere in the room becomes warm and containing. We are sucked into their narrative of how the group members meet after demonstrations, and how they debrief themselves. They always feel a great need to touch and hug each other afterwards. As Father Aldunate told us:

> The collective action had a powerful effect on all of us. It carried away individual desires. What we could call 'mysticism' also contributed to this. The mystical was part of the ethical and also religious significance of the action. It was an answer to a very strong ethical-religious demand. Our links with humanity and our links with the same God who had created mankind impelled us to react to the torture of our brother.

They try to avoid any kind of violence. As the Concepción group told us:

> Mostly we ask the ex-political prisoners not to participate in the demonstrations. They can react violently to the provocations from the police. The non-violence principle is extremely important to us – also if we are confronted with heavy police violence. Instead, we ask those of our comrades who are ex-political prisoners to mix with the crowd as 'observers' to record all the police aggressions and to note precisely what happens.

Afterwards they give us different material: photos, drawings, pamphlets. It requires several attempts to take a photo of the group because of all the laughing and joking. A strong healing power radiates from the whole group.

The Concentration Camp

The interior

In the concentration camp, there was a constant threat of interrogation, torture and death combined with a daily routine which was characterized by primitive living conditions, hard physical work and scarcity of food.

In contrast to the prison territory, the camp prisoners were not mixed with criminals. The inmates of the camps were defined as 'prisoners of war'. In the camps' barracks, it was possible to develop psychological counter-strategies by the formation of groups, and also of networks which connected the different barracks.

Many political factions were represented in the camps, and groups were often formed on the basis of these factions. The prisoners shared the harsh conditions in the camp, and in many places it was possible to develop a sense of group identity, which was an important factor for psychological survival and resistance.

The boundaries and their permeability

In general, the borderland between the concentration camps and the outer world was not very populated. In fact, the boundaries were nearly impermeable. The concentration camps were placed in remote areas in locations which were more or less clandestine, or in military areas. Even if visits were allowed, which they seldom were, except occasionally after great intervals of time, many family members were simply unable to afford the long journey.

If representatives of the human rights movement, priests or family members got the chance to approach the gate and ask after a particular person, his or her presence in the camp was often denied. Representatives of international bodies such as the Red Cross and UN organizations were, in fact, the only people who had any chance of getting in. Although it was difficult to get any truthful information about living conditions in the camps because of the cover-up perpetrated by the camp commanders, international pressure was an important element in highlighting the existence of the camps – and the later closure of these locations.

The exterior

After release from the camps, the former prisoners have developed healing strategies on the private, the professional and the political levels. *Testimonies* to reconstruct the truth about what happened have been elaborated (see the testimony about the camp on Dawson Island in Chapter 9) as part of professionally guided therapies (see Chapter 6 on the testimony method), and as part of a collective strategy on the part of the human rights organizations (see Chapter 9 for CODEPU documentation of the camp on Quiriquina Island).

Healing rituals have also been performed by some of the survivors' groups. For example, the Association of Ex-Political Prisoners of Pisagua and the Association of Family Members of the Disappeared and Executed made a collective visit to the grave of the disappeared in Pisagua. During this visit, the dead were mourned and honoured. Although the survivors' groups do not, themselves, see this ritual as primarily healing, it un-doubtedly does have such function.

In this *return to the place of the trauma*, the large group of former prisoners are confronted with the shadows of the past. Reality is confirmed – the camp was real, although today only traces of what happened remain. For many, there have been years of intrusive thoughts, flash-backs, nightmares and fantasies about the place, and the journey back can provoke new intrusive symptoms. However, it is also a real chance of starting the very necessary process of integrating the trauma.

The plans of the survivors' groups from Pisagua to build a *mausoleum/ memorial* can be seen as one more element in the public recognition of what really happened – and a rehabilitation of the victims of repression. The building of such memorials are, thus, also parts of the collective rituals of healing and purgation.

The Psychiatric Hospital

The interior

Behind the locked doors of the psychiatric department, the patients exist primarily as individuals – poor, socially marginalized and with a psychiatric illness. They are not organized at any level and have to fight their own battles. The gap between the skilled professionals and the poor patients is enormous. This gap was extended during the dictatorship. The dismissal of all – even moderately – left-wing professionals from the hospital system has contributed to the deterioration of social consciousness and solidarity, which is often an important part of engagement in this type of work.

In some countries, psychiatric hospitals have been directly involved in repressive strategies. Opponents have been placed in hospitals with diagnoses of schizophrenia or paranoia and been treated with psychopharmacological drugs. We have no information about the use of these strategies in Chilean psychiatry.

However, it has been repeatedly documented that medical doctors were involved in torture, and it is logical to expect that the torturers have also drawn on the experience of psychiatrists who have worked in the hospitals – public or military – in the development of more sophisticated psychological torture methods. Also, they may have learned about the use of drugs such as pentabarbital (a barbiturate) or reserpine (a major tranquillizer). The machine used for electrical torture seems to be very similar to the one used for ECT (electric shock) treatment at the psychiatric hospital. Furthermore, the denial of the psychological and psychiatric consequences of repression found in psychiatric hospitals adds to the suspicion that hospitals also took part in the repression.

We were told that some non-compliant psychiatrists were allowed in behind the locked doors if they accepted self-censorship and passed frequent questioning by the authorities about their political position. These groups of professionals were of some importance to the limited communication that was made with the outside world of resistance.

The boundaries and their permeability

Through clandestine cooperation with these professionals, some opponents were able to pass into hospital departments in emergency situations. However, the repressive experiences of the patients were not reported at meetings or put on file.

The professionals working with the human rights movement were able to connect to those inside of the hospital system through unofficial channels. Those psychiatrists who were dismissed after the coup still have no official access to the hospitals. They cannot get a job because of their 'criminal' records.

The exterior

The official mental health system has thus had only a very limited role in mental health support of the survivors of the repression – even after the election of the democratic government. The PRAIS teams are located in the general hospitals, but in several towns the mistrust of the hospitals and the professionals working in them hinders the population from joining these programmes. This is not surprising as it is well known that some of the doctors who participated in torture still have their hospital positions. Moreover, some hospitals were also used as torture centres!

The lack of confidence in the public system, and the reduction of support to the NGOs from international organizations, reduce the possibilities for survivors to get sufficient mental health assistance. In consequence, an important issue for the democratic government seems to be the development of new and alternative settings for mental health assistance. Another important issue would be to rehabilitate the dismissed (exonerated) professionals. We propose the following:

(1) *The development of community-oriented psychiatry settings* Initiatives towards developing community based psychiatry have been taken, for example in the area of Talcahuano where local mental health teams have been created. A psychiatrist supervises the teams, which are composed of a general practitioner, a nurse, a social worker and a psychologist. It seems important for these teams also to be trained in the treatment of traumata after repressive experiences and to include this aspect in their general work with psychiatry, alcoholism and poverty.

(2) *Rehabilitation of exonerated professionals* The professionals who were dismissed for political reasons should have their criminal records deleted. It is a sad and absurd fact that these professionals, even after the change

of system, are not allowed to work in the public health system due to 'political crimes and imprisonment' during the early days of the dictatorship. Since supporters of the former regime are still in charge of several institutions, it seems necessary to create alternative positions for the exonerated professionals through the following:

(a) An integration of NGO professionals within the official system (many of the exonerated professionals now work in the NGOs).

(b) Public economic support for the NGOs.

(c) Development of new public centres/hospitals, especially for the treatment of consequences of repression and social marginalization, in close collaboration with community psychiatric teams. Such centres would need international support.

(d) Development of an academic setting for prominent professionals from the mental health teams of the human rights movement. This setting should establish an environment for teaching other professionals about their ground-breaking work and offer space for theoretical studies. In this academic setting, experiences could be exchanged with other professionals and a research environment developed which would connect national experts in the international professional community. It would be especially important to establish a South–South dialogue between professionals. This is also only a realistic proposal if international economic support is provided.

(3) *Development of an ethical code*   In collaboration with the public authorities and the professional organizations, an ethical code should be developed, whereby professionals could be charged if they have assisted in direct repression. If this is proved, they should be expelled from the system.

The Ethnic Minority: The Mapuche

The interior

The Mapuche community, which has primarily been organized in family groups, without any political or military organization, has been an easy target for exploitation. The main community organization of the Mapuche has been connected to religious beliefs and ceremonies, the Mapuche language and cultural tradition. In fact the Mapuche are divided into several different tribes and communities as well. The Mapuche have their own healing strategies, which are quite different from the European tradition.

The body and soul cannot be separated

In the Mapuche world, the theme of mental health is central to the understanding of their global perspective on disease, and consequently also for their healing strategies. From the Mapuche perspective, most diseases have a psychological cause. Physical and mental health (and illness) are integrated and inseparable, because for the Mapuche the health of the body can never be separated from the health of the soul, and vice versa.

Several new Mapuche organizations have grown up during recent decades. A consciousness-raising process has started in which politically committed individuals and groups have tried to develop their infra-structure. The traditional resistance against organization is, however, still a problem. The 500th anniversary celebration of 'the time when the Mapuche discovered Columbus' was used for demonstrations for Mapuche rights. The Mapuche also occupied land and houses of large landowners to demonstrate their legal rights to this land. Some negotiations are in fact being carried out with the new government on this issue.

The boundaries and their permeability

In general, the Mapuche boundaries are nowadays easy to permeate for aggressors. This permeability has resulted in exploitation and a constant process of emotional withdrawal by the Mapuche community from the 'foreigners' (the Chileans). Also, geographically, they have withdrawn or been forced to withdraw to minor and distant villages. The mental health care system, the churches and the human rights movement have, however, succeeded in the establishment of some contact. Initiatives are being taken at the Faculty of Medicine of the University of Frontera in Temuco, where health care providers and anthropologists are working together to develop integrated programmes especially aimed at the Mapuche community.

How can Chilean mental health professionals learn from the Mapuche and vice versa?

At the Faculty of Medicine of the University of Frontera, Dr M.A. Solar is teaching the medical students about Mapuche culture. He wants to discuss similarities and differences between the traditional medicine of the Mapuche and traditional academic medicine. The means is a video presentation of a case of schizophrenia. A psychiatrist presents the case from his rather traditional point of view; the Mapuche parents tell their story about their ill son, and we see the *machi* (the female shaman) at work in the family context of a traditional Mapuche cottage.

The son is placed on a bed in the centre of the cottage and of the family. His head is wrapped in a cloth with an extract of herbs. The *machi* beats a small drum, *el kultrún*. She performs a series of rituals: she smokes and blows the smoke up into the air; she draws her head-scarf over her face while she sings and moves around in the cottage to the rhythm of the drum. Sometimes, the family follows her by clapping their hands. She is invoking the spirits. The ritual continues for hours. She throws small stones on a cloth and reads the mosaic they create. Her diagnosis is that somebody from another village envies the son and has stolen his soul. Now the task is to bring the soul back and get the evil out through the door.

At sunrise the battle against the evil reaches a climax. The whole family follows her and the drum out through the door; the soul has come back and the evil leaves the house. Later she talks to the members of the family about their situation. The mother is advised to have no more children. The *machi* prepares a way for the son to stay integrated within the family and do some work in the fields.

The rituals are, of course, rooted in Mapuche traditional culture. Good and evil are the two antagonistic and complementary forces: *Ngenechen* is the positive force; it is constructive and gives life. *Wekufu* is the spirit of the negative forces – destruction and death. There are two fundamental types of magic. One is the positive magic of the *machi*, and the other the negative magic of the *kalku*. Both call on natural and supernatural forces. The natural force is a 'biochemical' knowledge of herbs and traditional medicine. The supernatural force is the ability to act as a medium for contact with the spirits, and to be able to interpret messages from the good spirits (the *machi*) and from the evil ones (the *kalku*).

In order to become a *machi*, the woman must have innate qualities and also have had a hallucinatory (psychotic?) experience as a young girl. During this experience her power becomes visible to the community. She will then receive a very expensive education mastered by an older *machi*. In contrast, to be a *kalku* in the Mapuche community is a very painful condition which is lifelong. In most cases, the only possibility of escaping from the role of *kalku* is to escape from the community.

In his lecture Dr Solar points out how the old healing rituals and therapeutic strategies of the *machi* have similarities with psychotherapy and modern psychiatric work. Dreams play a very important role for the Mapuche, a fact which has not been integrated into any 'Western' therapeutic strategies with Mapuche individuals.

The Mapuche understanding of illness is not far removed from the bio-psycho-social model (Engel, 1953; Jensen, 1992) of understanding and treatment. According to this model, you need to encompass the interdependency of biological, psychological and social factors to understand and to heal most illnesses.

Nor is the involvement of the family and the local community far removed from modern theories of community psychiatry or family therapy. Dr Solar comments that one of the problems in public health care for the Mapuche is to get them to understand the necessity of rudimentary preventive and curative strategies against simple somatic problems, because they insist on a more complicated model of illness.

The strategy in the public health programmes sponsored by the university is to offer education for those Mapuche women whose status is a little lower than that of the *machis* (see Girardi et al., 1991). These women are respected in the Mapuche community because they have a certain knowledge about the use of herbs and traditional medicine. A leaflet, *Primer Manual de Medicina Casera para la Madre Campesina* (Basic Manual of Household Medicine for the Peasant Mother) (Solar, 1989), has been produced for this purpose. The churches also work in the Mapuche communities and offer social assistance, but this work is complicated by the churches' missionary efforts to convert the Mapuche to Christianity (see Rhee, 1992). The human rights movement has succeeded in the establishment of a certain connection to the Mapuche community. CODEPU in Temuco had an office for Mapuche affairs for a period. However, the anthropologist Roberto Morales (1991b) claims that a degree of racism also exists against the Mapuche within the human rights movement.

The exterior

One key problem in the Mapuche world is the problem of the land, and the lack of clear frontiers surrounding it. In fact, a land reform would be the most important collective contribution to the mental health care of the Mapuche. The rights of this minority to own their land should be respected and the development of organizational structures based on Mapuche culture should be supported, politically, culturally and professionally.

The Shanty Town

The interior

The interior climate is quite different in shanty towns with a solid infrastructure to that in those without one. In shanty towns such as La Victoria and El Progreso, the population is united in a highly organized structure which is an important counter-strategy against poverty and repression. In most of the shanty towns, however, the inhabitants live without an express political and collective commitment. These communities are mostly oriented towards survival at the individual or family level. The lack of a social and political network results in a scattered community without any internal solidarity and gives way to criminality, violence and severe alcohol and drug abuse.

Mental health work has a natural and important role in the resistance against social marginalization in the well-organized shanty towns. In the communities without much internal structure, however, health care professionals are primarily seen as representatives who provide emergency aid from the outside world.

The boundaries and their permeability

During the dictatorship, the shanty towns — especially the organized communities — were useful locations to which opponents could flee from persecution. The traditional connection between the shanty towns and the socially engaged priests and health workers was important in the initial formation of a human rights network.

Later, the survivors' groups could find space for some of their activities in the safe holding environment of, for example, the culture house of La Victoria. However, these territories were also invaded by the repressive forces — the bullet-holes in the walls are kept as memorials even today.

The NGOs did connect to some of these social structures. Church organizations such as FASIC, the Vicarage and others created aid programmes with free meals, social and religious support and also alcoholism programmes. Moreover, some of the professionals from the NGOs participated in the voluntary work of organizing the communities.

The exterior

For years before the coup, the Chilean medical tradition encompassed socially oriented work in the shanty towns as a natural area for physicians of all shades of political commitment. After the coup, this work was used against several professionals, who were charged with stimulating revolutionary activities through their social work there.

The revival of this tradition of social medicine, including a community psychiatry approach, seems obvious in the development of healing strategies within these communities. The fight against poverty remains, however, the most important concern in these areas. Thus, human rights and mental health play an important part in the psychological resistance against passivity and isolation and for the empowerment of the poor, without which they are not able to take their fate into their own hands.

Therapeutic strategies

In some poor areas, impressive therapeutic strategies have been developed in the collaboration between the survivors' groups and the mental health professionals of the human rights movement. In the following, we will give some examples of this work.

A house in the provinces

When the gate is opened to the yard in front of a small house, you hear the elegy of a woman accompanied by a guitar. Inside the house, there are posters with photos of the disappeared and the question 'Donde estan?' ('Where are they?'). Soledad greets us and starts telling us her story.

Her husband was detained and disappeared in 1973. Everything in the house was ransacked. She was left with five children. An adult son is now a political prisoner; a daughter was killed in an accident.

She is angry and has fantasies of revenge. It is her life-project right now to run this small house from which the activities of the local group of Family Members of the Disappeared are coordinated. She leads the activities on the political level and also the activities connected with the visit of the psychiatrist from the capital twice a month. We have the opportunity to meet with the psychiatrist on his visit today. Later the same day, when he has finished his individual consultations, it is time for the group.

First we have a small cup of coffee in the modest kitchen together with some of the group members while we wait for the others to arrive. The atmosphere is rather heavy.

One by one people are introduced. There is Pedro. He is a nice young man; he smiles and shakes hands. 'His parents disappeared, his sister was executed,' Soledad says. Seconds later Pedro himself 'disappears' behind a silent, sorrowful expression. Five other group members, all sons or daughters of the disappeared, are presented in the same way. We join the silence and wait for Carlos, the psychiatrist, to show up.

Besides these six participants, the group consists of Soledad, a social worker and a young doctor who runs the group every second week when Carlos is not there. Carlos takes over now. He asks everybody to write an answer to three questions on a piece of paper:

- 'Which feelings do you have right now in relation to the political situation and the event last week [the murder of the right-wing politician Jaime Guzman]. What does that mean to you?'
- 'Which feelings do you experience in the group right now concerning these events?'
- 'What is your main problem right now?'

The answers are written down and the papers collected. One of the group members reads all the responses to the group. In between, Carlos works with the comments and reactions from the group.

Suddenly, the young doctor gives a political speech which lasts for nearly fifteen minutes. In one sense, he obstructs the dynamics which have just developed – how can you express feelings when someone gives a political pep-talk? On the other hand, feelings of hopelessness were hanging heavily in the room. He wants them to wake up and fight.

His energy and engagement change the atmosphere of the group. They start talking and slowly they begin to express their feelings again; later they discuss what they could do next to keep the public aware of their problems. Carlos himself is supportive and seems to mediate between the private level of emotional pain experienced by the group members and the connection of their suffering to the political repression.

There is no doubt that Carlos is a skilled therapist, although the setting is somewhat 'against the academic rules'. We begin to understand how psychotherapy in this scenario becomes part of the resistance. It is a long way from this situation to discussions about psychotherapy as a luxury for the 'young, rich and beautiful'. In fact, we also understand why those in power have directed their attention towards the psychiatrists' work in the shanty towns. Carlos is not preparing a revolution, but he is supporting the development of their psychological resistance and human dignity, helping them overcome the feelings of being powerless.

The House of the Mothers

The next day, we accompany Carlos to another shanty town area. The procedure is similar, although the environment here in 'The House of the Mothers' is even poorer. We ask permission to place the tape-recorder in the middle of the circle when the group session is about to start. 'Yes, they are happy to have the session recorded. They want us to bring their pain out of the room so that their testimony can be heard.'

The scenario here is also different from the types of therapeutic setting that we are accustomed to. In a small kitchen, three woman bake *empanadas* (meat pies), and coffee and sandwiches are served. Dogs and small children run in and out of the door. At the same time, the group members participate very seriously in the therapy group. We observe a professional therapist at work in an uncommon setting where psychotherapy has a high level of meaning for the participants.

The professional and the survivors' groups

Madariaga (1990, pp. 1–11) has described psychotherapeutic work with the Association of Family Members of the Disappeared in a rural society. The group met once a week for one and a half hours with an average participation of eighteen individuals. He divides the therapy process into four periods.

The first period

The aim of the first period is to consolidate the committed, therapeutic bond, to stimulate the emotional relationships among the group members, to reduce fear and mistrust and to express and recognize their pain. Activating plays, dramatizations and role-playing are employed to further this objective. Quite soon, a group cohesion develops with the identification of shared realities and a feeling of belonging to the group.

The second period

The aim of the second period is to define the repressive experiences and get an overview of the problems of each of the group members. In particular, the aim is to focus on the privatization of the traumatic experiences and the necessity to reformulate these experiences. The means for doing so is to have group members bear testimony in the group. This is possible because of the atmosphere of confidence on both the social and therapeutic levels which has been established during the first period.

The initial fear of talking about the repressive experiences is followed by a shared feeling of solidarity and recognition of mutual pain. A cognitive level is introduced which gives members an opportunity to exchange opinions and views. A collective reflection is also encouraged in order to allow for a more profound understanding of reality.

One important theme is to get in touch with the basic conflict of all group members: the denial of the death of the disappeared. Nearly everyone in the group has a fantasy, a hope or a feeling of 'presence' of the disappeared ('Something tells me that he is alive ... I know he is alive. Of course it is possible that they have shot him, but something tells me in my heart that he is alive, and I am his mother).

The third period

The group have to address themselves to the new political reality. During the dictatorship, they were in a double-bind, a trap: if they accepted the death of the disappeared they would, on the emotional level, also accept the lies of the authorities.

In the new social and political situation following the publication of the report from the Commission of Truth and Reconciliation and the recognition of human rights violations, it is time to confront the fact that the disappeared are dead. In therapy, this is worked with on both the cognitive and the emotional level with the aim of connecting the personal traumatic experience to the new historical truth.

The intention is to develop a higher subjective level of consciousness in a search for new strategies which do not imply self-punishment. Two cognitive methods are used. First the group share all the psychological 'traps' which through the years, via fantasies, thoughts and speculations, have combined to create a 'false truth'. Some examples are:

- 'They could be on an island in the south, Dawson Island maybe, but it's a bit strange that they never send any messages.'
- 'People say that there are tunnels from the Dignidad Colony, very deep down below the earth, running all the way to Argentina. Maybe they have been taken there. I have been told that the disappeared live 200 metres below the earth on bread and water.'
- 'I think my husband is alive because the soldier told me that he had been set free and had probably run off with another woman.'

In a following session, the group works with all the facts and documentation which exist about the repression in the local area – for example, data from the Vicarage and other human rights organizations. This confrontation between fantasies and realities creates an intense dynamic in the group. Little by little, a deep sorrow and feelings of anxiety and fear develop, and the group members share their emotions and pain. The death of the beloved is becoming a reality.

The fourth period

In this last period of group work a reframing takes place. The combination of cognitive understanding and emotional work opens the way to new types of group work (for example, oriented towards social change) and to individual members' choice as to how they will continue. However, some of the damage is chronic, both psychologically and socially. Poverty and bad health are irreparable consequences of the repressive experiences (Madariaga, 1990).

Mental health work with the survivors' groups

During recent years the cooperation between the survivors' groups and the mental health institutions of the human rights movement has been further developed. Several of the institutions have units in the provinces with a local staff, typically a social worker and a psychologist and/or a physician. These local teams work closely together with the different survivors' groups.

Mostly, the trained psychotherapists come from the capital and, for example, run groups as described above, or they supervise the local staff. There are a very limited number of psychiatrists in the provinces and they are often neither engaged nor skilled in this field, as we have explained earlier.

The professionals from the 'old' mental health centres are, therefore, very much needed to supervise and initiate this type of work. Since 1991, the governmental PRAIS programme has been started in several of the towns. In some areas, the PRAIS teams include professionals from the human rights movement who have worked with the NGOs before, while in other areas the staff have only limited skills in this field. The PRAIS teams consider the survivors' groups to be an important source for referral of patients to the teams.

THE 'TRANSFERABLE'

The survivors groups share the trauma; they share the repressive experiences. They are both a private and a political entity, integrated in a movement. The groups constitute a new social network and a source of social and political consciousness-raising.

Professional aid from therapists to the survivors' groups counteracts the risk of groups getting 'trapped in the trauma'. By the introduction of professional/therapeutic dimensions in the groups' work, a more differentiated connection can be established between the private and the political levels of suffering. The committed bond and the therapists' view of psychological symptoms as sequels of repressive political experiences maintain, and even reinforce, the continuity between the private and political dimensions.

11

Issues of Social Reparation

'I name thee freedom'

The overall strategy of state terrorism is to change certain social power relations. Thus, individuals, families and groups that are hit by repressive political acts are targets because of the *social threats* they are believed to represent. The repressive strategies are thus aimed at gaining control of the whole social body of society, which is more than the sum of its individual members.

In the preceding chapters, we have attempted to capture some of the qualities of the conflicting forces which are at work under state terrorism. We have described how certain *meanings* and a certain *rationality* have developed within both the repressive and the resisting forces. An understanding of the political significance of these opposing meanings and rationalities is important for the healing of trauma suffered on the individual, family or group level, because it allows the survivors to reframe or de-privatize their traumatic experiences.

However, it is not only important for psychotherapy at different levels; it is also important for the healing and democratization of the society when the dictatorship is no longer in power. The term 'traumatized' is thus also applicable to a society which has been the object of state terrorism, because a set of meanings and a type of rationality have become socially sanctioned, legalized and normalized by those in power.

These meanings and types of rationality endorse acts which are 'usually' considered to be criminal – for example, torture, murder and the disappearance of people. 'Sick' acts are deemed 'good' and 'healthy' acts by those in power, and this suggests that in reality it is society that is 'sick', 'unhealthy', 'traumatized', according to internationally sanctioned ethics of human rights.

It is important to understand these shifts of meanings and rationality during the process of dictatorship. Likewise, it is paramount for the subsequent process of democratization that these shifts of meaning and rationality are reversed, so that normal human rights ethics can be re-established. A societal process of legal justice, in one form or another, is essential for this reversal to be accomplished.

RITUALS OF SOCIAL REPARATION

We are using the term 'rituals of social reparation' to refer to several interrelated processes; for example:

1. A public ethical process of revealing and condemning human rights violations by the former government.

2. Judicial and political processes in courts and parliament which relate to the human rights violations of the former government.

3. A process of healing on the part of the traumatized society and its individual members.

4. A process of preventing future human rights violations.

Rituals of social reparation will, as we will describe in more detail below, be influenced and limited by the power balance between the old and the new governments. Moreover, the strong emotional dynamics produced in the traumatized society after severe human rights violations may in fact lead to new human rights violations, thus impeding a development towards democracy. Experiences from European countries after the German occupation of the Second World War, and recent events in the Eastern European countries, demonstrate the strong feelings that are at work.

In Chile, it is emphasized by the report of the Commission of Truth and Reconciliation (1992) that a process of social reparation must contain the following elements:

1. The *truth* about what happened must become public knowledge.

2. The perpetrators must be brought to trial: *justice*.

3. The survivors must receive financial or other forms of *compensation*.

4. A *reconciliation* must take place between that part of the population which supported the dictatorship and the part which was persecuted. This reconciliation can only be achieved, however, after the first three requirements have been fulfilled.

5. *Education* about human rights must become part of general public education.

The concepts of truth, justice and reconciliation are, however, not easy to define. How much 'truth' is necessary, and how much 'truth' can the public take? From Argentina it is reported that people became overfed with horror stories and pictures in the media depicting the deeds of the former dictatorship. Instead of giving impetus to a new consciousness of human rights, it led instead to a general desire to *forget*. This tendency was also expressed by some of the people we met in Chile.

Likewise, the demand for justice is problematic to define. To whom does it apply? It is not possible to punish all of the soldiers and civilians who were connected to the violations. Many of them just followed orders and would, themselves, have been persecuted if they had not carried out the commands of their superiors.

The concept of reconciliation raises the same types of problem. Is it possible ever to forgive those who supported the murderers and torturers? A leading member of the human rights movement, a Catholic priest, told us the following about this dilemma:

This is a real problem in Chile today: the reconciliation. We cannot live this way as enemies; it will lead us into a vendetta where there is no justice. There must be some justice, that is our problem. It is not easy. The government tries to do all the justice they can do, but they are not strong. They are tied down by the constitution, by many laws created by the military. In a way, the military handed over the government to democracy by a peaceful transaction, but they took great care to define the limits of the democracy and to ensure that nothing would happen to themselves, and that no justice would be done. That is our problem. How can we do justice if the government does not have a majority in congress? The judges of the tribunals are not interested in real justice when the military forces are always threatening. So it is difficult to advance very fast.

But I think that we will do it, little by little, and I hope that we will get some justice – the justice that comes from truth. The judgement of History will be very severe for the military government.

I do not think it is really important simply to put a few more men in jail; what is really important is that the authors of all this should be denounced by public opinion, should be condemned, so that everyone knows who they are.

Some people can forget; almost no one has a real wish for revenge. They will not do to others what they did to them. They often say that they hate and cannot forgive. I have talked to many who have told me that to forgive is a wonderful experience, and that it for them was the real liberation: to be able to forgive, and not to hate. I think this is true. They do not get peace from revenge. To hate is to be still dependent on the persons who tortured them. It is a dependency that continues; they cannot forget or forgive. I still think that to forgive is to liberate oneself.

Not all of us can. A few days ago, I visited a mother. Her son disappeared in '74. She has been looking for him all these years. She got cancer. Many of them get cancer these days. I talked to her before she died. Her problem was that she could not forgive. She accepted the sacrament, so I guess she ended up by forgiving. I tell them that it is not necessary to renounce the demand for justice in order to forgive. Justice is something positive, because, in a way, justice also liberates the criminal. He needs justice to be able to become conscious of what he has done. If he does not suffer he will not recognize it. He will just stay the way he is. So, in a way, to get him back to humanity one needs to sanction him. I think it is good for them and for the country to bring the criminals to justice. To forgive is not to renounce justice. A father also punishes his son from love, not from hate, but to give up hate is not easy for many.

The process of justice has been very slow due to a number of factors, which we will describe in the following.

THE TRANSITION TOWARDS DEMOCRACY

President Patricio Aylwin took office on 11 March 1990, thus terminating seventeen years of military rule. The new government had a clear obligation to redress the wrongs of the past, and a long and arduous process of 'social reparation' has begun. However, there have been a number of obstacles in this process. The legal problems of the new government can be summarized in the following way (Medina, 1992):

1. Left-over legislation from the former regime has had a deleterious effect on the process of democratization. The electoral law sanctions a system in which Pinochet supporters are favoured. Nine senators have been appointed by the Supreme Court, the National Security Council and by General Pinochet. The result has been that the new government does not have a majority in both chambers, and therefore it cannot ensure that all amendments which are necessary for social reparation can be passed.

2. The Constitutional Court is composed of members appointed for eight years by General Pinochet. The Supreme Court is composed of members who also have been appointed by General Pinochet without an age limit for retirement. These bodies are not sympathetic to the process of legal justice.

3. A third perspective which permeates the situation is the position of the armed forces. The General is still Commander-in-Chief of the Army. Moreover, the former members of the junta – the heads of the Navy, the Air Force and the police – will remain in their positions until 1998.

At every step of the democratization process the government will, therefore, have to consider the reactions of the military. Many civilian employees are also adherents of the former regime and they will do what they can to slow down the process.

The Human Rights Movement in the Transitional Process

The political prisoners and social reparation

The two main challenges for the new government are the problem of the political prisoners, and the problem of social and economic reparation for the severe human rights violations committed by the former regime.

In March 1990 there were still about four hundred political prisoners who were either imprisoned or released on bail. None of them had been prosecuted in accordance with correct legal procedures, and many were still waiting for a final judicial decision.

A law of 1 April 1991 changed Article 9 of the 1980 Constitution, which prohibited amnesties, pardons and release on bail for those who were charged according to the Law of Terrorism. Now it was in the power of the President to grant pardons and amnesties for these types of crime. Several law amendments had already been introduced on 11 March 1990 to improve human rights conditions. Resistance from the right-wing, however, delayed the implementation of these laws.

One important element in the new law was to transfer trials for these types of crimes to ordinary judges or courts of appeal. Due to the opposition from the right wing, the changes did not become effective until March 1992.

The Commission Report

On 25 April 1990, the National Commission of Truth and Reconciliation was established. The Commission issued its important report on 9 February 1991 (in English, 1992). The content of this report has been discussed in detail throughout this book.

One major consequence of this report was the establishment of the National Corporation for Reparation and Reconciliation (31 January 1992), a temporary decentralized state organ under the supervision of the Ministry of the Interior whose task will be to carry out the recommendations made in the Commission Report. Important elements in the recommendations are pensions and economic compensation for the survivors of the human rights violations. There are also recommendations to establish aid programmes for health care (especially mental health/psychological aid), and programmes to reintegrate survivors and their families in society.

The Commission Report has also resulted in the foundation of the National Education Campaign for Truth and Human Rights: To Believe in Chile. This national educational campaign was created to disseminate the contents of the report – especially in an effort at empowerment and social education of the poor population.

The survivors' groups

Until the new president took office in March 1990, the different types of survivors' groups were among the core grassroots of the human rights movement. Since March 1990, and even more so after the publication of the Commission Report in 1991, this united front has seemed to be threatened by dissolution because of the differences in the social and economic compensation granted to the survivors.

The Associations of Family Members of the Disappeared and of the Executed have been recognized by the Commission Report, and they will receive an economic compensation and be morally rehabilitated. Before the publication of the Commission Report, however, these groups had a high status in the absurd 'trauma hierarchy' as those who had suffered most – and their dead were considered the real 'martyrs'.

The survivors of torture and political imprisonment are not recognized by any commission, however, and will receive neither economic compensation nor moral, public acknowledgement or rehabilitation. Still alive, but traumatized and marginalized, they are the losers on the individual and family level. They have to pay the immediate price of 'reconciliation'. Their torturers are not taken to court, but are free to continue in their positions in the military, while the survivors who are stigmatized by their criminal records are kept unemployed – and in poverty.

Many of the returnees from exile enjoy better economic conditions than those who stayed in the country, although many returned families also come back to unemployment and poverty. International economic support favours projects in which returnees are involved, and many returnees have a better educational status than those who stayed, maybe because they were able to get an education while they were in exile.

It becomes quite understandable why the returned families are sometimes met with envy and distance from their former political comrades. Of course, it is not the first time in history that two under-privileged groups have confronted each other instead of their aggressor. This internal conflict between survivors must, however, be seen as just one more symptom of traumatization on the group and collective level.

It seems important for the human rights movement to pay attention to this perspective and to work for solidary solutions. The different groups have all been exposed to various traumatizing events under the same type of regime, and in many cases they share continued marginalization on the individual and societal level, as well as poverty.

With or without the intention of the new government, the aftermath of the dictatorship has brought a dramatic reduction in the power of the human rights movement at the time of victory.

The NGO mental health teams and centres

The Chilean case study demonstrates that the main protective structures under state terrorism – the church and the international community – began reducing their aid to victims of human rights violations shortly after the change of system.

The Catholic church has closed its aid programmes for survivors. More traditional programmes are favoured, and it seems as if leading members of the church – in their attempt at reconciliation – want to forget that the survivors are still there, and that they are still traumatized.

International economic support to the NGO institutions has also been reduced. After the change of government, it has become increasingly difficult for these organizations to receive foreign economic support. The countries or international organizations which supported the NGOs argue that their aid is no longer necessary because of the change towards democratization. Economic support is now offered directly to the new government, which then has to make decisions and prioritize the use of these resources.

This is an argument which is not valid. Actually, the NGO centres and teams are even more necessary now than they were before. The trauma survivors are numerous, and many have not wanted or dared ask for help until now. Also, the mental health work of the NGOs is fundamental for social reparation and democratization. The expertise which has been built up in these mental health centres is, moreover, invaluable for training other professionals. The reduction of aid to these centres can, therefore, lead to the loss of a very important resource for the building of a new democratic society. The centres, do, however, need to accommodate to the new reality. As one psychologist told us:

> We organized our field of work, our ideology about reality, within the limits of a war. We were the enemies of the dictatorship. It was very simple. With this new government we have a complexity which is not very clear. Who the enemy is is no longer the main clue to the understanding of reality.... It is possible that we still have a few cases of torture, but we do not have torture as a system. It is possible that the secret police still functions – yes, but this is a political problem, not a problem with the same power as we had in the past.... Now, human rights are not the most important theme of the country.... The Commission Report said 'yes, this is the reality, in this country we had a lot of people affected by torture, by death and disappearances. These people need social and health service and need some money to live.' The activities of the government will stop at some moment, and the activities of the parliament will also stop, when the law of social reparation appears. And the organizations of affected people [the survivors' groups] – it is possible that they will remain for some time but not in the core of the society. The institutions related to the human rights programmes need, therefore, to re-conceptualize their activities.... I think this is the challenge to the human rights organizations – not to remain in the past, but to work with the past in the sense of the consequences of the past for the present life, for the future. This is very difficult for people, because they remain very close to the old identity.... We perceive that the human rights movement needs to re-elaborate their proposal to the country about human rights, but not to focus only on human rights as *violations* ... this was the most important aspect for us over seventeen years, but it is not the main problem of the country now.... We have the opportunity to work with this in a positive way, but we can also remain stuck in the past without any influence.

In the NGO mental health centres there are thus quite different opinions about how to react to the new situation. The reduction of international economic aid has increased the internal competition between the different centres for the scarce funding which is available, although there is enough work for many more centres. This competition is also expressed on the intellectual/academic level with a limited amount of collaboration between the different centres and teams.

However, already in the eighties, the mental health centres created CESAM (Coordinadora de Equipos de Salud Mental [the Coordinating Committee of Mental Health Teams]). The aim of this collaboration was to open up the boundaries between the teams, so that they could share with each other. Differences in opinion about the new reality are currently being discussed in CESAM. Members of some centres feel that CESAM has overly rigid boundaries towards the outside world, that it must establish contacts with other groups. The challenge is to open the boundaries, and at the same time to maintain one's identity, as one psychologist told us.

A very positive initiative has been the establishment of CESAM's Technical Commission in August 1990. The overall purpose of this commission was to register the experiences and needs of each team, and to attempt to define future objectives for their work. In April 1992, the Technical Commission published a register of what it found to be the most important publications of the mental health teams of the human rights movement (Kovalskys et al., 1992). A whole section is devoted to the topic of impunity and social reparation.

CESAM has also collaborated with the Ministry of Health in the development of a governmental programme of assistance to the survivors – the PRAIS.

The PRAIS teams

The PRAIS is a health programme established for people who have been affected by human rights violations. It started with a team in Iquique in 1991 and now also has teams in other towns: Temuco, Concepción, Santiago, Antofagasta and Valparaíso. A psychologist told us about the objectives of this programme:

You know, the mental health system is very under-developed in our world. We have some psychiatric hospitals and services, but these are not very well developed. So when the Concertation [for Democracy] organized its pro-grammes, we also established a mental health commission to write on this aspect. From that moment we began to think: 'What are we going to do about the victims of repression? What is our programme of "psycho-social reparation" going to be?' We really were not very clear what we were going to do at the state level. Because – you know – the institutions of the state were very contaminated by the last government. So for people – after a very long-lasting dictatorship – the confusion between state and government was very great. We do not think that state and government are the same. So we thought that we had to repair not only the effects of repression in the people, but also the institutions of the state.... In these state institutions, most of the people who are working there are people who did not participate in the former government – they were against the right wing, they were against all this sort of thing – they were people with democratic ideas. People on the higher levels were removed, but not the nurses, the midwives, the medical doctors, the social workers. So the idea is to undertake reparation through concrete actions in programmes that answer the many problems that people have. Not by first cleaning up the system and then doing things – but through the programmes. We thought that through this programme we could find a way to 'open the doors of the system to the people affected by the violations of human rights'.... So we decided that we were going to start. We didn't know how we were going to do this, but we started the experience in Iquique. And at the same time, the Ministry invited a commission of the directors of the NGO mental health centres to organize a working group – on the level of advisors to the Minister.

Once a month, we also have a meeting with CESAM and we discuss with it what we are doing. The idea is that CESAM advises the Ministry – but the Ministry also has its own rules.... The association between the Ministry and CESAM has not been an easy one. There have been several contradictions in these meetings. The first is: they have another time-scale, another rhythm. They want the Minister to give, at once, all the assistance to all the people everywhere free of charge. And this is not possible, because you have to get people to participate in the idea and to make the idea known.... Although human rights are very important, it is not the *most* important thing for a health system. If people, in order to see a doctor, have to get up at 5 in the morning and queue for several hours, and then have to bring the baby two hours later and then wait again for two hours – well, this is a problem you have to solve first.

So this is one of the contradictions. CESAM is saying that the Ministry is not doing anything.... But on the other hand I find – and this is very much a personal opinion – that the NGO organizations give a sort double message: 'You have to take this responsibility' is the first message. The second message is: 'We are the only ones who know how to do this.' So we discussed a lot.

The medical doctors, the nurses, are perfectly capable of doing this work if they receive training and supervision. And the idea is that it is good that *they* do the work – and that it is not the same kind of marginal structure that does it. We have to cooperate with the NGOs, but they [the people from the hospitals] need the opportunity to develop their own programme, because there we have the people who during all these years have been working for public health under terrible conditions, and they have to develop now also. They have to participate in the reparation. It is a reparation for themselves as well.

So this has been a contradiction which has not always been openly discussed.... But I think we have reached a point now where we have a sort of working alliance with CESAM, where the Ministry has its own programme and the NGO organizations are going to be the trainers of the people all over the country.... The major goal is that every service will have a team composed of a medical doctor, a psychiatrist, a psychologist, a nurse, a nursing auxiliary and a social worker. And this team is the way in to the system. This team gets in contact with the organizations of the affected people [the survivors' groups] ... or the church office which earlier assisted these people.... This is the first step: how will the patients be referred, and what is the role of the survivors' groups? And then the other step which is parallel with this: which NGOs do we have in this place, and how can they collaborate in the programme through training, through being present? Because they are the link between the people and the institutions of the state. If we collaborate with the NGOs we may be trusted by the people, who can then participate in the introductory meeting of the programme. Certain faces must be present to show what kind of initiative this is so that people can again rely on the hospital.

Thus, a major problem on all levels seems to be the re-establishment of trust in the system after seventeen years of 'systemic' violations of fundamental human rights.

RITUALS OF PURIFICATION

By way of a series of *jornadas de purificación* (acts of purification) held after the change of government, collective trust is being re-established in the popular places of assembly. From a mental health care perspective these rituals are interesting. They have been performed, for example, in the National Stadium in Santiago and in the Stadium of Chile (an indoor sports arena). Both stadiums were used as repressive territories just after the coup. Prisoners were held there; they were tortured in the gangways; and some were also murdered there.

The present rituals are being performed to 'wash the blood off', so that these places can again become what they originally were meant to be: sports stadiums. Rituals of purification have also been performed in several former torture houses.

'The Song of Freedom'

One of these rituals of purification was held on 9 April 1991 at the indoor Stadium of Chile in Santiago. The event was called 'Canto Libre' ('The Song of Freedom'). We were given tickets for it by one of our informants.

It is difficult to get in, due to a demonstration on its way into the stadium. We find our seats, and are placed in an honourable position among the Family Members of the Disappeared. They all wear pictures of their disappeared relatives attached to their chests. Small pieces of cloth in red, white and blue – the Chilean national colours – are distributed so that the audience can wave them during the ritual. In the stadium, there is a seething mass of people, and from the loudspeakers Victor Jara's voice is singing the hymns of freedom. In between, groups of people chant slogans.

The entrance of Victor Jara's widow signals the official start of the ritual. She stands in the middle of the arena; following the ovation to her, a poem by Bertolt Brecht is read. Then actors give a performance which is a mixture of theatre, song and dance using many Mapuche symbols. The dead are called back. The audience light candles in the dark and everyone sings the national anthem. A woman in front of us insists that we wave our 'flags' more vigorously! The audience say their farewell to the dead. The performance ends with a very concrete 'cleaning'/purification process: the actors sweep the stadium clean with brooms.

Just when the ritual is about to end, a young man in the row behind us stands up. He has a picture of his father on his chest. He is shouting his pain out to the audience. He calls for a 'NO!', a 'no to impunity' for the perpetrators. Others join him in a scream for truth and justice and the atmosphere grows tense. In the streets outside the stadium, the police are lined up with submachine guns and bullet-proof jackets.

12

From Latin America to the Balkans

A journey from one field to another

FROM ZAGREB TO CASA DE LA PAZ

Zagreb: January 1995

The sharp winter sun reaches us at the work table. The book about Chile has to be finished within a few days. We have been working here for more than a year as part of the humanitarian mission to the war-torn countries of former Yugoslavia. Overwhelmed by the work we have been involved in here, it has taken us a long time to prepare ourselves to go back to the Chilean world through our manuscript, which has been almost ready for two years now as a 'preliminary report' (Agger and Jensen, 1993b).

Sounds of a lazy Zagreb Sunday can be heard through the open window. Odours drift in from preparations for the traditional Croatian Sunday lunch at which families get together before the long afternoon siesta. The war seems far away – nearly unreal; but only two hours' drive from here, there is heavy fighting going on in the Bihac enclave. One hour's drive away, in the so-called United Nations Protected Areas (the UNPAs), most of the houses are destroyed and United Nations Protective Forces (UNPROFOR) are guarding the front lines separating Croats and Serbs.

A few days ago the Croatian government decided not to extend the mandate of UNPROFOR any longer. UNPROFOR are scheduled to leave in a few months. What will happen then? Will the peaceful Sundays in Zagreb soon be confronted with the reality of war, or is this decision of the government just part of psychological warfare?

We are struggling with the last chapter: we face a dilemma when we read the final conclusions and recommendations of our preliminary

213

report. We were so certain of our new knowledge, so convinced that the transferable elements of 'the Chilean model' were self-evident. Maybe it is too difficult to confront our theory with this new Balkan reality. On the other hand, it is also a challenge to ask if those conclusions offer any meaningful framework for understanding what happens here – under war conditions in a very different cultural and political context.

We also realized that we, once again, had nearly 'forgotten' what we had learned from the Chileans. In our attempts to understand what was going on in this reality, we started from scratch again. Revisiting our testimony, however, created a bridge to our own recent past. Our conclusions still provided a meaningful framework. However, our firm conclusions became subject to doubt and had to be rephrased as questions to which we have no definite answers.

The Pliva Club, Zagreb: 8 November 1994

The most important therapeutic tool for working with people who have suffered severe violations of human rights is to create a space which makes it possible for them to share their feelings.

Three months ago, the Chilean therapists Elizabeth Lira and David Becker came and worked with us at a WHO seminar about 'Families of the Disappeared and Killed'. About fifty mental health professionals from former Yugoslavia shared their experiences from their work with these families.

The atmosphere in the circle was tense and engaged. Somehow, Elizabeth's and David's narrative about their work during many years of dictatorship gave meaning to the situation here. A bridge of understanding was built between continents and across language barriers. A woman stood up and gave her emotional contribution. She represented the Association of Families of the Disappeared in Croatia. She talked in Croatian through an interpreter, but she could just as well have been speaking Spanish in a house in Parral, or in the Vicarage of Concepción.

Casa de la Paz, Santiago: 13 April 1993

Nearly two years ago, we went back to Chile to share the findings of our preliminary report at a seminar to which a major group of our informants were invited. Already at that time we knew that we would soon be posted to former Yugoslavia. We were, therefore, especially interested in discussing with the participants the transferability of 'the Chilean model'.

The seminar was entitled: 'Trauma and Healing Under State Terrorism', with the subtitle question: 'How can the Chilean experiences of human rights and mental health work during the dictatorship be applied to mental health work in other countries where human rights are violated or a process towards democracy has begun?' The participants had received an English version of our preliminary report beforehand.

Twenty-five of our informants attended the seminar and all major NGOs were represented. It was a moving experience to meet them again. Through the long interviews we had had with each of them, we had listened to their private and professional testimony, often for many hours, and we had been quite close to most of them. In the process of writing we had again been listening to their voices on the tape-recordings.

How would they now react to our narrative about their world? How would they react to the roles and words we had attributed to them? We were looking forward to sharing our work with them – and we were also a bit anxious when the circle became a reality at the seminar in the symbolic space of Casa de la Paz (the House of Peace).

AN OPEN WINDOW

So we are back in the Chilean autumn, where a heavy rainfall sets the scene this early April morning, when our participants – and former interviewees – arrive for the seminar. No secret police are outside the building now. Life is changing towards a new normality. The sounds from the Santiago morning rush-hour accompany the greetings. The participants here opened a window and allowed us to look into their private and professional lives. It is now our turn to share the narrative we wrote about them:

> Our narrative starts in exile. It was through the meeting with exiled Chileans and traumatized refugees from other countries that we first felt the urge to learn more about trauma and healing under state terrorism. When we started clinical work in this field, ten years ago, it was the papers and articles by Chilean professionals which were a primary source of inspiration. Thereafter came encounters with Chilean professionals at congresses and workshops which further developed our interest in your approach – 'the Chilean model', as we have named it in our narrative.
>
> When we participated in the first seminar on torture in Chile in 1989, the experience had a great emotional impact on both of us. It was, in fact, this meeting which gave us the idea to carry out a deeper investigation of the Chilean human rights movement.

When we made the proposal for this project we wanted to investigate two fundamental questions:

1. How are people able to develop psychological weapons of self-defence to protect their human rights?
2. How do they heal the psychological traumata caused by violations of their basic rights?

We attempted to find an answer to these two questions by studying your human rights movement in Chile. Therefore we tried in our research to draw a map of the psychological strategies of terror and the counter-strategies against them, seen through a Chilean 'prism'.

Through your prism we tried to understand how concepts of trauma, therapeutic strategies and therapeutic relationships are developed under state terrorism. From your Chilean case-example, we wanted to discover if this model is 'transferable' to other societies in which human rights are also abused.

We understood from the meeting with your reality the importance of knowing the objectives of state terrorism. We have found these objectives to be focused around the following theme:

The theme of silence and destruction.

We felt, ourselves, how fear creeps into a person who lives in a terrorist state, and we felt how this fear can lead to denial, mistrust and paranoid tendencies. Those in power try to keep control by damaging individuals and relationships that threaten their power. As we saw it, they do this primarily by the psychological and social dynamics of:

Splitting and victimization.

The strategies of splitting and victimization can be found on all social levels: on the individual level, on the family level, on the group level and on the societal level.

Consequently, the overall purpose of the human rights movement is the opposite. Its aim is to counteract silence and destruction by:

Denunciation and healing.

A human rights movement consists of social relations between people, and we found that it was the collective consciousness and moral community of this movement that were the primary denouncing and healing agents. It was this collectivity and this moral commitment that were primarily able to create a force that counteracted those in power.

We found that the strategies of destruction, which we have put under the headings 'splitting and victimization', were counteracted within the culture of the human rights movement by the opposite strategies of healing. These strategies can be subsumed under the headings of:

Integration and self-empowerment.

The trauma is integrated on an individual level by allowing it to be a part of the survivor's history whereby she or he gives up the exhausting attempts to split off the trauma from the conscious part of her- or himself. The trauma is integrated on the family and group levels by allowing it to be part of the family's and the group's common history, allowing energy to grow for the struggle against the abusive system. Instead of being divided and split up, the family and the group can even become stronger and more unified. On the societal level, the trauma is integrated by allowing it to be a part of the story of this society – thereby counteracting the social split between different parts of the population. To remember the violence is one of the most powerful tools of prevention.

Self-empowerment is a means of counteracting victimization. Empowerment is created by the membership of a movement – a human rights movement that validates your trauma and places the guilt and shame with the abusers. Of special importance are the establishment of survivors' groups – the groups of family members – and the close cooperation between these groups and the NGO mental health institutions. The whole human rights movement acted as such an empowering tool in Chile.

As we see, then, 'the Chilean model' comprises a human rights movement which works on all levels: the private level, the professional level and the political level. The work could also be described as focusing both the individual and the family, as well as the survivors' groups and all of society. The totality of and the interaction between these different levels we see as the characteristic of 'the Chilean model'.

Between therapists working in the movement there may be theoretical differences as to which strategy is best – a psychoanalytic, a systemic, an existentialist approach; but we see these as minor differences compared to the overall attitude which recognizes that the private, professional and political levels cannot be separated. Our report is our map of how these different levels interact in the Chilean human rights movement. It is, however, also our attempt at giving a name to a hypothetical truth about human resistance to power abuse. This truth was something we read 'between the lines' – something which was not said directly to us. This truth is moveable. It is not local, although it grew out of your experiences which were gained at a certain time in Chile's history.

As we were our own informants also, our experiences of fear during our fieldwork in Chile led us to understand some of your reality. From the interviews with forty mental health professionals, we were astonished to learn that three out of four among you had suffered major traumatic events.

We realized from these discoveries that under conditions of state terrorism this is a 'normal' event. Naturally, both professionals and patients will become traumatized by the repression. This fact led us to ask many questions about 'wounded healers' and counter-transference reactions, and we think it is one of our most important findings that this fact must be acknowledged. Under conditions of state terrorism everyone becomes affected by it. This, however, also creates the basis for an alliance between therapists and patients which can be more difficult to establish under normal circumstances.

What comes back to us as a question – and from our report you can see that it was there all the way through our fieldwork – is the problem of silence and speech. In a dictatorship silence is supported. After the dictatorship has ended, many members of the new government want to forget. The survivors of abuse feel that speech is painful. Researchers and therapists who ask questions about the trauma story easily become new violators. When should there be silence, and when should there be speech? Or maybe the question could rather be put in another way: under which circumstances should the unspeakable be spoken?

The video: Casa de la Paz, Santiago: 13 April 1993

There is a break between our presentations. Coffee is served in the middle of the circle, while the video-recorder is still on. In retrospect, we realize that it is not often that this group meets in the same room. Times are changing. This might be a historic moment. The camera moves around and catches Dr Paz Rojas (DITT-CODEPU) and her sister Maria Eugenia Rojas (PIDEE); Dr Fanny Pollarollo, who started FASIC's medical team and is now a full-time politician; her husband Dr Mario Vidal (CINTRAS); Dr Hector Faúndez and his wife Sara Balogi from (CODEPU Terapia Familiar). The camera moves from Eliza Neuman (FASIC) and Carlos Madariaga (CINTRAS) to Juana Kovalskys (ILAS) and Rosario Dominguez (PRAIS). It moves further, and records the 'two other women in Paris', Dr Patricia Barceló and Dr Katia Reszczynski (DITT-CODEPU), Beatriz Brinchmann (CINTRAS) and the two colleagues from Promesa in Punta Arenas, Pastor Benjamin Rodrigues and Mauro Orloff. The voices and thoughts of these people and many more have now become part of our inner video of Chile and the human rights movement.

We share one of those moments where you feel a sense of what makes life meaningful and worth all the effort. However, this moment also contains the pain related to a transient life where we can only for a brief moment share such sense of belonging.

From One Field to Another?

Back on 'stage' in the Balkans we try to share what we have seen as the transferable elements, that is, those factors in the Chilean model we found important to consider in the development of counter-strategies during state terrorism.

From the symbolic space of Casa de la Paz, we try to open a new window to the world outside: how can the Chilean experience contribute to our understanding of human rights and mental health in other repressive contexts?

From our new perspective in the midst of an ongoing European war scenario, we turn our preliminary conclusions into open questions for this context:

1. The establishment of – or further development of – a human rights movement?
   - Is there a powerful human rights movement?
   - How could such a movement be strengthened – on both sides – to create a basis for development of a strong resistance against the war and the war atrocities?

2. Must core elements in the human rights movement include the 'DITE' factors? (Denunciation, Investigation, Treatment and Education)

   Denunciation:
   - Is there a public outcry, blaming those in power – on both sides – for the violations of human rights?

   Investigation and Documentation:
   - Are human rights violations investigated and denounced (when? where? who? what? – to permit the analysis of why?) through testimonies that verify that reality which is denied?

   Treatment:
   - Are mental health and judicial aspects of violations of human rights part of the treatment? Do the professionals pay equal attention to psychological, social, medical and judicial problems?

   Education:
   - Do people know enough about their human rights?

3. Is there an appropriate organizational structure to support survivors?
   - Are there survivors' groups and networks on a grass-roots level?
   - Are there solidary professional organizations or institutions to support survivors?
   - Are there any 'protective shields' to support human rights work?

4. Have structures and traumatic experiences been systematically analysed?

5. Have appropriate therapeutic contexts and strategies been established?

6. Have appropriate structures been established to take care of the care-givers?

7. How can the process of social reparation be supported in a way that respects human rights?

Casa de la Paz, Santiago: 14 April 1993

The final session of the seminar is in progress. The circle has diminished but most of us are still there. We talk about 'the transferable' and each participant is asked two questions: 'What is your best advice to us for our future work in former Yugoslavia?' 'What surprised you most when you read our report?' Everyone in the circle gives his or her opinion. Some are in doubt if the Chilean work can be at all useful for the very different cultural context and the war conditions in the Balkans. Juana Kovalskys from ILAS tells the group about her work in El Salvador and argues strongly for the idea of transferability, although one must modify the interventions according to specific needs and circumstances.

Other voices tell us:

It was a surprise you were able to carry out this project at all – to get access to our world.... We are here nearly all of us.

It was astonishing suddenly to see ourselves through your prism. Before I felt I was working alone. Now I see myself more as part of a movement.

You have made us visible, showing us our own dimension.

The wounded healer may be seduced by the patient. Could you possibly as researchers have been seduced by us? Maybe we 'forgot' to tell you something.

One sentence stands out clearly, a last word from Maria Eugenia Rojas, Director of PIDEE, and author of the book from 1987 documenting the repression (Rojas, 1987). Her husband disappeared, her son in law had his throat cut. While all this happened, she remained a strong figure in the movement:

Tell them that they have to document everything!

The participants are about to depart, and while they put on their coats and find their umbrellas, they say their goodbyes.

We associate to the veranda of 'The Blue Room' (Agger, 1994), with the refugee women breaking up the healing circle and going out into the borderland of exile. The researcher must also depart, but 'even though she has written her narrative, it still remains a part of her' (p. 127).

This voyage has ended. It is time to go back and write our testimony.

A JOURNEY THROUGH ANOTHER FIELD

Excerpts from Field Diary III: Humanitarian Aid Work, February 1994–January 1995

'Because of the bird in the cage...'

On the Zagreb terrace in a corner warmed by the early spring sun, the canary sings his call for love and tenderness. Through a window somewhere on the opposite side of the yard a weak response is heard. The bird disappeared one day when the door was left open.

A girl on the Dalmatian island: April 1994

We arrive by ferry at the beautiful Dalmatian island. Minutes later we are at the entrance of a large mental hospital. A committee of patients receive us at the gate, begging for cigarettes. Within seconds the peaceful scenario turns into shouting and fighting about who has the right to beg first. The psychotic anger makes the atmosphere tense. Sharp voices of command from two nurses approaching in their caps and cloaks create sufficient space to let us in. The Dalmatian spring is soon contrasted with the indoor darkness of the wards. We walk our round amidst the smell of urine, insanity and poverty. In the women's ward we ask if we may look behind a closed door which we were supposed to pass. In the 6 by 2 metre space two women are locked inside a net 'cage' surrounding their beds. The youngest woman is in a strait-jacket. She is angry, but obviously not psychotic. Her bad teeth are evidence of poverty, and her voice sounds drugged. She has been threatening the nurse so as to get a cigarette. 'She has to stay there until she learns to behave,' the nurse explains.

'Because of my friend, who is in prison'

In a refugee camp, Croatia: September 1994

Aged 46, she had recently arrived at a small refugee camp neighbouring her country with her son Amir, aged 9, daughter Sanela, 13, and mother Indira, who is 78. When the enemy troops invaded her village, they took her husband and two older sons away at gunpoint. She has not seen or heard from them in seven weeks and fears the worst. She and her husband were farmers and owned a modern home, several outbuildings, a car and two tractors. Her mother has been totally blind for twenty years due to a degenerative eye condition. She needs some instruction and assistance to orient her to her new surroundings, a room in an old army barracks, which the family shares with four other adults and two children. Amir has not attended school, as there is no room in the local school near the camp, and the refugee school is five kilometres away, too far to walk. A month prior to being forced to flee their home, Sanela was diagnosed with leukaemia, a potentially fatal disease with, however, a good prognosis for cure with early detection and treatment.[1]

Bihac Hospital: October 1994

The psychiatric ward is full of young men, soldiers back from the front with severe traumatic stress reactions. Their eyes express despair, an outcry for help without any hope of getting it. In the orthopaedic ward the scenario is similar except for the physical wounds.

A checkpoint in Bosnia: October 1994.

We are waiting to pass the checkpoint on a mountain outside Sarajevo. The drive up here took much longer than we expected. It is growing dark. Four heavily armed soldiers surround the car. We stay very quiet, remaining inside the car ready to show our blue cards. They look at us and ask the driver to get out. They want to search the luggage. We are nearly invisible behind the windows and the silence is total. We remember all the stories we have heard about what can happen, but do not dare to share them. Suddenly we hear shouting and laughing. Our driver and the guards apparently have relatives in the same village, so 'nema problema' ('no problem'). Suddenly everything is OK. Nothing really happened.

Two days later, both of us are wide awake in the middle of the night and share the fear we felt while on that mountain.

'Because of the tortured bodies'

The WHO office, Zagreb: October 1994

We have tried to calculate the number of people who are suffering from severe traumatization due to war-related events. Based on a series of assumptions we end up with the extreme number of more than 1 million severely traumatized people. To treat these people would require 5,000 full-time professional experts. The present capacity only covers 1–2% of the needs.

A psychiatric department near the front line: January 1995

The soldiers live at home with their families when they are not at the front line. At the psychiatric ward, more than four hundred reactive traumatic psychoses have been treated during the last year. Domestic violence has become a serious problem in the main town. There has been a massive increase in suicides. Within the last year more than one hundred homicides were committed here without reason. All were connected to alcohol intake and easy access to weapons.

Medical Centre for Human Rights, Zagreb: January 1995

Four young doctors are sharing their preliminary findings from fifty-five testimonies of sexually violated men. They have collected the testimonies systematically and the data have been analysed on their computers. The quantitative and qualitative data create a mosaic reminding us of the Chilean testimonies about sexual torture. The similarities are astonishing. Where did the torturers learn how to do this, or is it just instinctual?

The tortured men meet for group counselling; gradually they have begun to share their feelings and break the conspiracy of silence. The barrier against this seems to be even stronger than among raped women.

'Because of the flowers that were torn up...'

The Mothers of Vukovar, Zagreb: May 1994

Outside the UN barracks, the 'Mothers of Vukovar' have built a wall of bricks. On each brick is written the name of a disappeared person. These mothers are still searching for their loved ones who disappeared when the city of Vukovar fell to the Serbs. The wall is impressive and the UNPROFOR soldiers have to understand their message: they are the ones to blame!

This survivor group of mothers is active, but seems not to be especially oriented to a human rights perspective. Their approach is more nationalistic.

Mostar: August 1994

The black widows of 'killed Croatian defenders of the fatherland' are meeting in the women's house created by an international NGO on the West Bank. The widows have organized themselves as a survivor group giving each other support. They are talking about their anger against the Muslims living in *their* houses on the other side of the river – the houses they were expelled from. In the group, the facilitator tries to arouse their interest in meeting the widows from the other side. Maybe they will cross the river some day?

Sarajevo: August 1994

A young woman is telling us her story. She was happily married until a year ago. However, she was also in a what is now called a 'mixed marriage' since she and her husband do not belong to the same 'ethnic' group. She is a Serb, he a Muslim. Her husband went abroad to avoid going to the front and took one of their two children with him. The couple have had no contact in the last three months. The other child, who was wounded by a shell, is staying with her. What happens to this boy when he discovers that mother's people are fighting father's people, and how does he solve the problem of choosing which group he belongs to?

'Because of the trees that were pruned...'

Sarajevo: October 1994

The participants in the training course are working in groups. Each of them has made a drawing of a traumatic event which happened in their own life. At this moment there is a space, a safe-holding environment where it is possible to share, to talk, to mourn and to be listened to. These 'wounded healers' are temporarily taking care of themselves. We share this strong experience, too strong maybe for some of them, although the overall outcome seems to be a general feeling of relief.

'Because of the fish in its bowl...'

On the eighth floor, Sarajevo: August 1994

This is the first evening in town where we got a feeling of Sarajevo life before the war. We are back at the hotel before the curfew at 22.00. A few minutes later, the first rounds of shooting are heard. We feel scared and are considering what to do on the eighth floor of the Holiday Inn hotel. Should one lay down on the floor in the bathroom or run down to the reception? We just wait and surprisingly we fall asleep. The next morning the shooting continues. We learn in a security briefing that the situation is 'relatively calm; only small weapons fire and sniper-shootings'.

From the window a group of boys can be seen playing football on the lawn just outside the hotel. An armoured car always brings us through this same area.

Sarajevo: October 1994

A few hours before we arrived, people were shot by snipers just in front of the hotel. We are advised to stay indoors. Through the windows people can be seen walking along the so called 'Sniper Avenue' as if nothing had happened. A collective denial? 'No,' says one of the inhabitants, 'we've become accustomed to the fear, and we're also a bit superstitious. Destiny will decide when it is my turn to be hit. You can't fight destiny, can you?'

'Because of the grass that was downtrodden...'

A tent in Mostar: April 1994

In Mostar for the first time; we are walking through the devastated city along the River Neretva. In Chile, we saw the need for a protective shield (in that case, the church and the international community) to protect a human rights movement.

The role of the church here is more complicated. The Muslims are on the Bosnian East Bank of the river, the Catholics are on the Croatian West Bank, and the Orthodox church supports the Serbs on the mountains around the town. However, the same ambivalence on the part of the church as we found in Chile is also found here. Some of the priests are engaged in social work. Others are strong supporters of a nationalistic approach. The international shelter is represented by the humanitarian agencies and the blue-helmeted UN soldiers guarding the front line, which has just recently fallen silent.

In a tent in the midst of the ruins on the old front line, fifty persons from each side meet. They have been allowed to cross over and be together in the UNPROFOR tent for the first time in two years. Goods and emotions are shared in a mixture of tears, anger, smiles and plastic bags. Moments ago we were walking through the streets of destruction on the East Bank where the collection of water and waiting for humanitarian aid seem to be the major activities. No electricity, no shops, no infrastructure are functioning.

We do not understand the words, but the scenario takes us back to the prison in Temuco, Chile, with the armed guards overseeing events. UN guards are placed in strategic positions in the ruins around the tent. No circles of political speeches or resistance are noticeable, just pain. We walk across the battered bridge to the West Bank. Five minutes later we are sitting on the main street having a cappuccino accompanied by disco rhythms.

We meet a man from the human rights movement. They are collecting testimonies, he tells us. For a moment we feel relieved. Somebody is trying to document what is happening. Seconds later we understand that only violations from the other side are of any interest.

The post-traumatic training group, Sarajevo: October 1994

Thirty-two psychiatrists from Sarajevo are participating in a training course. We meet 'the problem of the wounded healer' once again. Most of those who stayed here have suffered severe private trauma. Their professional commitment was part of their survival strategy. The inhabitants trust them: 'You stayed here with us.' The professionals try to assist everybody, including those from the other side. The professional ethic is useful and strong, but not always strong enough to overcome the mistrust – on both sides.

'I name thee freedom...'

A café in Zagreb, February 1994

We understand our new roles when we visit the professionals here. We are no longer 'the Danes', the researchers arriving and asking questions 'in the name of science'. We are representing two large international organizations and are expected to represent power structures, and we are therefore potential sources of funding. It is difficult, however, to use our Chilean experience and try to look at the situation through a 'research prism'. However, at least one significant working tool is still appropriate: to take our initial reaction of astonishment seriously.

One such instance of astonishment is shared in an outdoor café on the main square in Zagreb. People are standing, waiting for the tram, for friends, or just waiting to see if something will happen. Men in uniform pass by with their arms around elegant wives and girlfriends. UN soldiers on leave take pictures of each other, and the white UN cars are common features in the traffic. Croatian national symbols are for sale everywhere. 'There is no human rights movement here,' one woman says, 'only nationalism. Most of the opposition is even more right wing than those in power.'

We learn later that human rights groups do in fact exist. However, they seem to be marginal and small. There are also 'anti-war' groups, but most of these are having a hard time. 'When your country is at war, anti-war groups are easily labelled as traitors,' one man says. Apparently, there have been a few vague attempts to create meetings of human rights people from both sides of the front lines, but with only limited power to counteract the 'war fever'.

From the other side, Belgrade: September 1994

We can cross front lines and listen to narratives about violence from all sides. We realize how easy it is to become influenced by propaganda. Here in Belgrade, we are quite surprised that people seem normal. We meet the same spectrum of people as on the other sides: people who are tired of the war, people who are suffering, and people telling us a very nationalistic story. We realize that all sides have committed human rights violations. We see similar methods of repression on all sides. Maybe there are quantitative differences, but are there any qualitative differences? The methods of torture are astonishingly similar to those we already know about. Some of the testimonies are maybe even more gruesome and terrifying.

European Community Task Force office, Zagreb: January 1995

We have recorded 185 ongoing psycho-social projects in Bosnia-Herzegovina and Croatia (Agger, 1995). An overview illustrates that a lot of creative projects have been set up especially for traumatized women and children. In spite of the number of projects, probably only a minimum of the needs for psycho-social assistance are covered.

Mostar seminar, January 1995: peace-building?

A seminar on 'Mostar and Mental Health' has been set up. Seventy professionals from both sides are participating. From each side they tell us their story of what happened during the war. The context is professional and structured. Between the talks they joke with each other: 'Why did you send all these shells at us? Why didn't you send us chocolates instead?'

Later, during the group work, they tell each other about what really happened. They want to continue talking in the groups. Much more has to be spoken about. Later they agree to participate on both sides in a mutual training programme for the next six months.

Psycho-social projects are set up on both sides of the river. They may be developing into peace-building activities. Professional roles may be used for creating a dialogue and for building new bridges – including in Mostar.

'Because they spoke...'

Trauma, testimony and social memory

Silent and invisible people are easier to manipulate and dominate. Testimony is one way to ensure that the silent victims are given voice. Testimony documents *social memory*. However, testimony can also become an important part of a *reconciliation* process.

Reconciliation involves re-creating trust between people who are divided by hatred and fear of each other; social remembrance and testimony require keeping all that happened – both the good and the evil – in the collective memory of these same people, in our memory.

Must we forget old grievances in order to build peace? Or is it necessary to remember the evil that happened in order to ensure that it does not happen again?

Here, we argue for the necessity of combining the processes of reconciliation with the construction of social memory. More specifically, we want to propose these issues as the basis for discussion in the search for new methods and aims in trauma therapy. How can the divergent perspectives of reconciliation and social memory be integrated?

Reconciliation

- Reconciliation involves identification of and support for those groups in the local communities who are striving for peace.
- Reconciliation is the creation of peace from below, involving work at the grass-roots, community level with the specific aim of re-creating trust between members of the warring factions.
- Reconciliation works at establishing a dialogue between the divided groups – overcoming the 'spiritual division' between the groups and creating new hope for a peaceful future.
- Reconciliation works at changing local power structures so that those factions that advocate war and violent solutions become marginal.
- Reconciliation works at changing *the demonic/satanic image* of the enemy into a more realistic conception: not everyone belonging to the enemy group is bad, although some are.

- Reconciliation, therefore, also involves getting to know the feelings and the thoughts of ordinary people belonging to 'the other' side. Ordinary people on all sides are victims of the war, victims of human rights violations.

- Reconciliation, however, also implies a search for justice and truth.

Reconciliation is thus a process which follows two paths: changing the demonic image of 'the others', getting acquainted with *their* suffering, their feelings and thoughts; and remembering the truth about what some of those others have done.

Social memory

History exists as an unavoidable fact. The individual woman, man, child, family have lived through this history. Before the violence began there was also a history of having lived together with 'the others', having married them, having had children with them, having been good neighbours with them. Social memory also contains this good and positive aspect.

There is also the evil part of social memory. The local community has suffered this experience, has become uprooted, destroyed, traumatized, divided and betrayed in every imaginable way. It has happened and there are thousands of stories that need to be told about those bad times. Violence is part of the social memory of the war; there are events that cannot be denied or forgotten. They will continue to live in the social memory of the community and the individual people who suffered them. They will also continue to live in the memory of those who witnessed them – and those who perpetrated them.

So social memory contains these two aspects: the stories of both the good and the evil experiences. As often happens when people are under severe stress, the image of the other is split into a good and a bad part: either they are completely bad or completely good. Under war conditions, the enemy group will usually be perceived as completely bad, while members of our own group are completely good. It becomes threatening to remember the positive part of history, the times when it was possible to live together with members of the other groups. If peace is restored only by directives from the leadership level, we might see a reversal of this picture: now the bad part of history must be 'forgotten' – it must be denied, repressed or silenced.

What happens if this social memory is repressed, or cut off and dissociated? What happens if this unresolved past is preserved in the icebox of history? What happens if it is not integrated into the collective consciousness of the people? What happens if the survivors of violence and abuse are silenced? What happens if the rapes become a shameful secret that lives on in the victims as their individual problem, their dark past?

As therapists we know very well what can happen if individuals carry a heavy burden of past traumatic experiences that have not been integrated and worked through. From dictatorships we have also learned that destruction of social memory is an important means of domination.

In the social memory of a group, an experience which has been hidden for a long time, has been cut off, repressed, dissociated – but never fully forgotten – supplies constant fuel for further conflicts if ignited by a new traumatizing experience. The shame and anger coming from the narcissistic wound will supply more fuel.

Again and again during our stay in the countries of former Yugoslavia, we are confronted with the social memory of the Second World War. Old, evil memories from this war have surfaced and are being relived. Some of the older people also have painful memories from the First World War. In the collective unconsciousness, wars from even earlier times are surfacing and supply fuel for new and continued violence.

We have seen how this present war has revealed hidden memories of the Second World War in other countries. In Germany, thousands of women who were raped by the invading troops after the fall of the Nazi regime are beginning to speak out after having kept the abuse as a shameful secret for nearly fifty years. For many of us working as humanitarian aid-workers, this war has confronted us with what happened in our own countries during the Second World War, and it has shaken our sense of security and trust.

The efforts at reconciliation and constructing social memory will touch all of us, all the people who have witnessed the disaster of war and state terrorism. In the individual and collective healing of the trauma, how do we create ritual spaces where testimony can be given, and where the truth can become an established part of social memory?

NOTE

1. Adapted from Agger et al., 1995.

References

Agger, I. (1989) 'Sexual Torture of Political Prisoners: An Overview', *Journal of Traumatic Stress*, Vol. 2, 305–18.

Agger, I. (1994) *The Blue Room. Trauma and Testimony Among Refugee Women: A Psycho-Social Exploration*. Zed Books, London.

Agger, I. (ed.) (1995) *Theory and Practice of Psycho-Social Projects in Bosnia-Herzegovina and Croatia*. ECHO/ECTF, Zagreb.

Agger, I. and Jensen, S.B. (1990a) 'Testimony as Ritual and Evidence in Psychotherapy for Political Refugees', *Journal of Traumatic Stress*, Vol. 3, 115–30.

Agger, I. and Jensen, S.B. (1990b) 'Trauma, Encuentro y Significado' ('Trauma, Meeting and Meaning'), in S. Pesutic (ed.) *Tortura: Aspectos Medicos, Psicológos y Sociale. Prevención y Tratamiento* (Torture: Medical, Psychological and Social Aspects. Prevention and Treatment). CODEPU, Santiago de Chile.

Agger, I. and Jensen, S.B. (1991) 'An Open Window', in E. Neumann (ed.) *III International Conference: Health, Political Repression and Human Rights*. Proceedings, 24–29 November. FASIC, Santiago de Chile.

Agger, I. and Jensen, S.B. (1992) 'Human Rights and Post-Traumatic Stress', in K. Achté, M. Henriksson, M. Ponteva, S. Hietanen and J. Hares (eds) *Traumatic Stress: Psychology and Psychopathology*. Psychiatrica Fennica Supplementum, Helsinki.

Agger, I. and Jensen, S.B. (1993a) 'The Psychosexual Trauma of Torture', in J.P. Wilson and B. Raphael (eds) *International Handbook of Traumatic Stress Syndromes*. Plenum Press, New York.

Agger, I. and Jensen, S.B. (1993b) *Trauma and Healing Under State Terrorism: Human Rights and Mental Health in Chile During Military Dictatorship: A Case Example*. Preliminary report to the Council for Developmental Research, The Ministry of Foreign Affairs, Copenhagen.

Agger, I. and Jensen, S.B. (1994) 'Determinant Factors for Countertransference Reactions Under State Terrorism', in J.P. Wilson and J. Lindy (eds) *Countertransference in the Treatment of Post-Traumatic Stress Disorder*. Guilford Press, New York.

Agger, I., Jensen, S.B. and Jacobs, M. (1995) 'Under War Conditions: What

Defines a Psycho-Social Project?', in I. Agger (ed.) *Theory and Practice of Psycho-Social Projects in Bosnia-Herzegovina and Croatia*. ECHO/ECTF, Zagreb.

Aránguiz, M.T., Palavicino, M. and Poffald, L. (1990) *Tratamiento Psicoterapéutico en Personas Afectadas por la Represión: Una Experiencia en la IX. Region* (Psycho-therapeutic Treatment of Individuals Affected by the Repression: An Experience from the IX. Region). Cresam, Temuco.

Balogi, S. and Hering, M. (1992) '...*y Entonces, Me Dediqué a Mis Hijos'* ('...And Then, I Dedicated Myself to My Children'). CODEPU TF, Santiago de Chile.

Barudy, J. (1990a) 'El Dolor Invisible de la Tortura en las Familias de Exiliados en Europa' ('The Invisible Pain of Torture in the Families of the Exiled in Europe'), in S. Pesutic (ed.) *Tortura: Aspectos Médicos, Psicológicos y Sociales. Prevención y Tratamiento* (Torture: Medical, Psychological and Social Aspects. Prevention and Treatment). CODEPU, Santiago de Chile.

Barudy, J. (1990b) 'La Psicoterapia de la Tortura: El Valor Terapéutico de la Solidaridad, la Esperanza y la Justicia' ('Psychotherapy of Torture: The Thera-peutic Value of Solidarity, Hope and Justice'), in S. Pesutic (ed.) *Tortura: Aspectos Médicos, Psicológicos y Sociales. Prevención y Tratamiento* (Torture: Medical, Psychological and Social Aspects. Prevention and Treatment). CODEPU, Santiago de Chile.

Bateson, G. and Bateson, M.C. (1987) *Angels Fear: Towards an Epistemology of the Sacred*. Bantam Books, Toronto.

Becker, D. (forthcoming) 'The Deficiency of the PTSD-Concept When Dealing with Victims of Human Rights Violations and Other Forms of Organized Violence', in R. Kleber et al. (eds) *Beyond the Trauma*. Plenum Press, New York.

Becker, D. and Kovalskys, J. (1990) 'Dentro y Fuera de la Cárcel: El Problema de Conquistar la Libertad' (Inside and Outside the Prison: The Problem of How to Conquer Freedom'), in M. Baró (ed.) *Psicología Social de la Guerra: Trauma y Terapia* (Social Psychology of War: Trauma and Therapy). UCA Editorial, El Salvador.

Becker, D., Castillo, M.I., Gómez E., Kovalskys, J. and Lira, E. (1989) 'Subjec-tivity and Politics: The Psychotherapy of Extreme Traumatization in Chile', *International Journal of Mental Health*, Vol. 18, 80–87.

Becker, D., Maggi, A. and Domínguez, R. (1987) 'Tortura y Daño Familiar' ('Torture and Damage to the Family'), in E. Weinstein, E. Lira, M.E. Rojas et al. (eds) *Trauma, Duelo y Reparación: Una Experiencia de Trabajo Psicosocial en Chile* (Trauma, Mourning and Reparation: An Experience of Psycho-Social Work in Chile). FASIC/Interamericana, Santiago de Chile.

Becker, D., Lira, E., Castillo, M. et al. (1990) 'Therapy with Victims of Political Repression. The Challenge of Social Reparation', *Journal of Social Issues*, Vol. 46, 133–49.

Bowlby, J. (1980) *Attachment and Loss*. Basic Books, New York.

Bustos, E. and Ruggiero L.R. (1986) 'Latin American Youth in Exile: Is It a Lost Generation?' Paper presented at the International Seminar of Refugee Cen-tres, Frankfurt/Main, 8–11 May.

Castaldi, L. and Ibacache Silva, L. (1991) 'Terapia de Torturados: Un Reconstruirnos Mutamente' ('Therapy of the Tortured: A Mutual Recon-struction of Ourselves'). Paper presented at the III International Conference:

Health, Political Repression and Human Rights, Santiago de Chile, 24–29 November.

Cienfuegos, A.J. and Monelli, C. (1983) 'The Testimony of Political Repression as a Therapeutic Instrument', *American Journal of Orthopsychiatry*, Vol. 53, 43–51.

CODEPU (1989) 'The Effects of Torture and Political Repression in a Sample of Chilean Families', *Social Science and Medicine*, Vol. 28, 735–40.

CODEPU (1992) *Isla Quiriquina* (Quiriquina Island). CODEPU, Concepción.

Comas-Díaz, L. and Padilla, A.M. (1990) 'Countertransference in Working with Victims of Political Repression', *American Journal of Orthopsychiatry*, Vol. 60, 125–34.

Commission of Truth and Reconciliation (1992) *'To Believe in Chile': National Education Campaign for Truth and Human Rights*. Chilean Human Rights Commission/Centro IDEAS, Ministry of Foreign Affairs of Chile, Santiago de Chile.

Constable, P. and Valenzuela, A. (1991) *Chile Under Pinochet: A Nation of Enemies*. Norton, New York.

Corvalán, C. (1990) 'Experiencia de Trabajo en el Centro Psicosocial de Frankfurt, Alemania' ('Experiences from the Work of the Psychosocial Center in Frankfurt, Germany'), in S. Pesutic (ed.) *Tortura: Aspectos Médicos, Psicológicos y Sociales. Prevención y Tratamiento* (Torture: Medical, Psychological and Social Aspects. Prevention and Treatment). CODEPU, Santiago de Chile.

Departamento Pastoral de Derechos Humanos Arzobispado de Concepción (1988) *Por la Sagrada Dignidad del Hombre* (For the Sacred Dignity of Man). Concepción.

Engel, G.L. (1953) 'The Clinical Application of the Biopsychosocial Model', *American Journal of Psychiatry*, Vol. 137, 535–44.

Escorza, E. and Maureira, G. (1989) 'Talleres Experienciales con Jóvenes' ('Experimental Workshops with Adolescents'). Paper. PIDEE, Santiago de Chile.

Faúndez, H., Estrada, A., Balogi, S. and Hering M. (1991) 'Cuando el Fantasma es un Totem' ('When the Phantom is a Totem'). Paper. CODEPU TF, Santiago de Chile.

Girardi, C., Rodino, M. and Citarella, L. (1991) 'Una Visión Antropológica del Problema de la Salud Mental: El Caso Mapuche' ('An Anthropological Perspective on the Problem of Mental Health: The Mapuche Case'). Paper. University of Frontera, Project APS, Faculty of Medicine, Temuco.

Hastrup, K. (1992) *Det Antropologiske Projekt: Om Forblöffelse* (The Anthropological Project: About Astonishment). Gyldendal, Copenhagen.

Jensen, S.B. (1992) 'Sexuality and Chronic Illness: A Bio-Psycho-Social Approach', *Seminars in Neurology*, Vol. 12, 135–40.

Jensen, S.B. and Agger, I. (1990) 'El Método Testimonial como Ritual y Evidencia en Psicoterapia para Refugiados Políticos' ('The Testimony Method as Ritual and Evidence in Psychotherapy for Political Refugees'), in S. Pesutic (ed.) *Tortura: Aspectos Médicos, Psicológicos y Sociales. Prevención y Tratamiento* (Torture: Medical, Psychological and Social Aspects. Prevention and Treatment). CODEPU, Santiago de Chile.

Jensen, S.B. and Agger, I. (1992) 'In the Borderland Between Insanity and Evil: Political Refugees Meet Psychiatry', in K. Achté, M. Henriksson, M. Ponteva,

S. Hietanen and J. Hares (eds) *Traumatic Stress: Psychology and Psychopathology*. Psychiatrica Fennica Supplementum, Helsinki.

Jung, C.G. (1983) *Memories, Dreams, Reflections*. Flamingo, London. (Originally published in 1963.)

Kernberg, O., Selzer, M., Koenigsberg H., Carr A. and Appelbaum A. (1989) *Psychodynamic Psychotherapy of Borderline Patients*. Yale University Press, New Haven.

Kleinman, A. (1988) *The Illness Narratives: Suffering, Healing, and the Human Condition*. Basic Books, New York.

Kordon, D.R., Edelman, L.I., Lagos, D.M. et al. (1986) *Efectos Psicológicos de la Represión Política* (Psychological Effects of Political Repression). Sudamericana, Buenos Aires.

Kovalskys, J., Faúndez, H., Jordán, C. and Aguilar, M.I. (1992) 'Catastro de Publicaciones de los Equipos de Salud Mental y Derechos Humanos' ('Catalogue of Publications by the Mental Health and Human Rights Teams'). Paper. CESAM, Santiago de Chile.

Lansen, J. (1992) 'A Critical View of the Concept: Post-Traumatic Stress Disorder', in Ministry of Welfare, Health and Cultural Affairs (ed.) *Health Situation of Refugees and Victims of Organized Violence*. Rijswijk, Netherlands:

Lifton, R.J. (1988) 'Understanding the Traumatized Self: Imagery, Symbolization and Transformation', in J.P. Wilson, Z. Harel and B. Kahana (eds) *Human Adaptation to Extreme Stress*. Plenum Press, New York.

Lira, E. (1983) 'The Chilean Experience in the Psychological Work of Political Repression and Torture'. Paper. FASIC, Santiago de Chile.

Lira, E. (forthcoming) 'The Development of a Therapeutic Approach for Treatment of Victims of Human Rights Violations in Chile: The Impact on Therapists', in R. Kleber et al. (eds) *Beyond the Trauma*. Plenum Press, New York.

Lira, E. and Castillo, M. (1991) *Psicologia de la Amenaza Política y del Miedo* (Psychology of Political Threat and Fear). CESOC, Santiago de Chile.

Lira, E., Becker, D. and Castillo, M.I. (1989) 'Psicoterapia de Víctimas de Represión Política bajo Dictadura: Un Desafío Terapéutico, Teórico, y Político' (Psychotherapy with Victims of Political Repression under Dictatorship: A Therapeutic, Theoretical and Political Challenge'), in E. Lira and D. Becker (eds) *Derechos Humanos: Todo es Según el Dolor con que se Mira* (Human Rights: Everything Depends on the Pain with which You Look at It). ILAS, Santiago de Chile.

Longman. (1991) *Dictionary of Contemporary English*. Longman Group UK Limited, Essex.

McCann, I.L. and Pearlman, L.A. (1990) *Psychological Trauma and the Adult Survivor: Theory, Therapy and Transformation*. Brunner/Mazel, New York.

Madariaga, C. (1990) 'Detenidos Desaparecidos en una Comunidad Rural: Daño Psicológico y Psicosocial' ('Detained and Disappeared People in a Rural Community: Psychological and Psycho-Social Damage'). Paper. CINTRAS, Santiago de Chile.

Maeder, T. (1989) 'Wounded Healers', *The Atlantic Monthly*, January, 37–47.

Medina, C. (1992) 'Chile: Obstacles and Challenges for Human Rights', *Netherlands Quarterly of Human Rights*, Vol. 10, 109–29.

Milgram, N.A. (1990) 'Secondary Victims of Traumatic Stress: Their Plight and Public Policy'. Paper presented at the Annual Meeting of the International

Society for Traumatic Stress Studies, New Orleans, 29 October–2 November.

Minuchin, S., Rosman B.L. and Baker, L. (1978) *Psychosomatic Families*. Harvard University Press, Cambridge, MA.

Morales, R. (1990) 'Informe de Investigación de Derechos Humanos y Opresión Etnico-Nacional de Los Mapuches en Cautín' ('Report on an Investigation of Human Rights and Ethnic-National Repression of the Mapuche in Cautín'). Paper. Institute of Anthropology, Temuco.

Morales, R. (1991a) 'Violaciones al Derecho a la Vida de los Mapuches' (Violations of the Right to Life of the Mapuche'), *Nütram*, Vol. 8, 24–56.

Morales, R. (1991b) 'Pueblo Mapuche y Represión Política' (The Mapuche People and Political Repression'). Paper presented at the III International Conference: Health, Political Repression and Human Rights, Santiago de Chile, 24–29 November.

Neumann, E., Monréal A., Bel, B., Gallardo, V. and Macchiavello, C. (1990) *Para Romper el Silencio* (To Break the Silence). FASIC, Santiago de Chile.

Ochberg, F.M. (ed.) (1988) *Post-Traumatic Therapy and Victims of Violence*. Brunner/ Mazel, New York.

Orellana, P. (1989) *Violaciones a los Derechos Humanos e Información: La Experiencia Chilena* (Violations of Human Rights and Information: The Chilean Experience). FASIC, Santiago de Chile.

Pesutic, S. (ed.) (1989) *Persona, Estado, Poder* (Individual, State, Power). CODEPU, Santiago de Chile.

Pesutic, S. (ed.) (1990) *Tortura: Aspectos Médicos, Psicológicos y Sociales. Prevención y Tratamiento* (Torture: Medical, Psychological and Social Aspects. Prevention and Treatment). CODEPU, Santiago de Chile.

Pinochet, A. (1980) *El Día Decisivo*. Andrés Bello, Santiago de Chile.

Pollarollo, F. (1983) 'La Tortura, un Problema Médico' ('Torture, a Medical Problem'). Paper. FASIC, Santiago de Chile.

Reszczynski, K., Rojas, P. and Barcelo, P. (1991) *Tortura y Resistencia en Chile: Estudio Médico-Político* (Torture and Resistance in Chile: A Medical-Political Study). Editorial Emisión, Santiago de Chile.

Rhee, K. (1992) 'Religion, Symbols and Social Consciousness in Contemporary Mapuche Cultures'. Paper. Institute of Anthropology, Temuco.

Riquelme, H. (1994) *Era in Twilight: The Psychocultural Situation Under State Terrorism in Latin America*. Instituto Horizonte SL, Bilbao.

Rojas, M.E. (1988) *La Represión Política en Chile: Los Hechos* (The Political Repression in Chile: The Deeds). IEPALA, Madrid.

Rojas, P. (1981) 'Resistir la Detención–Tortura–Interrogatorio' ('How to Resist Detention–Torture–Interrogation'). Paper. CODEPU, Santiago de Chile.

Solar, M.A. (1989) *Primer Manual de Medicina Casera para la Madre Campesina* (Basic Manual of Household Medicine for the Peasant Mother). University of Frontera, Faculty of Medicine, Temuco.

Summerfield, D. (1992) 'Charting Human Response to Extreme Violence and the Limitations of Western Psychiatric Models: An Overview'. Paper presented at the World Conference of the International Society for Traumatic Stress Studies, June, Amsterdam.

Traverso, A. (1989) 'The Mourning Process: Traumatic Stress Reactions. Prevention, Coping and Treatment'. Paper presented at the II International

Conference: Mental Health, Political Repression and Human Rights, December, San José.

Vicaría de la Solidaridad (1983) *Así lo Hemos Vivido... Detenidos Desaparecidos* (This Was How We Experienced It... The Detained and Disappeared). Vicaría de la Solidaridad, Santiago de Chile.

Vicaría de la Solidaridad (1990) *Algunas Cifras Sobre Atentados a los Derechos Humanos Durante el Régimen Militar* (Some Data about Violations of Human Rights during the Military Regime). Vicaría de la Solidaridad, Santiago de Chile.

Vicaría de la Solidaridad (1991) *Historia de su Trabajo Social* (The Story of Our Social Work). Ediciones Paulinas, Santiago de Chile.

Vidal, M. (1990) 'Daño Psicológico y Represión Política: Un Modelo de Atención Integral' (Psychological Damage and Political Repression: An Integrative Model of Treatment'), *Reflexión,* December, 10–14.

Weinstein, E., Lira, E., Rojas, M.E. et al. (1987) (eds) *Trauma, Duelo y Reparación: Una Experiencia de Trabajo Psicosocial en Chile* (Trauma, Mourning and Reparation: An Experience of Psycho-Social Work in Chile). FASIC/Interamericana, Santiago de Chile.

Weinstein, E. and Lira, E. (1987) 'La Tortura' ('Torture'), in E. Weinstein, E. Lira, M.E. Rojas et al. (eds) *Trauma, Duelo y Reparación: Una Experiencia de Trabajo Psicosocial en Chile* (Trauma, Mourning and Reparation: An Experience of Psycho-Social Work in Chile). FASIC/Interamericana, Santiago de Chile.

Wilson, J.P. (1989) *Trauma, Transformation and Healing.* Brunner/Mazel, New York.

Wilson, J.P. and Lindy, J. (1994) 'Empathic Strain and Countertransference', in J.P. Wilson and J. Lindy (eds) *Countertransference in the Treatment of Post-Traumatic Stress Disorder.* Guilford Press, New York.

Wilson, J.P., Lindy. J.D. and Raphael, B. (1994) 'Empathic Strain and Therapist Defense: Type I and II CTRs', in J.P. Wilson and J. Lindy (eds) *Countertransference in the Treatment of Post-Traumatic Stress Disorder.* Guilford Press, New York.

Index

237